THE URBAN LEGACY OF OLYMPIC VILLAGES

THE URBAN LEGACY OF OLYMPIC VILLAGES

FROM PARIS TO BEIJING (1924-2022)

VALERIO DELLA SALA

COMMON GROUND

First published in 2025
as part of Sports & Society Book Imprint
Common Ground Research Networks

University of Illinois Research Park
2001 South First St, Suite 201 L
Champaign, IL 61820 USA

Library of Congress Cataloging-in-Publication Data

Names: Della Sala, Valerio, 1990- author
Title: The urban legacy of Olympic villages : from Paris to Beijing
  (1924-2022) / Valerio della Sala.
Description: Champaign, IL : Common Ground Research Networks, 2026.
Identifiers: LCCN 2024058358 (print) | LCCN 2024058359 (ebook) | ISBN
  9781966214137 hardback | ISBN 9781966214144 paperback | ISBN
  9781966214151 adobe pdf
Subjects: LCSH: Olympics--Planning | Olympic host city selection--Social
  aspects | Olympics--Economic aspects
Classification: LCC GV721.5 D4477 2026 (print) | LCC GV721.5 (ebook) |
  DDC 307.1/4--dc23/eng/20250224
LC record available at https://lccn.loc.gov/2024058358
LC ebook record available at https://lccn.loc.gov/2024058359

ISBN: 978-1-966214-13-7 (HBK)
ISBN: 978-1-966214-14-4 (PBK)
ISBN: 978-1-966214-15-1 (pdf)
DOI: 10.18848/978-1-966214-15-1/CGP

Cover Design: Phillip Kalantzis Cope
Cover Image: Valerio Della Sala

TABLE OF CONTENTS

TABLE OF TABLES

TABLE OF FIGURES

FOREWORD

Egidio Dansero

The Olympics represent a topic of great interest from many points of view, starting, of course, from the sporting one, to the geopolitical one, both at the international scale and at the internal scale of individual countries, to the economic one, due to the consequent impacts, to the social, cultural, and, in particular, identity ones, to those concerning the spatial transformations directly or indirectly connected with the mega-event.

On each of these aspects, a literature has accumulated over time, both on a scientific level, in an international academic community, with different disciplinary points of view and different parts of the problem being investigated (the entire mega-event, or individual aspects), and on an operational level, in IOC circles and in companies specialized in consulting and event organization.

The growing and increasingly robust international literature has well highlighted not only the various lights but also the many shadows that each Olympic edition and, more generally, the Olympic mega-event entails.

Every Olympic Games, whether summer or winter, and more generally every mega-event (above all the International Expos, the Football World Cup), can be considered as a moment concentrated in time and space, requiring a rather long phase of preparation, and which manifests itself by drawing increasingly global attention on the host location, only to move to other places, leaving the host location (in a diversity of local-regional-national relationships that vary for each event) to manage a complex, material and immaterial, often cumbersome legacy.

Every single Olympic event has its own history and, above all, its own geography, which sees a different spatial organization for its event, including competition and training facilities, reception facilities for athletes and the vast Olympic family, and supporting infrastructure. One of the key locations of each edition is the Olympic Village, which can have very different configurations both for the operation of the event and especially in the post-event period.

This book makes an innovative and original contribution to the debate on transformations related to the Olympics, focusing on the Olympic Village, its relationship to the spatial structure specific to the individual edition, and its fate in the management of the post-event legacy, in an international comparative analysis.

The Olympic Village is the symbol of inhabiting the Games, a city (or cities) within the host cities, welcoming a truly global community during the 15 days of the event. McLuhan was probably not thinking of this when he spoke of the Global Village, but this one, even if only for a short time, really is. How does each city organize itself to set up the Village? What remains of these places once the five circles stop illuminating them?

This text is an important contribution both for those who work on the organization of the future Games, from their political and social legitimization to their operationalization, and for those who take a critical look at a transformation for an ephemeral event that leaves lasting and not infrequently problematic transformations on the ground.

ACKNOWLEDGEMENTS

This book was made possible thanks to a doctoral research project in international co-tutorship between the Autonomous University of Barcelona, the Polytechnic University of Turin, and the University of Turin. Over time, the following study has received support from many specialists who continue to support me in my research work.

First, I thank Professor Francesc Muñoz and Professor Egidio Dansero, sources of inspiration and daily encouragement. Likewise, I would like to thank all the Centre for Olympic Studies members at the Autonomous University of Barcelona, the Institute of Sport Research (IRE-UAB), and the OMERO Interdepartmental Centre for Urban Studies at the University of Turin.

Collaborating with the following research centres has allowed me to produce different publications that are fundamental to my research experience.

Finally, I would like to thank my family, my father Roberto, and my mother Katia for always having supported and sustained me. Special thanks also go to my partner, Chiara, who has always tried to help me with my choices from the very first moment. I want to emphasise that this book is also the result of extensive research in the Piedmont region, made possible thanks to the suggestions of some very special people in the OMERO group.

Grazie!

INTRODUCTION

The following book presents the background and context for an advanced multidisciplinary study to shed light on the different dynamics and models of the Olympic Village observed during the 20th and 21st centuries. The main objective will be to provide a comprehensive overview of the topic, understanding its difficulties by delineating key questions given the development of future Olympic accommodation.

Mega-events have attracted a great deal of attention in recent years. They are considered a unique phenomenon that can promote the spread of smaller events on a local or continental level. Large metropolitan areas are interested in the competition of global events to catalyze other significant processes within the host city. London, Paris, New York, Moscow, Boston, Madrid, Melbourne, Rome, Milan, Beijing, Los Angeles, and Barcelona are just some of the modern metropolises interested in hosting a global sports mega-event. The interest shown by the following metropolises over time can take on different meanings and have discordant results.

Furthermore, throughout Olympic history, we have been able to observe different experiences with different objectives from the sporting practice itself. The interest in mega-events can generate different outcomes in different contexts and each specific situation. Throughout Olympic history, we have had different experiences proposing the restructuring of urban functions, the improvement of materials or the affirmation of possibilities to open up to the world. Therefore, other catalyzing elements within the Olympic cities can be observed by observing spatial patterns and the object territory. To observe the different summer and winter editions, the following book uses a quantitative methodology by introducing some standard parameters that allow the different Olympic experiences to be compared, considering their specificities. The data were catalogued and assimilated using geospatial analysis techniques using the open-source QGIS software. Furthermore, all the data used are part of the author's archive.

For the descriptive information, the official sources of the International Olympic Committee present in the online library or within Barcelona, Turin, and Lausanne archives were used.

As we will observe within the book, the chosen approach is a territorial one, starting from a first question posed by way of introduction: What types of urban functions have the Olympic Villages assumed throughout history, considering their use in the post-Olympic period?

The following question will allow us to observe how different Olympic accommodation models have developed throughout the 20th and 21st centuries.

While considering the planning of host cities, we will analyze the different spatial models in order to answer the following question: Can the Olympic Village be considered a catalyst for urban expansion and/or transformation?

This question will advance the introduction of the spatial processes that may result from applying one model rather than another.

Therefore, we will introduce some critical references to understand the different local, metropolitan, regional, and national dimensions that the event can catalyze within the context territory. From a local point of view, the event is a catalyst for new processes that can plan, propose, and reduce the territorial dimension of the candidate cities. Moreover, thanks to the reuse of housing models, the Olympic cities in the post-Olympic period can be endowed with an active heritage for the community. Operational assets that can be transformed into a new model of local development to be implemented within the territory in the medium and long term.

Therefore, all the resources can constitute a territorial legacy that can be a positive experience for the entire community. Experience that becomes part of the heritage and territorial resources of the host city.

However, the Olympic experience can represent a negative element that can favor the destruction of the territory with the consequent consumption of land. In the 21st century, we have observed several Olympic experiences that have represented a negative element capable of fostering the evolution of phenomena such as territorial fragmentation, segregation, gentrification, and other phenomena that may constitute an unnecessary cost for the host community. Therefore, the definition of adequate and long-term planning can favor the realization of projects that respect citizens' priorities and needs. One of the book's objectives is to explore the different Olympic Village experiences that constitute the fundamental Olympic heritage for introducing new housing practices. Therefore, reading the other models and territorial transformations will focus on the evolution of both Olympic editions (Summer and Winter) to observe the different evolutionary phases of housing.

Subsequently, after observing the different evolutionary phases, the models of permanently built Olympic Villages during the 20th and 21st centuries will be introduced. Therefore, the following contribution will consider the Olympic territory as a phenomenon of extraordinary territory production that implies a reconsideration of the ordinary production of territory. Furthermore, considering the event as a remarkable production requires observing rules, processes, and obligations of a different institutional nature.

The book considers all the resources, materials, relationships, directions, and contractual obligations the Olympic event provides. The Olympic event permanently transforms and compromises the territory. By complexifying and modifying territorial dynamics, it becomes difficult to reconstruct and observe the tangible and intangible values related to the development and protection of local systems. With this in mind, we can introduce a clear distinction between project territory and context territory. Let us consider the project territory as a temporary territory configured through the Olympic project and the compulsory works to host the mega-event. On the contrary, the context territory, whether or not it is included in the Olympic event, follows its rules and ordinary transformation paths. Therefore, the representation of a material, perceptive and symbolic transformation of the territorial space through a mega-event can be observed as a production of values typical of contemporary society.

Only by observing the planning models of the Olympic Villages will it be possible to anticipate common patterns in terms of urban typology. Classifiable and comparable urban typology throughout the history and future of Olympic accommodation.

The following book aims to analyze the different spatial transformations induced by the Olympic event. Spatial transformations have allowed the evolution of the other models of Olympic accommodations that remain an active and available heritage at the disposal of most host cities throughout history.

The functions and modes of reuse of the Olympic Village in the post-Olympic period will then be analyzed, considering the different territorial contexts. Furthermore, the different territorial contexts that can absorb or reject temporary situations will be regarded as in observance of the summer and winter events. Metropolises are subjects that can digest and absorb transient events such as universal expositions, the capital of culture, and the Olympic Games. All events involve a cycle of territorialization.

The following manuscript can be divided into three parts.

The first part deals with conceptual issues related to Olympic cities and the theoretical history of Olympic Villages. Therefore, the first chapter attempts to advance an overview of the development of Olympic cities and Olympic Villages during the 20th and 21st centuries. The second chapter will analyze the phenomenon of Olympic town planning and the spatial organization of Olympic cities. First, Olympic territorialization will be introduced, and an overview of the different impacts on the territory during the Olympic process will be provided. Next, considering local development, local development policies will be introduced to introduce the different planning scales for the Olympic event. Finally, after an overview of the history and evolution of the territorial dimension, the other spatial models of the Olympic Villages built throughout Olympic history will be observed. Furthermore, in this chapter, we will keep the substantial differences in the summer and winter editions of the global event.

The third chapter will observe the different evolutionary phases of the summer and winter Olympic Villages. We will advance some considerations on the spatial dimension and spatial patterns observed during the 20th and 21st centuries.

By introducing the different evolutionary phases of the two editions, the reader will be able to observe the dimensions and types advanced by each Olympic city about the territory.

The fourth chapter allows all the Olympic Villages to be analyzed, considering the parameters used for the comparative analysis. Thanks to the observation of the accommodation facilities, the reader will be able to observe the main changes and quantitative differences with the help of the common elements proposed in the 2022 PhD study.

Finally, the last chapter will discuss the evolution of Olympic accommodation between the 20th and 21st centuries in consideration of the study's findings.

Furthermore, the final chapter will provide some fundamental indications of the future implications given the implementation or reconsideration of Olympic accommodation.

Through the results obtained from the 2022 doctoral study, the following book will offer an innovative vision for the research and implementation of future Olympic Villages.

Finally, the last chapter will discuss the evolution of Olympic accommodation between the 20th and 21st centuries, considering the results obtained from the study. In addition, the next chapter will provide some insights into the future implications of implementing or reconsidering Olympic accommodation. The following text, with the results obtained from the PhD study, will offer an innovative vision for the research and implementation of Olympic Villages.

CHAPTER 1

The Olympic Village: A Brief History

1.1 Introduction to Olympic cities

The Beijing Olympics in August 2008 ushered in a shift in the global audience for mega-events, generating record revenues from audiovisual rights sales and marketing.[1] For this reason, the event's revenue and audience numbers have continued to evolve since 2008 through new digital platforms that significantly contribute to the event's global audience. The International Olympic Committee's (IOC) 2021 report shows that the 2012 London Games and the 2016 Rio Games had around 5 billion spectators worldwide. Meanwhile, the 2014 Sochi Winter Olympics and the 2018 Pyeongchang Winter Olympics had a combined audience of 2.5 billion viewers.[2] These data allow us to significantly differentiate between the summer and winter editions.[3] This puts the Winter Olympics at a disadvantage due to the difference in audience and funding provided by the IOC and Olympic sponsors, forcing the organizing Committee to deliver a highly complex project with little financial flexibility. A hypothesis is born. Therefore, the dependence between cities and the Olympics is an element that remains only in the summer version. As we will see in Chapter 3, since 2006, the winter edition has seen significant changes in The size, scale, and utilization model of Olympic events. Previously, in October 2009, two economists, Mark Spiegel of the Federal Reserve Bank of San Francisco and Andrew Rose of the

---

[1] Sands, L. M. (2008, July -August). The 2008 Olympics' impact on China. *The China Business Review*.

[2] IOC. (2021). *Marketing fact* (pp. 8-21).

[3] In addition, there is a 100% difference in the marketing of audiovisual rights between the two editions.

University of Berkeley, studied the Olympic legacy of host cities.[4] The study focuses on the facilities and infrastructure created to host the Olympics. Like many other researchers, they focus on strategic planning issues and emphasize the centrality of strategic planning in all aspects of the success of the Olympic Games. Therefore, given the significant investments in infrastructure, it is crucial to emphasize the importance of developing strategic plans in collaboration with all stakeholders at local, national, and international levels. This strategic plan allows for a legacy to be left in the local community.[5] In terms of venues, facilities, parks, and everything designed for the Olympics (Rose & Spiegel, 2009). Developing an excellent strategic plan requires maintaining long-term communication with all stakeholders and planning for 10 to 20 years. This is because it is an essential factor in promoting mixed management of public and private companies.[6] For example, in the case of Barcelona, in 1976, as part of an agreement with the government, a General Metropolitan Plan[7] for the city was developed for hosting the 1992 Olympic Games.[8] The Barcelona case serves as a model.[9] For the management and organization of these "*Mega-Events*," unfortunately, not all states have the same capabilities and human resources.[10] However, political, social, and cultural contexts influence and determine the success of Olympic events. In this sense, this theory has been proven that not all cities worldwide can hold these events and achieve the same results.[11] Every event must be analyzed according to its historical moment. Only through post-Olympic planning can a consistent focus on the city's image

---

[4.] Rose, Andrew K., & Spiegel, Mark M. (2009, October). *The Olympic effect*. National Bureau of Economic Research.

[5.] However, citizens being the central part of the strategic planning, the Organizing Committee, without the support and involvement of the host community, will not be able to take advantage of all the intangible benefits associated with this type of "*Mega-event*."

[6.] PwC. (2010, June). *Public-private partnerships: The US perspective*.

[7.] Plan general metropolitano de ordenación urbana, de la entidad municipal metropolitana de Barcelona, Economic Study (February 1976), Corporacio Metropolitana de Barcelona (CMB), Barcelona, January 1976.

[8.] The urban project of the new Barcelona began in 1976 with the approval of the Metropolitan Plan which included 26 municipalities considering them as part of a total urban planning, using the communication and service roads as integration tools.

[9.] For example, Turin in 2006 and Rio in 2016 were two cities inspired by the Barcelona model for the exploitation of the Olympic event and have obtained entirely different results.

[10.] World Economic Forum. (2010, January). *Global Risks 2020: A Global Risk Network Report*.

[11.] To host the two events (World Cup and Olympic Games), Brazil has received 83 billion in public and private funds for the development of new infrastructures, connections, communication, technology and other works that had to help the State solve some problems.

and marketing be established. Cities such as Sydney,[12] New York, Barcelona, Atlanta, and Sochi invested heavily in marketing before, during, and after the event. There is no doubt that tourism is the most significant tangible value that we can associate with the image of a city (Preuss, 2000).

Barcelona has become one of the leading cities in Europe in terms of the number of tourists, sporting events, and international conferences. The primary funding sources are managed through joint ventures specialized in various operations. Tables 1 and 2 show the candidate cities for the Summer and Winter Olympic Games. Moreover, Michael Payne, who has worked for the International Olympic Committee for more than 20 years, believes that the optimal management of this type of "*Mega-Event*" should be left to a joint venture with business sector experts.[13] Bidding for the Olympics can, therefore, be an opportunity for host cities to develop and change their operating philosophy.[14] Organizing committees must keep in mind the importance of citizens and locally sustainable practices and must consider all current and future risks.[15] Furthermore, facility planning should integrate urban social policies and promote long-term urban development. Integrating events into regional or national strategic plans can turn them into long-term, dynamic processes. As Gold (2008, 2016) and Roche (1992, 2002, 2003, 2006) have pointed out, if successful in organizing and promoting a city's image, mega-events can create a new international image and identity for the city (Viehoff, 2018).

Table 1: Candidate cities for the Summer Olympic Games, 1896–2032

Year	Year of adjudication	Host city	Host country	Other candidates
1896	1894	Athens	Greece	London
1900	1894	Paris	France	
1904	1901	St. Louis*	The US	Chicago

(*Continued*)

[12.] NSW Treasury: Office of Financial Management. (1997, November). *The economic impact of the Sydney Olympic Games*. PwC. (2001). *Business and economic benefits of the Sydney 2000 Games: A collation of evidence.*

[13.] Payne, Michael. (2007, Spring). "A gold-medal partnership." *Strategy+Business.*

[14.] PwC. (2010). *Public-Private partnerships: The US perspective.*

[15.] Reassessing existing structures over time has become essential.

Year	Year of adjudication	Host city	Host country	Other candidates
1908	1904	London**	Great Britain	Berlin, Milan, Rome
1912	1909	Stockholm	Sweden	
1916	1912	Berlin	Germany	Berlin, Alexandria (Egypt), Budapest, Cleveland, Brussels
1920	1914	Antwerp	Belgium	Amsterdam, Atlanta, Brussels, Budapest, Budapest, Cleveland, Lyon, Havana, Philadelphia
1924	1921	Paris	France	Los Angeles, Atlantic City, Chicago, Pasadena, Rome, Barcelona, Amsterdam, Lyon
1928	1921	Amsterdam	The Netherlands	Los Angeles
1932	1923	Los Angeles	The US	
1936	1931	Berlin	Germany	Barcelona, Buenos Aires, Rome
1940	1936	Tokyo	Japan	Tokyo, Helsinki, Rome
1944	1939	London	Great Britain	London, Athens, Budapest, Lausanne, Helsinki, Rome, Detroit
1948	1946	London	Great Britain	Baltimore, Lausanne, Los Angeles, Minneapolis, Philadelphia
1952	1947	Helsinki	Finland	Amsterdam, Chicago, Detroit, Detroit, Los Angeles, Minneapolis, Philadelphia

Year	Year of adjudication	Host city	Host country	Other candidates
1956	1949	Melbourne	Australia	Buenos Aires, Chicago, Detroit, Los Angeles, Los Angeles, Mexico City, Minneapolis, Montreal, Philadelphia
1960	1955	Roma	Italy	Budapest, Brussels, Detroit, Lausanne, Mexico City, Tokyo
1964	1959	Tokyo	Japan	Brussels, Detroit, Vienna
1968	1963	Mexico City	Mexico	Buenos Aires, Lyon, Detroit
1972	1966	Munich	Germany	Detroit, Madrid, Montreal
1976	1970	Montreal	Canada	Los Angeles, Moscow
1980	1974	Moscow	Soviet Union	Los Angeles
1984	1978	Los Angeles	The US	Tehran
1988	1981	Seoul	South Korea	Nagoya (Japan)
1992	1986	Barcelona	Spain	Amsterdam, Belgrade, Birmingham, Brisbane, Paris
1996	1990	Atlanta	The US	Athens, Belgrade, Manchester, Melbourne, Toronto
2000	1993	Sydney	Australia	Brasilia, Beijing, Berlin, Istanbul, Manchester, Milan, Tashkent

(*Continued*)

Year	Year of adjudication	Host city	Host country	Other candidates
2004	1997	Athens	Greece	Buenos Aires, Cape Town, Istanbul, Lille, Rio de Janeiro, Rome, San Juan, St. Petersburg, Seville, Stockholm
2008	2001	Beijing	China	Bangkok, Cairo, Havana, Istanbul, Kuala Lumpur, Osaka, Paris, Seville, Toronto
2012	2005	London	The UK	Istanbul, Havana, Leipzig, Paris, Madrid Moscow, New York, Rio de Janeiro
2016	2009	Rio de Janeiro	Brazil	Baku, Chicago, Doha, Madrid, Prague, Tokyo
2020	2013	Tokyo	Japan	Baku, Doha, Istanbul, Madrid
2024	2017	Paris	France	Unanimous
2028	2017	Los Angeles	The US	Unanimous
2032	2021	Brisbane	Australia	72 Yes, 5 No, 3 abstention (93.5% of valid votes)

* Tensions caused by the Russo-Japanese War and difficulties in travelling to St. Louis resulted in very few top-class athletes from outside the United States and Canada participating in the 1904 Games. Only 69–74 of the 651 athletes who competed came from outside North America, and only between 12 and 15 nations were represented.
** The 1908 Games were originally scheduled to be held in Rome but were relocated on financial grounds following the violent eruption of Mount Vesuvius in 1906, which claimed over 100 lives.

Source: Compiled by author from IOC, 2022

Table 2: Candidate cities for the Olympic Winter Games, 1924–2026

Year	Host city	Host country	Other candidates
1924	Chamonix	France	
1928	St. Moritz	Swiss	Davos, Engelberg (Switzerland)
1932	Lake Placid	The US	Montreal (Canada), Bear Mountain, Yosemite Valley, Lake Tahoe, Duluth, Minneapolis, Denver (the US)
1936	Garmisch-Partenkirchen	Germany	St. Moritz (Switzerland)
1948	St. Moritz	Switzerland	Lake Placid (the US)
1952	Oslo	Norway	Cortina (Italy), Lake Placid (the US)
1956	Cortina	Italy	Colorado Springs, Lake Placid (the US), Montreal (Canada)
1960	Squaw Valley	The US	Innsbruck (Austria), St. Moritz (Switzerland), Garmisch-Partenkirchen (Germany)
1964	Innsbruck	Austria	Calgary (Canada), Lahti (Sweden)
1968	Grenoble	France	Calgary (Canada), Lahti/Are (Sweden), Sapporo (Japan), Oslo (Norway), Lake Placid (the US)
1972	Sapporo	Japan	Banff (Canada), Lahti/Are (Sweden), Salt Lake City (US)
1976	Innsbruck	Austria	Denver (the US), Sion (Switzerland), Tampere/Are (Finland), Vancouver (Canada)
1980	Lake Placid	The US	Vancouver—Garibaldi (Canada): withdrew before the final vote
1984	Sarajevo	Yugoslavia	Sapporo (Japan), Gothenburg (Sweden)

(*Continued*)

Year	Host city	Host country	Other candidates
1988	Calgary	Canada	Falun (Sweden), Cortina (Italy)
1992	Albertville	France	Anchorage (the US), Berchtesgaden (Germany), Cortina (Italy), Lillehammer (Norway), Falun (Sweden), Sofia (Bulgaria)
1994	Lillehammer	Norway	Anchorage (the US), Östersund/Are (Sweden), Sofia (Bulgaria)
1998	Nagano	Japan	Aoste (Italy), Jaca (Spain), Östersund (Sweden), Salt Lake City (the US)
2002	Salt Lake City	The US	Östersund (Sweden), Quebec City (Canada), Sion (Switzerland)
2006	Turin	Italy	Helsinki (Finland), Klagenfurt (Austria), Poprad—Tatry (Slovakia), Sion (Switzerland), Zakopane (Poland)
2010	Vancouver	Canada	Pyeongchang (South Korea), Salzburg (Austria)
2014	Sochi	Russia	Pyeongchang (South Korea), Salzburg (Austria)
2018	Pyeongchang	South Korea	Annecy (France), Munich (Germany)
2022	Beijing	China	Almaty (Kazakhstan)
2026	Milan and Cortina d'Ampezzo	Italy	Stockholm

Source: Compiled by author from IOC, 2022

1.1.1 The impact of the Olympic Games

As we will observe subsequently, from the first modern Olympic Games in Athens in 1896 to Tokyo in 2020, the Summer Olympics have been held 29 times, with 24 held in different cities in 17 countries. Meanwhile, the first Winter Olympics was held in Chamonix in 1924, and by Beijing 2022, 24 Games have been held in 21 different cities in 12 countries. Therefore, we can observe the Olympics' impact in multiple areas by looking at various projects in different socioeconomic contexts. Authors such as Andranovich and Burbank (2001) analyze the effects on cities and identify spatial transformation as the most visible impact and one of the most important legacies of the post-phase.[16] Subsequently, authors such as Kasimati (2003, 2006) and Kassen-Noor (2013) identify infrastructure as the most tangible and dangerous legacy for the future of candidate cities. Additionally, editions such as Rome, Tokyo, Mexico, Munich, Barcelona, Sydney, Turin, Vancouver, and London will allow you to observe how these mega-events remain an active and dynamic legacy of their host cities today. Therefore, the transformation of urban spaces, streets, and infrastructure requires new strategies to create synergies with existing urban forms without endangering the future of citizens.[17] Therefore, considering the visibility of urban impacts and physical changes in Olympic cities, we observe a first classification of urban intensity through the contribution of Essex and Chalkley (1998).

- Low impact: Athens 1896, Paris 1900, St. Louis 1904, London 1948, Mexico 1968, Los Angeles 1984.
- Games that have focused on the development of sports facilities: London 1908, Stockholm 1912, Los Angeles 1932, Berlin 1936, Helsinki 1952, Melbourne 1956, Atlanta 1996.
- Games that have transformed the city's urban identity: Rome 1960, Tokyo 1964, Munich 1972, Montreal 1976, Moscow 1980, Seoul 1988, Barcelona 1992, Sydney 2000.

However, the following group only refers to summer editions up to 2000. Table 3 lists the Olympic Games held so far and were not observable then. Table 4 shows the classification of urban impacts for the winter edition.

[16.] Andranovich, G., Burbank, M. J., & Heying, C. H. (2001). Olympic cities: Lessons learned from the politics of mega-events. *Journal of Urban Affairs, 23*(2), 113–131. Arsen, D. (1997). Is there really a link between infrastructure and economic development? In R. D. Bingham & R. Mier (Eds.), *Dilemmas of urban economic development: Issues in theory and practice* (pp. 82–98). Sage Publishing. Auruskeviciene, V., Pundziene, A., Skudiene, V., Gripsud, G., Nes, E. B., & Olsson, U. H. (2010). Change of attitudes and country image after hosting major sports events. *Inzinerine Ekonomika [Engeneering Economics], 21* (1), 53–59.

[17.] Bale, J., & Christensen, M. K. (2004). *Post-Olympic? Questioning sport in the Twenty-First Century.* BERG.

Table 3: Urban impact of the 2004-2028 Summer Olympics

Low impact	Sports facilities	Urban transformation
Paris 2024*	Beijing 2008	London 2012
Los Angeles 2028**	Rio 2016	Athens 2004
		Tokyo 2020

* The Paris 2024 edition will have 95% temporary or existing structures.
** The 2028 edition of Los Angeles will be an event with 100% temporary or existing structures.

Source: The following elaboration was provided from the groups provided by Essex and Chalkley in 1998

The winter version, on the other hand, requires the transformation of mountainous areas, specific facilities, and, ultimately, the transportation system, and we see it evolve differently over time than the summer version. Table 4 shows the different editions in three other groups based on the effects created.

Table 4: Urban impact of the Winter Olympics 1924-2026

Low impact	Sports facilities	Urban transformation
Chamonix 1924	Cortina 1956	Oslo 1952
Saint Moritz 1928	Squaw Valley 1960	Innsbruck 1964
Lake Placid 1932	Lake Placid 1980	Grenoble 1968
Garnish 1936	Sarajevo 1984	Sapporo 1972
Saint Moritz 1948	Lillehammer 1994	Innsbruck 1976
Calgary 1988	PyeongChang 2018	Albertville 1992
Salt Lake 2002		Nagano 1998
Milano Cortina 2026		Turin 2006
		Vancouver 2010
		Sochi 2014
		Beijing 2022

Source: Own implementation

Therefore, urban transformation and spatial design are of great importance for cities' social and economic aspects. Considering the natural conditions, planning and constructing new sports facilities in mountainous areas is a sensitive issue. In addition, ski jumping facilities and bobsled tracks are among the most problematic facilities that still raise questions and criticism for the IOC. However, spatial changes need to be integrated into dynamic structures based on long-term planning.

Authors Chalkley and Essex agree with Preuss (2004) and stress the importance of effective design of facilities in the post-Olympic period,[18] which fosters the development of sports practice and tends to secure accommodation for the poorest citizens (Chalkley, 1999).

Then, in 2014, with a view to mega-events in urban processes, Hiller identified the following phenomena that could be realized in candidate cities:

- The catalyst for urban change.
- Land-use change in urban space.
- Stimulation of creativity in spatial planning.
- They mobilize funding (private and public).
- Support in projects is considered to be very ambitious or costly.
- Requires completion by the date of the event.
- Structural improvements in specific sectors (e.g., transport).
- It produces specific structures that redefine urban space and territory.

However, urban transformation can impact different sociocultural, political, and economic areas. Furthermore, since the 2006 Turin edition, environmental impact has become a fundamental factor in selecting candidate cities. Subsequently, changing the image of a town through lifestyle promotion can help increase national pride and have a sociocultural impact on host communities. Meanwhile, Preuss, in her 2000 study, identifies tourism as the most essential socioeconomic impact on Olympic cities after the Olympics. Moreover, the international promotion of an Olympic city should motivate businesses and investors to visit the city and take advantage of new services developed for the post-Olympic future (Billings, 2012). For example, Barcelona's post-Olympic plans are based on creating

---

[18] Chalkley, B., & Essex, S. (1999). Urban development through hosting international events: A history of Olympic Games. *Planning Perspectives, 14*, 369–394.

new sectors dedicated to technological development. Therefore, investments in telecommunications are included in the budget to provide companies with new services of high technical value (Brunet, 2005). In Sydney, pre-Olympic planning was an example of an international company's advertising campaign. The city and State conducted a targeted campaign to encourage global companies to hold conferences and events in the city that hosted the 2000 Olympics. This promotional effort allowed the City of Sydney to host events continuously over 4 years. The next significant achievement was Sydney's entry into the international meetings, conventions and events market, which was surprising and perhaps unprecedented.[19]

The Olympic Games can only guarantee their own development if the quality of management and planning is close to perfection (Chalkley, 1999; Essex, 1998; Gratton, 2002; Preuss, 2000, 2004). Why do cities want to host the Olympics? Over time, we have observed different political motivations that remain important for host countries. Additionally, in recent years, the bidding process has completely changed to include submissions by each country's prime minister.[20] At the political level,[21] hosting the Olympics is often presented as an opportunity to stimulate new job creation and increase countries' gross domestic product.[22]

Starting around 2000, the number of protest groups[23] against the hosting of the Olympic Games increased dramatically and became an active movement.[24] To force the government to decline political candidacy (Heine, 2018). However, the phenomenon of referendum remains a fundamental element for recognizing and confirming a joint development model for all *stakeholders* in this event.

---

[19] To achieve the following result, the Sydney Organising Committee involved the top experts in Olympic planning, ensuring a unique development for the entire community.

[20] In 2021, for the first time, Australia's prime minister presented the official Melbourne 2032 bid 11 years before the Olympic event, something that had never happened before.

[21] Political interest focuses on the possibility of attracting new foreign investors and increasing the capital available to meet or attempt to meet the real needs of citizens.

[22] Matheson, V. A. (2006). *Mega-events: The effect of the world's most significant sporting events on local, regional, and national economies.* College of the Holy Cross, Department of Economics. Matheson, V. A., & Baade, R. A. (2004). Mega- sporting events in developing nations: Playing the way to prosperity? *South African Journal of Economics, 72*(5), 1084–1095. McDonogh, G. (1991). Discourses of the City: Policy and response in post-transitional Barcelona. *City and Society, 5*(1), 40–63.

[23] For example, Munich in 2018 was forced to withdraw its bid because citizens, through a popular referendum, did not want any events in those locations chosen by third parties.

[24] NOlympics is recognized as one of the most functional movements internationally.

On the other hand, the economic impact of the Olympics is highly debatable. Some of the authors have conducted detailed studies on funding structures, public capital investments, marketing studies, and the strategic organization of *stakeholders* for the future of candidate cities.

Therefore, quantifying the actual economic benefits of candidate cities remains very difficult. For example, in his 2004 study, Preuss cited tourism as the most significant financial benefit that Olympic cities could achieve over the long term.[25]

Furthermore, in 2000[26] Preuss identified two central points when considering economic aspects:

- *Increased demand*→ Increased the number of employees, increased the domestic economy, and increased employees and profits. Preuss foresees rapid inflation after the Olympics as a possible downside if the economic restructuring plan is not planned or does not work.
- *International attractiveness*→ Increased numbers of tourists who, if they leave positive feedback, can contribute to incalculable long-term benefits. In addition, the increase in tourists and travelers will enable the city to acquire a new image in the global community.

Indeed, according to Preuss, the economic analysis of an event should be divided into event-related spectator spending and non-Olympic spending. Other values, such as unemployment rates in Olympic host cities, should not be compared to when the Olympics were held. Logically, during the construction of Olympic works the unemployment rate will decrease due to practical needs. Still, in the post-Olympic period, the situation is different. Preuss (2000) then identified price increases.[27] As the most relevant negative impact associated with increased tourism in candidate cities, price increases can quickly cause temporary inflation in host communities, inevitably leading to social inequality. Finally, transforming a city's image and building a brand will help attract millions of tourists and businesses willing to invest in the host city in the long run. However, increasing tourist flows and business pressures on cities can affect the development of host societies and create new inequalities over time (Smith, 2009).

[25.] Preuss, H. (2004). *The economics of staging the Olympics: A comparison of the Games, 1972–2008.* Edward Elgar Publishing Limited.

[26.] Preuss, H. (2000). *Economics of the Olympic Games.* Walla Walla Press.

[27.] For example, in Barcelona in 1993, one year after the event, prices increased by 240% compared to the pre-Olympic period.

In conclusion, the physical transformation of a city and its image is a sensitive issue that should be dynamically programmed between the town and its inhabitants. In a city like Barcelona, for example, tourism is a fundamental element of the entire region's economy and has developed over the years, always to the detriment of its citizens. In Barcelona, the loss of emblematic places, the transformation of new districts, the creation of new offices, rising prices, and the planning of unique hotels are causing residents to move from the center to the periphery. Furthermore, rising prices and job insecurity are considered to be the main effects of gentrification in Barcelona. In 2012, London's bid for the Olympics led to the gentrification of Olympic venues due to rising prices and changes in the labor market. In recent years, research on the impact of the Olympic Games has increasingly focused on the use of new mixed models for post-Olympic management and organization.

1.2 Planning the Olympic Village

1.2.1 Introduction to the Olympic Villages

"The Olympic Games through the candidate cities represent the image of the strategy for the promotion of the space with the achievement of a competitive advantage over other cities."
(Whitson & Macintosh, 1996)

In modern times, candidate cities are seeing potential for large-scale sporting events. The host city used the event to strengthen its image in the world and accelerate the process of globalization. According to Hiller (2000, 2003), from an urban perspective, any large-scale event can be considered a mega-event if it has significant and lasting urban development effects on the urban fabric. Moreover, this event is regarded as a new priority for the city council. In that case, the urban planning agenda will inevitably prioritize including the Olympic project in the overall transformation plan. Future work involving spatial modifications and changes will further the urban legacy of the Olympic Games (Hiller, 2014). According to Harvey, one of the critical elements of post-industrial cities is urban revitalization through gentrification, leisure, and entertainment (Harvey, 1991).

Furthermore, new urban entertainment structures are created in the central spaces of post-industrial cities. Further, specific urban entertainment districts

(UEDs) are developed (Sorkin, 1992). Therefore, mega-events preferentially intervene in normal urban processes and require long-term and large-scale preparations to facilitate shared resources of realization and expectations. Considering the construction process and reuse of the Olympic Village, therefore, Olympic urbanization in general and the Olympic Village in particular represent a concrete case of urban transformation (Muñoz, 1996). The Olympic Village is considered to be the heart of the Olympic project, both in terms of its function during the Games and, above all, in its subsequent use (Muñoz, 1996). In this way, Olympic events help observe the host city's urban development by renovating spaces in the urban fabric and creating new urban areas. However, research on the Olympic Village includes the study of the city and the planning and processes of specific interventions for the temporary accommodation of athletes. The origin of the Olympic Village concept is based on the ideas of Baron Pierre de Coubertin. The idea of creating a new "modern Olympia" was openly presented to a group of architects by the Baron as early as 1910 (Muñoz, 1996). The Olympic Village is defined as a complex organized in different locations to celebrate the Olympic event and was inspired by the internationalism and desire for world peace that was characteristic of the thinking of European intellectuals in the first half of the 20th century (Gresleri, 1994). The Baron's idea was to create territorial space through sport and education to achieve other goals, reflecting the philosophy of Thomas Arnold in 1830. From this point of view, Coubertin's proposals had many similarities with modern proposals, such as the "cosmopolitan city" envisioned by architect Ernest Hébrard in 1910.[28] Suppose this cosmopolitan city can be defined as the new capital of peace and ideas. In that case, Coubertin's Olympic city can be described as the capital of peace and sport (Muñoz, 1996). Therefore, the concentration of athletes, officials and visitors began to force the IOC to consider the issue of accommodation as a priority, taking into account the host city and its availability. However, at that time it was not easy to manage accommodation independently, especially since the IOC had not yet been defined in terms of national budgets (Muñoz, 1996). The initial solution was to spread the event across cities with available hotels and negotiate rates for all participants. The accommodation situation was characterized by complete improvisation,

---

[28] Muñoz, F. (1996). Historic evolution and urban planning typology of Olympic Villages. In Miquel de Moragas, Montserrat Llinés, & Bruce Kidd (Eds.), *Olympic Villages: A hundred years of urban planning and shared experiences: International Symposium on Olympic Villages, Lausanne* (p. 28). IOC.

with some countries using boats to transport and accommodate their delegations.[29] Over time, the organizing Committee had to look for other locations that could be converted into temporary accommodation, such as hospitals, schools, military camps, and rental boats. The first decade was marked by the need to find accommodation for the participants. However, the regulation of the Games and the construction of the first Olympic Village in Paris in 1924 provided a clear signal for the debate about the status of future Olympic accommodation. Therefore, the first phenomenon observed in the first Olympic Village in Paris in 1924 is definitely an emergency (Muñoz, 2006). Due to temporary obligations to accommodate Olympic athletes, timely decisions had to be made to secure accommodation for the duration of the event. The Olympic Village in Paris was planned as barracks on uninhabited land near the Olympic Stadium. It provided essential services but had few elements in common with the first Olympic Village built for Los Angeles. It is crucial to point out that Event 1932. During the 1930 Berlin Conference, IOC members began discussing new accommodation solutions. Zach Farmer promised a new way to solve the accommodation problem, offering a solution that included food for two dollars a day.[30] Then, in 1936, Berlin began building permanent villages, taking shape as a construction site with a significant physical impact on the territory. As stated in the organizing committee for the Olympic Games' (OCOG) 1936 official report, the Berlin Organizing Committee's desire was to recreate the Olympic Village in Los Angeles to emphasize and recreate the modern city of Elis (OCOG, 1936). Therefore, the organizing Committee proposed a permanent solution using the Döberitz military camp, approximately 21 km from the Olympic venue. However, as in Los Angeles in 1932, the women were interned separately. The villages of Los Angeles and Berlin were the type that promoted and inspired the housing model that would lay the foundation for villages throughout the century. From this moment on, this residential building formed a new image of the "Olympic City" by incorporating sports facilities into its architectural ensemble. The concept of Olympia Residences is, therefore, much more than just a temporary location for Olympia accommodation. The Olympic Village began to evolve by defining new proposals to realize and redefine spaces beyond specific sports spaces. Over time, the Olympic Village

---

[29.] The issue of travel and accommodation costs for delegations will be one of the main topics of discussion in connection with the increase in the number of participants.

[30.] The American offer of accommodation, meals, and use of local transport took a lot of work to refuse. Therefore, the Village of Los Angeles will become an inspirational model for future candidate cities.

will become an essential element in promoting the structural modernization of the city and, in some cases, a model for the future development of the host city. Looking at successful models such as Rome (1960), Munich (1972), Barcelona (1992), Sydney (2000), Vancouver (2010), and London (2012), cities of the future will need to shape themselves to take on new roles via the city network. The summer version of the Olympic City Plan consists of the Village, Olympic Stadium and Olympic Pool. Undoubtedly, the following buildings form the architectural heritage of the Olympic Games in the host city. Urban heritage, which considers each host country's cultural, social, political, economic and sporting history, can be an essential element in creating new socioeconomic dynamics. However, the Olympic Games and the Olympic Village have played a fundamental role in restructuring urban space since Rome in 1960, prompting a reconsideration of the project's scope for future interventions.[31] In Oslo, Rome, Mexico, Grenoble, Munich, Barcelona, Sydney, Turin, Vancouver, and London, we demonstrate how the Olympic Village remains an active and dynamic heritage site, permeating the fabric and form of cities. Therefore, when building new housing or new projects in a city, it is necessary to consider the possibility of an Olympic village and thoroughly evaluate all possibilities for the city's future. Therefore, the Olympic Village is the cornerstone of the urban regeneration project through the Olympic Games. Urban styles, material choices, and the use of new construction techniques, supported by changes in infrastructure, present unique opportunities for candidate cities, which should be considered in light of the cities' existing plans and future projects. It must be done. As explained in the next section, the typologies of Olympic Villages adopted by candidate cities in the history of the Olympic Games can be analyzed through various permanent and temporary models. Constructing an Olympic village can only be considered prudent to fulfil the Olympic Committee's obligations. Cities need to see the Olympic Village as an integral part of a new urban development philosophy that can promote healthy lifestyles through sport. Only by considering the actual needs of residents can permanent projects meet host communities' expectations. Otherwise, interim solutions are the best way to avoid jeopardizing the long-term future of the candidate city. For example, the Olympic villages of Athens, Turin, Sochi, Rio, and Pyeongchang still jeopardize the future of the host cities. This State of neglect resulted from choosing a permanent model, which was not included in the

---

[31.] In 1960, Rome was the first Olympic city to use the Olympic event as a catalyst for other urban and infrastructural transformations proposed by the city's post-war reconstruction.

post-Olympic accommodation plans. These examples of abandoned buildings allow us to consider the importance of Olympic urban planning to ensure that the host city's land is not permanently jeopardized. Over time, various projects involving the transformation or renovation of urban spaces have been observed.

Recognition of the impact of the Olympic Village has led to the introduction of a new mixed model for the realization of accommodation. Building an Olympic village in the center of a city would change the range of services, increase prices, and accelerate the process of gentrification in the new area. In addition, identifying land in some countries, including Sydney, Athens, Beijing, and Rio, has led to people's relocation to construct the Olympic Village. At the same time, Beijing's regional changes will lead to changes in land prices and, as a result, changes in its uses in the post-Olympic phase (Zou et al., 2015). In the long term, the Olympic Village will play a central role in the physical transformation of the space. Land-use changes need to be considered and incorporated into the overall master plan to revamp the socio-urban and economic fabric of the city. On the other hand, changes in land-use values may lead to real estate speculation and gentrification.

On the other hand, organizing the Olympic Games with multiple Olympic Villages contributes to spatial changes in different areas of the region. Regarding the Olympic Village, it is necessary to refer to Millet's 1996 contribution to its relationship with the city. According to Millet (1996), due to the complexity of developing an Olympic village with mixed financing in some towns, cities need to justify the construction of accommodation facilities in other ways. However, choosing a different venue can improve the layout of facilities across the area without negatively impacting the host city. Millet (1996) and Muñoz (1996) argue that no standard development model can be identified in the history of Olympic Villages. Therefore, the Olympic Village model mainly depends on the urban context and the master plan in each host city.

Millet (1996), in his analysis, identifies four generic cases that represent the planning of the Olympic Village:

- *Zero impact*→ Where the Olympic effect does not cause much structural change. Los Angeles, Calgary, Atlanta, and Salt Lake are examples of the use of student accommodation).
- *Urban spread*→ The Munich Olympic Village of 1972 respected the general strategy of the city's master plan, developing new neighborhoods with access to infrastructure, and parks and using the Olympic Village as a model.

- *Urban renewal*→ Rome, Tokyo, Barcelona, and Turin are the most important examples. The Olympic Village was developed with more qualitative than quantitative aspects in mind, allowing a temporal revaluation of the area.
- *Mixed option*→ In Seoul 88, we can see how the Olympic Village was in the middle of relocating factories on its territory (Millet, 1996).

After having introduced the Olympic Villages, in the following sections, we will look at the IOC standards for the construction of the Olympic Village, the typology, the spatial model and the formal language of Olympic accommodation in the summer and winter editions. By analyzing the different evolutionary stages of Olympic accommodation, we will provide some food for thought about future new projects to be planned by the candidate cities.

1.2.2 The Olympic Village Symposium

The 1996 Symposium on the Olympic Village in Lausanne is considered the first Olympic symposium organized on the initiative of the *Centre d'Estudis Olimpics [Olympic Studies Centre (CEO-UAB)]*, the International Olympic Committee and the Lausanne Olympic Museum. To this day, this symposium is considered the only moment to reflect on the projects carried out and the future development of this subject at an academic level. The contributions of experts at this symposium showed that the Olympic Village raises several essential questions about the relationship between the Olympic Village and the Olympic Games.

- Planning/market.
- Redevelopment/extension.
- Public sector/private initiative.
- Social policies/private profit.
- Integration/segregation.
- Innovation/tradition.
- Environmental concerns/economic growth.
- Utopia/reality.

Based on the relationships below, the planning and location of the Olympic Village could determine rather than influence the housing market. They could lead to uncertainty about the future of housing in the host city.

Architectural design, area redevelopment and service enhancements will be some of the most influential factors in determining how the village functions post-Olympic. Additionally, the symposium emphasizes the importance of the Olympic Village as a central location for transmitting the Olympic experience between all cultures worldwide. The seminar highlighted the importance of viewing the Olympic Village as a central place where athletes from all over the world live together before and during the Games, thereby fostering a sublime sense of understanding and camaraderie between participants from each country. We could promote our ideals and contribute to the international community's development. Olympic sports. Currently, Olympic Villages are required to accommodate the following numbers of participants, depending on the edition:

- Summer: approximately 20,000 people
- Winter: approximately 5,000 people

Additionally, to comply with IOC requirements, housing proposals must be planned using the following housing typologies:

- New housing development in the host city
- Use existing housing, such as hotels, student dormitories, resorts, and barracks.
- Temporary facilities such as *bungalows* or demountable trailers

This symposium, therefore, aims to provide an overview of the various phenomena observed up to 1996 and to provide considerations for future discussions regarding Olympic accommodation (Moragas, 1996). During the symposium, Muñoz (1996) presented new observations on the different solutions of the host city and analyzed the other urban models and formal languages that had a lasting impact on the history of the summer edition. Throughout the history of the Olympic Village, we have seen different solutions in the typology and integration of permanent facilities into the urban fabric of the host city. Other solutions for host cities allow you to think about the stages of development of Olympic housing, as described in the following paragraphs. The symposium will also consider the importance of transportation systems during the Olympic Games. From this moment on, the planning and temporal redefinition of a viable system will be regarded as a fundamentally important element for the transportation of

Olympic athletes. In 1996, the IOC first introduced its own feasibility typology for athlete routes during events:

- Within the Village (carbon-neutral)
- From the Village to the competition sites
- From the Village to the city center
- Between the airport and the Village

Introducing a new dedicated route will undoubtedly require a reconsideration of the design plan of the Olympic Village and the operational plan of its functions from an urban planning perspective (Kassen-Knoll, 2016). After profitability problems were seen in Atlanta in 1996, the IOC did not want to jeopardize the Olympics by postponing sports competitions. Therefore, regarding the management of the Olympic Village, the IOC requires the Organizing Committee to establish a steering committee for the planning and management of the Olympic Village operations at least 4 years before the Games (IOC, 1996). Village management should be involved in the conception, strategic planning, and execution of the event during its implementation. IOC 1996 identifies the next steps for planning the design of Olympic accommodation.

- Planning assumptions
- Identify and acquire
- Block planning
- Permanent design and construction
- Design, construction, and temporary fitting-out

In addition, factors to consider when determining the permanent design should be:

- Physical constraints of the Olympic Village site
- Requirements defined in the Olympic Village technical manual
- Requirements specified during block planning
- Use of permanent buildings after the games
- Infrastructure requirements (sewerage, waste, water, energy)

The IOC then acknowledged that funding for the permanent construction of the Olympic Village would generally come from government sources and identified several possibilities for future host cities.

- Private investors
- Public companies
- The future owners of the site
- The construction company itself

Finally, scientific considerations point out that the Olympic Village must necessarily include training and service facilities in the international area. Furthermore, as explained in the specific section, the Olympic Village must be implemented in accordance with IOC guidelines and technical manuals, respecting the construction and operation specifications for the entire Olympic Village area. When constructing sports facilities, host cities comply with the instructions contained in their respective technical manuals. The IOC, therefore, makes the following distinctions regarding the sports facilities included in the Olympic Village:

- Winter→ Gymnasium, men's and women's changing rooms
- Summer→ Gymnasium, jogging route inside the Olympic Village (1 km minimum), Saunas, male and female changing rooms.

Based on the following factors, the 1996 Olympic Symposium is a starting point for reflection and research on the development of summer and winter Olympic villages. Furthermore, the next section describes the basic requirements and characteristics a city must meet to plan and organize an Olympic village. However, as the research results show, holding a new symposium is essential to understanding the new urban phenomena that have appeared on the stage of the new Olympic Games of the 21st century.

1.2.3 Main Requirements

The following section describes the commitments required by the IOC in relation to the construction of the Olympic Village in the host city.

- The predisposition of the areas is as follows: Residential Area (athletes' accommodation) and International Area (services, shops, and cultural facilities). The Olympic Village must remain open 24 hours a day for authorized persons.

- Dimension: Summer (20,000 athletes) (see Figure 1), Winter (5,000 athletes) (see Figure 2)
- Typology: New development, existing dwellings, temporary dwellings
- Additional staff 1,550 (1,000 rooms) and 800 for Winter Games (300 rooms)
- Dimension of accommodation: for two athletes, a minimum size of 15 m^2 and a private bathroom must be respected. Meanwhile, for officials, eight-person flats can be provided with at least three toilets and three showers.

The organization of the area international

- Administrative headquarters of the delegations: Summer Olympic Games: 10,000 m^2; Winter Olympic Games: 2,200 m^2.
- Restaurants: Summer Olympic Games 5,000-6,000 seats + kitchens, shops = 12,000 m^2; Winter Olympic Games 1,200-1,400 seats + kitchens, shops = 2,800 m^2.
- Delegation offices: Summer Olympics: 10,000 m^2; Winter Olympics: 2,500 m^2.
- Changing rooms: Summer Olympic Games 6,000 m^2 (for 9,000 people); Winter Olympic Games 1,500 m^2 (for 2,100 people)
- Training areas: Summer Olympics 30,000 m^2; Winter Olympics 5,000 m^2.
- Leisure center: Summer Olympic Games 2,000 m^2; Winter Olympic Games 700 m^2.
- Shopping center: Summer YOG 2,000 m^2; Winter YOG 500 m^2.
- Logistics center: Summer Olympics 10,000 m^2; Winter Olympics: 2,200 m^2.

Services inside the Olympic Village

- National Olympic Committee (NOC) Service Center
- NOC Sports Information Center
- Shopping center
- Laundry service, dry cleaning
- Office service center with language and secretarial services on request, photocopiers, service station and/or sports equipment repair shop
- TV room with capacity for live or delayed coverage of Olympic events on request
- Games rooms, discotheques, and other leisure facilities
- Relaxation facilities such as sauna and swimming pool

- Cafés and bars
- Photographic laboratories, flower shops, hairdressing salons, beauty salons
- Post office
- Bank, travel agency, and tourist office
- Various religious centers and meditation halls
- Meeting and conference rooms for team use
- Key features of the Paralympic Village
- The geographical location of the largest Village
- Topography
- Relationship to the nearest city
- Nature of buildings
- Rooms
- Toilet/bathrooms
- Food service—24 hours
- Security
- Internal services
- Support services
- Information system
- Circulation in the village/space
- Climatic factors
- Specialized medicine

1.2.4 Olympic Village Technical Manual

The Olympic Village Technical Manual[32] is one of the mandatory documents that host cities must adhere to when planning and managing Olympic events. According to Rule 39 of the Olympic Charter, organizers must build an Olympic Village as temporary accommodation for athletes and Olympic officials. The Olympic Village is considered a strategic location for knowledge transfer that fosters cultural exchange between participants. However, some obligations must be met to benefit the participant experience. The Olympic Village is required to:

[32.] The Olympic Village technical manual is a document that was updated in 2015 and is one of the 33 technical manuals that host cities are obliged to consider for the planning and organization of the event.

Figure 1: Dimension of the area of the Summer Olympic Village

Annex : Relational Plan of Surface Areas
(Scale 1:10,000)

Games of the Olympiad

(The surface areas indicated give the approximate number of m² of raw floor space developed).

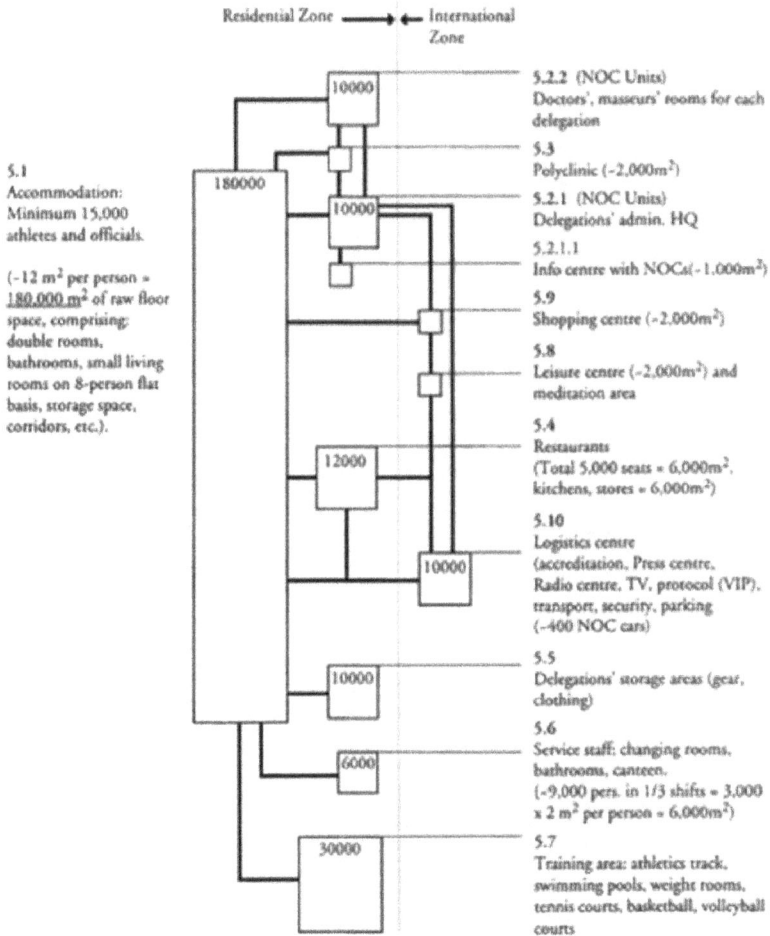

Residential Zone ⟶ ⟵ International Zone

5.1
Accommodation:
Minimum 15,000
athletes and officials.

(~12 m² per person =
180,000 m² of raw floor
space, comprising:
double rooms,
bathrooms, small living
rooms on 8-person flat
basis, storage space,
corridors, etc.).

180000

10000

10000

12000

10000

10000

6000

30000

5.2.2 (NOC Units)
Doctors', masseurs' rooms for each
delegation

5.3
Polyclinic (~2,000m²)

5.2.1 (NOC Units)
Delegations' admin. HQ

5.2.1.1
Info centre with NOCs(~1,000m²)

5.9
Shopping centre (~2,000m²)

5.8
Leisure centre (~2,000m²) and
meditation area

5.4
Restaurants
(Total 5,000 seats = 6,000m²,
kitchens, stores = 6,000m²)

5.10
Logistics centre
(accreditation, Press centre,
Radio centre, TV, protocol (VIP),
transport, security, parking
(~400 NOC cars)

5.5
Delegations' storage areas (gear,
clothing)

5.6
Service staff: changing rooms,
bathrooms, canteen.
(~9,000 pers. in 1/3 shifts = 3,000
x 2 m² per person = 6,000m²)

5.7
Training area: athletics track,
swimming pools, weight rooms,
tennis courts, basketball, volleyball
courts

Source: IOC, 1996

Figure 2: Dimension of the area of the Winter Olympic Village

Annex : Relational Plan of Surface Areas
(Scale 1:10,000)

Olympic Winter Games

(The surface areas indicated give the approximate number of m² of raw floor space developed).

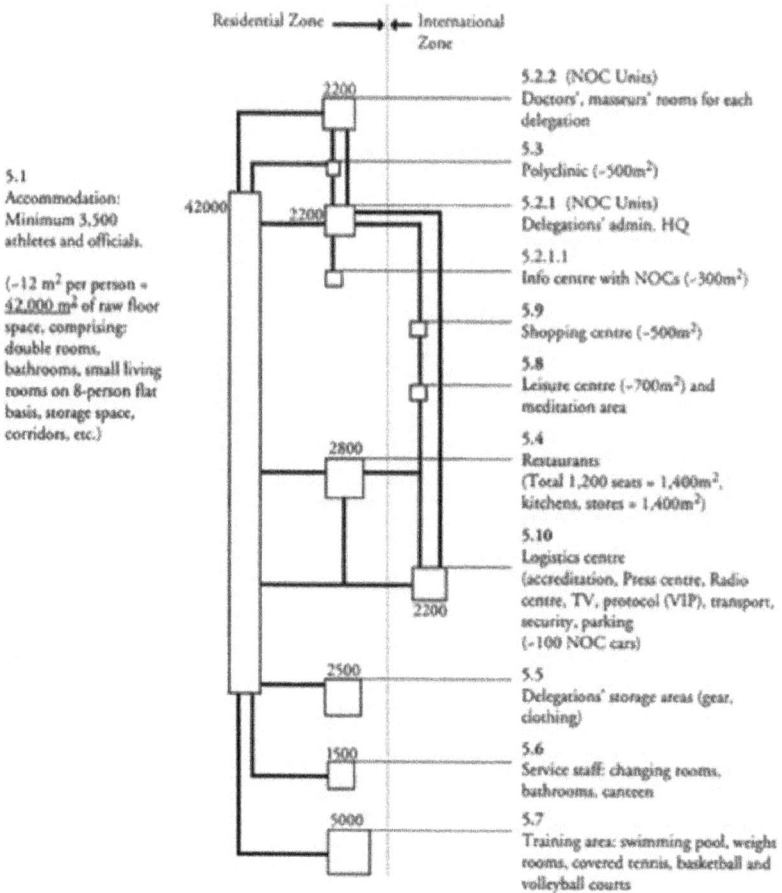

Residential Zone ⟶ ⟵ International Zone

5.1
Accommodation:
Minimum 3,500
athletes and officials.

(~12 m² per person =
42,000 m² of raw floor
space, comprising:
double rooms,
bathrooms, small living
rooms on 8-person flat
basis, storage space,
corridors, etc.)

42000

2200

2200

2800

2200

2500

1500

5000

5.2.2 (NOC Units)
Doctors', masseurs' rooms for each
delegation

5.3
Polyclinic (~500m²)

5.2.1 (NOC Units)
Delegations' admin. HQ

5.2.1.1
Info centre with NOCs (~300m²)

5.9
Shopping centre (~500m²)

5.8
Leisure centre (~700m²) and
meditation area

5.4
Restaurants
(Total 1,200 seats = 1,400m²,
kitchens, stores = 1,400m²)

5.10
Logistics centre
(accreditation, Press centre, Radio
centre, TV, protocol (VIP), transport,
security, parking
(~100 NOC cars)

5.5
Delegations' storage areas (gear,
clothing)

5.6
Service staff: changing rooms,
bathrooms, canteen

5.7
Training area: swimming pool, weight
rooms, covered tennis, basketball and
volleyball courts

Source: IOC, 1996

- Operate 24 hours a day.
- To be protected from the general public and the media.
- Provide the necessary facilities for athletes and officials.

The objectives of the technical manual on the Olympic Village are:

- Provide applicant and candidate cities with information to develop their Olympic Village plans.
- Provide the OCOGs with the structural information to plan and build the Olympic Village.
- Provide information on the planning and operational requirements of the Paralympic Village.
- Guide an OCOG to design, plan, construct and operate an Olympic Village for the Olympic Games, Winter Games and Paralympic Games.

Olympic village requirements must, therefore, be tailored to the host city and respective location. However, the Olympic Village Technical Manual requirements are standard requirements that are subject to change following discussions with the IOC and its stakeholders (IOC, 2005a). While the event plan is being refined, planning and construction of the permanent building can begin. The endless construction authority usually leads the planning and construction phase of athletes' accommodation. It requires the regular participation of the Olympic Village management. Factors to consider when determining the permanent design are (IOC, 2015d):

- The physical limitations of the Olympic Village;
- The requirements are defined in the IOC Technical Manual on Olympic Village (IOC, 2005b);
- The requirements defined during the planning of the block;
- Use of permanent buildings after the Games;
- Infrastructure requirements (sewerage, waste, water, energy).

Continuous communication between the authorities responsible for construction and the management of the Olympic Village is an essential prerequisite for its successful design. The IOC notes that past experience should be considered when determining the consumption of water, electricity, waste and other utilities to reconstruct villages after the Olympics. Therefore, it must be taken into account that the Olympic Village requires much more supply resources than a typical residential complex. It would be beneficial to study the technical requirements of the Olympic Village and incorporate these to reduce temporary costs and bring intangible benefits to the Olympic City. Additionally, consider the need for quick construction (such as electricity and water) to ensure the Olympic Village can accommodate additional demand during the Games.

1.2.5 Olympic Village obligations

The Olympic Village Technical Manual outlines the following obligations for host cities:

- In the case of several Olympic Villages, the proposal must be submitted to the IOC for approval;
- The OCOG only has to offer the general layout of the Olympic Village to the IOC for approval;
- Specific visits should be allowed throughout the construction phases of the Olympic Village;
- At the start of the exclusive use, the management of the Olympic Village must carry out a walk-through of the site with the owners;
- Area control points, access control points and vehicle checkpoints must be operational;
- The accommodation must have at most two persons per room.
- No more than four persons per bathroom;
- All NOCs must have adequate accommodation, office space, medical space and storage space;
- The OCOG should provide a media center in the Village to allow the media a working area in the Olympic Village;
- The OCOG must complete and establish block planning, policies and procedures in the Olympic Village;
- The pre-opening period of the Olympic Games starts 7 days before the official opening of the Olympic Village;
- It officially opens 14 days before the opening ceremony for summer and 10 days before for Winter;
- The Olympic Village closes 3 days after the closing ceremony;

- The OCOG must complete a housing allocation process in the Olympic Village;
- Transport must be operated by the OCOG (IOC, 2005c).

1.2.6 Olympic Village managements

In its Olympic Village Technical Manual, the IOC defines the basic organizational structure of the Olympic Village as follows:

Figure 3: Organization of the Olympic Village

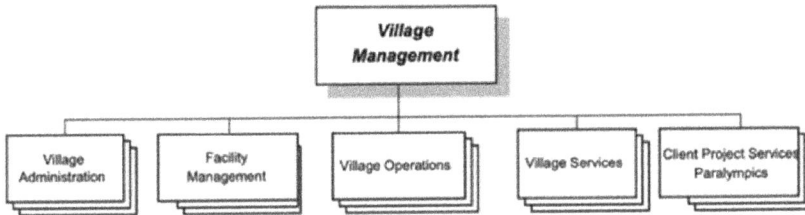

Source: IOC, 2015d

Meanwhile, regarding the operational management of the Village, the Committee should direct the following:

- The design of the Olympic Village;
- The strategic planning of the Olympic Village;
- The functioning of the Olympic Village;
- In addition, the Village management must cooperate with;
- THE IOC;
- THE CIP;
- The owners of the Village;
- Public security;
- Several municipalities/local governments;
- Construction companies/architects;
- Contractors;
- Government agencies, health and safety, and environmental organizations.

In addition, specific visits should be allowed throughout the construction phases of the Olympic Village.

Olympic Square

The Olympic Village Plaza[33] (OVP) shall host the following activities and venues:

- Welcome ceremonies for the teams;
- Retail services;
- Recreational services;
- Meeting rooms;
- Village management offices (optional).

1.2.7 Olympic Village planning

The operational plan is considered the basis for the operation of the Olympic Village. It should be organized into four primary phases:

- Strategic planning;
- Concept planning;
- Operational planning;
- Operational readiness.

At this stage, the Village Department must:

- Strategic scenarios;
- Working meetings;
- Contingency plans and crisis scenarios;
- Actual testing of functions and services;
- Identify the specific roles and responsibilities of all staff, volunteers and contractors.

[33.] The Olympic Plaza was first introduced in Los Angeles in 1932. Since then, it has become the central venue for the medal celebrations of Olympic athletes.

Figure 4: Layout of the Olympic Village area

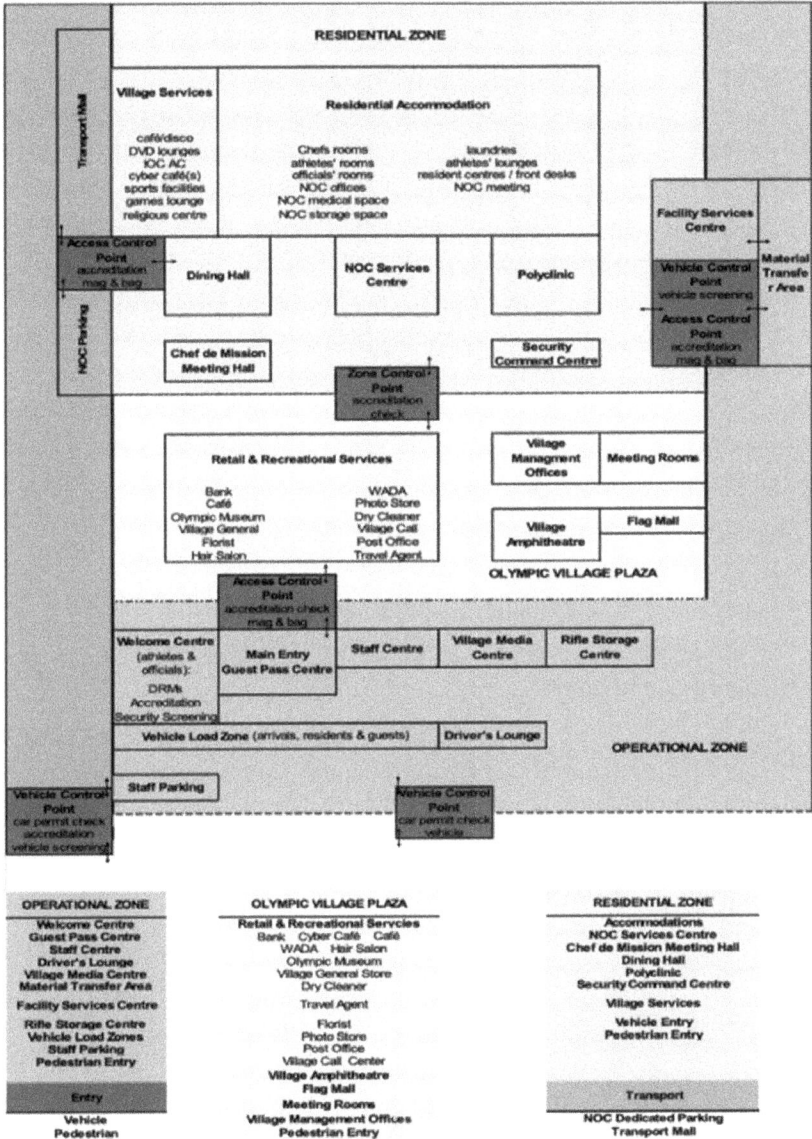

RESIDENTIAL ZONE

Transport Mall

Village Services

café/disco
DVD lounges
IOC AC
cyber café(s)
sports facilities
games lounge
religious centre

Residential Accommodation

Chefs rooms
athletes' rooms
officials' rooms
NOC offices
NOC medical space
NOC storage space

laundries
athletes' lounges
resident centres / front desks
NOC meeting

Facility Services Centre

NOC Parking

Access Control Point
accreditation
mag & bag

Dining Hall

NOC Services Centre

Polyclinic

Vehicle Control Point
vehicle screening

Material Transfer Area

Access Control Point
accreditation
mag & bag

Chef de Mission Meeting Hall

Zone Control Point
accreditation
check

Security Command Centre

Retail & Recreational Services

Bank
Café
Olympic Museum
Village General
Florist
Hair Salon

WADA
Photo Store
Dry Cleaner
Village Call
Post Office
Travel Agent

Village Managment Offices

Meeting Rooms

Village Amphitheatre

Flag Mall

OLYMPIC VILLAGE PLAZA

Access Control Point
accreditation check
mag & bag

Welcome Centre
(athletes & officials):
DRM&
Accreditation
Security Screening

Main Entry
Guest Pass Centre

Staff Centre

Village Media Centre

Rifle Storage Centre

Vehicle Load Zone (arrivals, residents & guests)

Driver's Lounge

OPERATIONAL ZONE

Staff Parking

Vehicle Control Point
car permit check
accreditation
vehicle screening

Vehicle Control Point
car permit check
vehicle

OPERATIONAL ZONE	OLYMPIC VILLAGE PLAZA	RESIDENTIAL ZONE
Welcome Centre	Retail & Recreational Servcies	Accommodations
Guest Pass Centre	Bank Cyber Café Café	NOC Services Centre
Staff Centre	WADA Hair Salon	Chef de Mission Meeting Hall
Driver's Lounge	Olympic Museum	Dining Hall
Village Media Centre	Village General Store	Polyclinic
Material Transfer Area	Dry Cleaner	Security Command Centre
Facility Services Centre	Travel Agent	Village Services
Rifle Storage Centre	Florist	Vehicle Entry
Vehicle Load Zones	Photo Store	Pedestrian Entry
Staff Parking	Post Office	
Pedestrian Entry	Village Call Center	
	Village Amphitheatre	
Entry	Flag Mall	Transport
	Meeting Rooms	
Vehicle	Village Management Offices	NOC Dedicated Parking
Pedestrian	Pedestrian Entry	Transport Mall

Source: IOC, 2005b

The Olympic Village is typically the largest construction project of the Olympic Games and usually involves large investments (IOC, 2005c). Agencies other than the organizing Committee are involved in the construction phase. However, ongoing plans for the Olympic Village should be the responsibility of appropriate construction companies to bid through an open and transparent tendering process. If the Olympics are to be held in the European Union, this process must respect both EU and national laws. Importantly for the OCOG, bidding decisions are not necessarily based on the lowest bid but on what is best suited for the Olympic Village and post-Games use.

Regarding exterior planning, architects are often part of the construction group or authority responsible for construction. In this case, the OCOG has less control over the design, but the post-game usage is more detailed. It is important that there is constant communication between the permanent construction authority and the Olympic Village management and that the OCOG monitors construction to ensure that what is planned is being built.

The OCOG shall define the construction requirements for:

- Utilities (e.g., water, electricity, sewerage);
- Technology (e.g., computer network and information system);
- Telecommunications;
- CATV;
- Foundation and soil requirements;
- Heating/cooling requirements; safety considerations;
- Main service buildings of the Village; access roads and internal roads; fences;
- Lifts;
- Lighting;
- Parking;
- Ensuring accuracy and quality of construction;
- Liaison with builders/architects (design team).

Design and temporary construction will be determined by the design of the permanent structure and the location of existing buildings on the site. Olympic Village services must be appropriately housed and function effectively within a permanent structure to be more economically efficient than the temporary construction of an OCOG. Temporary structures must be used to provide services to the Olympic Village that cannot be accommodated in permanent buildings but are mandatory for the IOC.

- Temporary structures depending on the operational needs of each area;
- Procurement policy and needs;
- Design of temporary structures;
- Terrain, type and size;
- Construction and installation methods;
- Technological and installation requirements;
- Power supply and temperature control requirements;
- Portable toilets;
- Temporary modular constructions;
- Structural tents.

However, the Winter Olympics will require significantly more temporary buildings and tents for the Olympic Village. Therefore, temporary buildings and structures for the Winter Olympics must be heated.

At the same time, the Comité d'Organisation des Jeux Olympiques (OCOG) must:

- Define the perimeter of the site;
- Secure financing before construction;
- Define in more detail the actual perimeter of the Olympic Village site, including security needs and access points.

Regarding the location of the Olympic Village's outdoor facilities, village transportation entrances, and parking areas, the OCOG should consider critical services within the Olympic Village (OVP, canteens, shopping centers, etc.). In addition, the IOC recommends a preliminary study to assess the environmental impact on the site area. Site evaluation should consider the following factors:

- Toxic waste;
- Contamination at the site;
- Hazardous materials (e.g. asbestos);
- Land quality;
- Soil composition;
- Vegetation and woodland;
- Water drainage and waterways;
- Soil erosion;
- Wildlife habitat;
- The potential impact of construction on the site;

- Emissions/pollution (roads, factories);
- Noise pollution.

Possible environmentally friendly projects for the Olympic Village may include:

- Recycling of materials (e.g., food, waste);
- Reusable energy sources;
- Solar energy (e.g., for heating),
- Minimize wrapping/packaging of deliveries/construction material;
- Recycling of water from the Olympic Village;
- Environmentally friendly Olympic Village vehicles (e.g.; natural gas, electric);
- Protection or integration of fauna and vegetation on the site.

Athletes and officials are provided with a unique shuttle service to and from the Village:

- All competition venues;
- All training venues;
- Airport;
- City center;
- Additional accommodation for officers.

To date, Olympic host cities must meet the following obligations. However, failure to comply with the commitments below will not result in sanctions or fines. The next section describes the IOC Evaluation Commission's evaluation criteria for constructing the Olympic Village.

1.2.8 Evaluation criteria for the Olympic Villages

Taking into account the evaluation criteria of the Olympic Committee of the IOC Working Group, accommodation structures are evaluated using three criteria and weightings:

a) Location 40%.
    ◦ Travel distance to competition venues, excluding football and sailing preliminary venues when outside of the host city.

(b) Concept 40%.
- Number of villages;
- Type of accommodation;
- Available land area;
- Surrounding environment;
- Temporary or permanent;
- Additional accommodation for athletes.

Village concepts are assigned a feasibility factor based on the likelihood that the proposed project will come to fruition.

(c) Bequest 20%.
- Post-Games use;
- Funding.

As mentioned earlier, the Olympic Village is one of the most essential locations for athletes and is the heart of the Games. The location of the Village relative to the competition venue is paramount. During the bidding stage, the IOC will ask for general information. Meanwhile, in the second phase, candidate cities must demonstrate how they will address the highly complex issues surrounding the scope and scale of such projects, both from an operational and legacy perspective. According to the IOC, most cities understand the requirements for an Olympic Village, including the project's heritage (IOC, 2008).

CHAPTER 2

Spatial Organization and Urban Planning of Olympic Villages

2.1   Olympic territorialization

"An urban structure entirely generated by the laws of economic growth; with a strongly dissipative and entropic character; without boundaries or limits to growth; unbalancing and strongly hierarchical; homogenising the territory it occupies; eco catastrophic; devaluing the individual qualities of places; lacking in aesthetic quality."
(Magnaghi, 2001)

The area is defined as historical products and artifacts resulting from long-term development between human settlements and the environment. Therefore, this territory is considered a living and very complex organism. It is a product of the encounter between culture and nature, a constantly changing ecosystem of places with identities, histories, and characteristics that form territorial and urban "*typologies*" (Magnaghi, 2001).

The first decade of the 20th century was dominated by Fordism and mass production, and the territory's organization became more complex regarding regional economic growth. Therefore, significant events such as the Olympics or World Fairs require different areas depending on the location's economic development.[1] As mentioned above, analyzing mega-events through territorial analysis requires viewing territory through two different geographical expressions in terms of form, control, governance, symbols, and values. The first expression refers to the "*project area*" where the structures and functions necessary to host an event, typified by Olympic venues, will be constructed. The second expression refers to "*contextual areas*," which are considered existing parts of the area at

---

[1] The identification of the Olympic territories imposes the analysis of different territories in a geographical space, which in the Beijing 2022 edition will reach up to 200 km from the Olympic city.

different scales (regional, national, local).[2] At both levels, potentially conflicting local–global relationships can be observed (Dansero, 2002). However, the dispute will continue until the closing ceremony of the Paralympic edition. Defining and constructing the Olympic region as a spatiotemporal system requires a regional effort that is a *stress test* of local organizations and communities. As we will observe in Chapter 3, the spatial structure of the Olympic Games continues to transform into a multipolar system, becoming more complex and extensive every day. During the Olympic Games, the region will have to provide new dedicated communication channels for the movement of a large number of stakeholders (athletes, technicians, media, members of the public, organizers, volunteers, sponsors).[3] As mentioned in the previous section, in all modern Olympic Games, transportation management has become an integral part of the success of the Games. Moreover, the organization of temporary transport systems changes the form of regional systems, creating new trips and overloading traditional transport systems.

Thus, maps of Olympic games depict regions that differ from the geographical representation of the host region. During the event, temporary operators and officials will manage and control Olympic venues. Additionally, some areas of Olympic venues will be inaccessible to most citizens.[4] The closest complex and temporary spatial structures are contained in the domain of the host community, a domain with its own logic and operational rules.

Analyzing host regions while planning mega-events reveals that Olympic events imply constructing a spatial structure promoted internationally that emphasizes or excludes specific locations and de-emphasizes others. You can see. Therefore, the Olympics' spatial structure presupposes a transformation of the regional scale to adapt the region to its temporal needs. However, the construction of Olympic spaces represents a homogeneous and standardized theory with its own rules for generating Olympic areas based on the experience of past editions. Significant events seek and consume spatial differences, ultimately producing them (Dansero, 2007). The outcome depends entirely on local and national administrations and

---

[2] The boundaries of the project territory should be considered temporarily only for the exploitation of the event, while the boundaries of the context territory during the Olympic event may compromise territorial control and governance.

[3] The contribution of Professor Eva Kassens-Noor (2017) is recommended for Olympic transport systems.

[4] For example, the Olympic Village and the International Venue are areas with rigorous and limited access for most Olympic operators.

requires negotiation and mediation between the International Olympic Committee's (IOC) recognized tendencies and supralocal actors. As we shall see, it is difficult for local communities and organizers to implement strategies that do not result from a conflict between national and global visions. Therefore, the possibility of changing territory during mega-events requires complex management during and after the event. However, the results will only be known after the Olympics are over. Parallel to the Olympic territory, there is a "*context area*" consisting of the Olympic city, the surrounding area and all the areas through which the main event slightly "*passes*." Contextual regions can be affected by changes that have a lasting impact on the area red, define local scenarios, and place hierarchies in the regional framework. Unlike the Olympic region, the context area is controlled, organized, and managed by a complete public administration consisting of all local governments and private capital in the area of interest. The relationship between the two regions requires thorough work to realize the various structures that add to the urban and territorial image of the Olympic venue. In this context, participatory planning helps define strategies for building new collective photos. Thanks to the coordination and contribution of all local actors, benefits can be obtained at the local level without compromising the region's promotion at the global level.

2.1.1 Territorialization

"We can imagine territorialisation in a strictly chronological perspective, as sequences of acts that begin in a distant prehistory."
(Turco, 1988)

As mentioned in the previous chapter, the Agricultural and Industrial Revolutions represent fundamental points in abolishing behavioral boundaries and, in short, stages in constructing the human environment. In the last paragraph, territory results from applying a work within a defined space. Territory can be seen as a privileged extension of a particular parcel of land on which human activities occur.

The acts of territorialization[5] represent the totality of the territorial mass in the universe. The morphology of a region, a particular part of the Earth's surface,

---

[5] Considering Raffestin, C. (1981). *Per una geografia del potere* and Turco, A. (1988). *Verso una teoria geografica della complessità* contributions, territorialization is regarded as the production of territory in a space produced by the actions of territorial actors.

is subject to various extrinsic and endogenous changes that depend on various natural factors. Thus, earthquakes, wars, etc., and territorialization are essential processes by which a space acquires anthropological value (Turco, 1988).

Thus, territorialization must be seen as a continuous growth of territory constantly being reconfigured and adapted to the needs and habits of local communities.

An analysis of territorial legal acts should start with three basic categories: naming, reification, and structuring (Turco, 1988). As a result, Olympic territorialization, understood as the production of new temporal domains, is intertwined with normal transformational dynamics through the T-R-D cycle, which contrasts the encounter between different acts of territorialization at work (Turco, 1988):

- Designation
- Reification
- Structuring

Applying the territorialization process to major events begins with the bidding and venue selection stage and goes through a deterritorialization phase after the event, coinciding with the Olympic venue's demolition. The reterritorialization phase is closely linked to the mission and Olympic infrastructure, which must be reconfigured for use over time. The final stage only appears in the post-Olympic stage and permanently changes heritage sites and state capitals (Figure 5).

Figure 5: Space and territory: Acts of territorialization

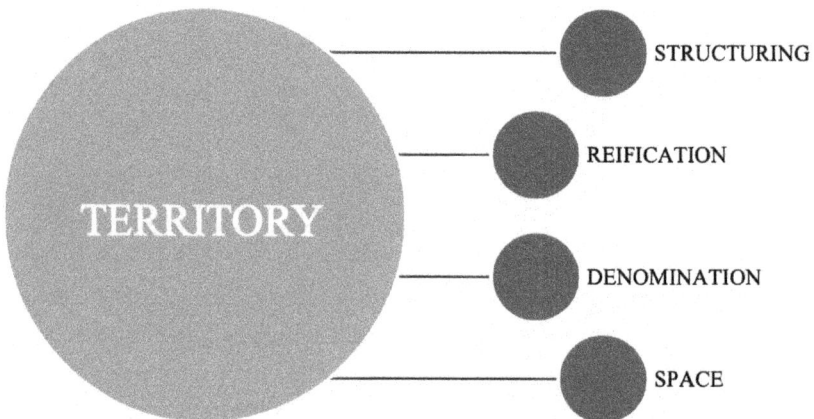

Source: Turco, 1988, p. 78

Therefore, one can hypothesize that the Olympic's territorialization–deterritorialization–territorialization (TDR) cycle contradicts the TDR process in the contextual realm. Turco (1988) states that place naming is a social work accomplished through cognitive and communicative strategies. Assigning a specific name to a temporary place allows that place to penetrate into the global and spiritual realm of the community. On the other hand, the second form of control is revealed through reification, which consists of the occupation of space through the use of resources. Symbolization is followed by material control of acts of territorialization. The final form of control is sequential structural. Structuring is, therefore, regulated and organized through administrative processes by authorities who manage and organize territories using norms and rules according to the objectives of a particular territorial situation (della Sala, 2023c).

2.1.2 Production in the territory: The denomination

In the previous section, we found that the territorialization of mega-events is strongly associated with the territorial symbols related to that event. For example, at the Olympic Games, there are the Olympic Rings, Olympic Village, Olympic Stadium, Olympic Square, Olympic Trampoline, etc.). Therefore, this designation could be temporary, existing only for the duration of the Games, or it could persist in the region and serve as an excuse to develop new strategies for various tangible and intangible purposes.[6] For this reason, it is stated that the financing of medium- to long-term localization is directly linked to the use of events (della Sala, 2022b). For example, in Barcelona (1992), the Olympic Village and Olympic Port were part of a regional marketing strategy that emphasized the importance of the Olympic heritage in the region to this day. Place naming is, therefore, the first act of territorial production.

As a result, the naming of the Olympic Games begins with a bidding process, where the event's region is defined, and the event date is confirmed to be associated with the host city (Barcelona 1992, Sydney 2000, Turin 2006, London, 2012, Rio 2016, etc.). The temporary and symbolic designation becomes a permanent fact over time through legitimation and aims to attract a new global image of

---

[6.] We have observed different models of preserving the Olympic name throughout Olympic history. For example, Barcelona has created an Olympic Quarter, a port, and a metro line. London and Beijing have turned the Olympic space into a large sports park, which changed its name after the Olympic event.

the Olympic area. The long-term legitimacy of a name is about constructing an identity communicated globally over a more extended period. Similarly, the symbolic control of a territory complicates the outcomes and legacy of mega-events of that territory's memes.[7] Regarding the Olympic Games, it is essential to remember that only the host city can use the Olympic symbol to promote its region during the bidding phase and during the organization of the Games. However, when naming Olympic venues, it is necessary to renew the image of the area and landscape to raise the city's profile on a global scale through technological tools such as television, the internet, SS, and photography. Therefore, only some Olympic areas and Olympic productions are at risk of being affected by permanent venue designation. For example, the area passed by the temporary modification of the Olympic space will disappear after the closing ceremony of the Paralympic Games. Therefore, this naming facilitates new communication strategies to develop the tourism market as a result of mega-events.[8]

Over time, there has been much criticism of the interim legislation that venues must adopt regarding the sale and marketing of advertising space at Olympic venues: for example, *"È significativo ricordare come il Comune e il CIO abbiano sollecitato i media internazionali a utilizzare il nome 'Torino' al posto dell'internazionale 'Turin'"* [*Significantly, the municipality and the IOC urged the international media to use the name 'Turin' instead of the global 'Turin'*] (Dansero & De Leonardis, 2006).

2.1.3 Production in the territory: Reification

The second process, reification, is considered the material transformation of territory and is the most evident and long-lasting aspect of territorialization. The construction of Olympic facilities, infrastructure, sports facilities directly related to the event, and all the works associated with the event's organization represent a significant change in the contextual area. Time can be a catalyst for other artifacts. Structures and infrastructure constitute themselves the material heritage of a place and hint at new future transformations in the use of space (della Sala, 2023b).

---

[7] The temporary production of information can lead to the disappearance of the Olympic effects in the post-Olympic period.

[8] It is essential to affirm that, during the Olympic event, the Olympic territory is protected under the control of the IOC concerning the space for billboards in the whole Olympic area.

For this reason, the materialization of the Olympic Games consists of an extraordinary material transformation by leading international architectural firms, which can be facilitated through the realization of Olympic works.

Material transformation may be accompanied by technological innovations, which will catalyze new processes in the construction and organization of infrastructure. For example, in 2000, Sydney proposed building a sustainable Olympic village using renewable energy sources. This continues to help reduce electricity generation from other nonrenewable energy sources. Meanwhile, in 2006, Turin proposed building the Olympic Village using recycled materials that could be reused. Therefore, the materialization of the Olympics is a very complex stage with different consequences in the post-Olympic period.

2.1.4 Production in the territory: Structuring

Structuring, as we have seen, represents the final stage of the territorialization cycle, introducing sensory or structural control, selecting a domain, and creating a program or program. It is a process that facilitates the creation of a domain structure that ensures implementation. Strategy that can be done (Turco, 1988). This phase could manifest as a significant post-Olympic event. Two possible levels can be identified:

- Subregional level (Olympic map)
- Local level (Olympic venues)

However, the locations included in the Olympic spatial system are influenced over time by *glocal* locations.

Therefore, Olympic venues may be affected during the event by integrating multiple organizing bodies working with different strategies and pursuing other goals. In this sense, regional and strategic planning are fundamental for organizing and defining common goals representing all parties involved in the Olympic Project. Strategic spatial planning reduces the risk of conflicts in the spatial system and strengthens the system to function in the post-event phase. On the one hand, territorial structuring can reinvigorate new economic, social, and urban processes that last longer (della Sala, 2023a). The territorial structures promoted by significant events can take different forms and effects, depending on territorial actors' objectives and activities regarding the post-Olympic legacy (Dansero, 2010).

The territorialization phase is followed by the deterritorialization phase of the space–time system developed for the Olympic event. The deterritorialization phase may include a reterritorialization phase in which the transformation of the contextual territory is resolved or intensified. Over time, we have observed various options for the subsequent redevelopment of the Olympic venue:

- Dismantling.
- Reuse.
- Reconversion.
- Abandonment.[9]

Throughout the history of the Olympics, we have observed that various projects often need to be more valued, resulting in overterritorialization in territorial contexts and remaining as artifacts without identity. Therefore, potential assessment risks can impact many communities (della Sala, 2023b). Lack of experience and resources can lead to conflicts between cities and Olympic venues (Jennings, 2012). For example, at the 2006 Turin Games, the ski jumping facilities and bobsled track left a crack in Piedmont that could never be rebuilt, as qualitative interview results show (della Sala, 2022).

Furthermore, these operations may lead to conflicts between regional territories and the central government. Therefore, constructing overvalued facilities, structures, and infrastructure to host mega-events is a goal of central governments that use mega-events to promote other symbols, monuments, or images. It is an expression of will (Poynter, 2015). It must also be said that the IOC has different interests than the host country. The form of Olympic territorialization is often quite different from the original plan of the organizing committee (see Table 5). Redesigning candidate city rules and Olympic contracts can reduce unnecessary territorialization processes for post-Olympic host communities (della Sala, 2023d).

---

[9] Abandonment is seen as defeating the territorial Project and destroying the contextual territory.

Table 5: The cycle of territorialization in Mega-events

	Territorialization	Deterritorialization	Reterritorialization
Designation	• Venue of the event • The territory of the event • Facilities • Structures • Infrastructure • Squares, monuments		• Places, structures, and artifacts that still retain the adjective "Olympic." • Creation of a territorial brand • International events market
Reification	• Sports facilities • Accommodation/hotels • Olympic Village • Olympic structures • Infrastructure	• Dismantling • Abandonment	• Public facilities • Multifunctional facilities • University Campus • Popular residences • Hotels • Infrastructure • Urban spaces, theme parks • Tourist accommodation
Structuring	• Regional territory • National territory • Local territory • Glocal territory	• Reuse • Reconversion • Liquidation of the organizing committee	• Reorganization of territorial promotion bodies • New spaces for international audiences • New post-event organizational structure • Setting up a volunteer event organizer • Creation of a specific structure for mega-events

Source: Own elaboration on Turco (1988)

As we have observed in the previous section, it describes some of the theories and possibilities mega-events offer for creating new territorial systems that can transform mega-events into concrete resources for exploitation. To consider the development of local systems, it is helpful to introduce Magnaghi's contribution to local projects (Magnaghi, 2000) and the prospects for their development. This is followed by a brief introduction to the Local Territorial Systems (SLoT) theoretical model (Dematteis, 2005), which attempts to identify the different development perspectives that mega-events can reveal. Finally, we consider some opportunities for local communities to capitalize on mega-events legacy.

2.1.5 The local project: Local development policies

"The local project is the political manifestation of a demand, a need, an idea to respond to the challenge of globalisation."
(Magnaghi, 2000)

In the 21st century, local projects are seen as a way for communities to resist the exclusivity of metropolises and preserve their identity, traditions, culture, and landscape without jeopardizing social relations and a sense of community. On the other hand, in the post-Olympic period, the local system of Olympic cities will conflict with the goals of the capital and will be subject to different rules of the global mega-event market (della Sala, 2022b). After World War II and the end of post-Fordism, this territory became a place of value production. This value is not only an economic consideration. Recognition, symbols and recognition, therefore, enable community recognition and enhance the value of local heritage in creating lasting and long-term prosperity. The structure of local projects is based on agreements between several stakeholders (Magnaghi, 2000). Defining a local project is a complex process of clarifying contradictions, defining goals and redefining projects to implement a joint project that creates cultural heritage values for the community. However, the construction of local projects should be financed and supported by local ordinances aimed at overcoming the collective individuality of places and proposing common goals through new forms of participation and direct democracy. Local communities support territorial transformation by enacting common laws and regulations, norms, and agreements they uphold. This way, local projects can promote self-employment, crafts, cultural areas, and micro-enterprises.

> The local project presupposes the growth of the powers and competencies of municipalities and supra-municipal territorial entities, expressions of the municipality as a higher local authority.
>
> (Magnaghi, 2000)

Establishing and promoting internal democratic institutions (local development institutions, agreements, dialogue tables, participatory workshops, living labs) can form a solid foundation for fostering local policies and networks at the local level. Therefore, the governance and control of internal democratic institutions at different levels has become a current and essential issue for the sustainable development of local communities.

> In the glocalist hypothesis, local development takes shape to the extent that the local community is contaminated by the global, bringing to the local the innovations coming from the opening of relations between long and short networks; local development occurs when local society can build horizontal networks in the global system.
>
> (Magnaghi, 2000)

Network forms are more deeply integrated into existing local areas, with local populations unable to withdraw from global projects. The intersection of new global networks for local communities and hosting mega-events is one of the most significant risks to maintaining local community trust and autonomy. As a result, local areas of mega-events become embedded in global networks of local communities and strengthen themselves through new relationships and networks that contrast with current centralized forms of economic globalization.

Local communities can establish:

I. Inter-local information relations and solidarity networks that interconnect with global networks.
II. The proliferation of cities capable of building nonhierarchical global relationships through the diffusion of services in peripheral regional networks in response to concentration processes.
III. Eco-solidarity business and financial relationships that develop local networks and transfer to the global market.
IV. Self-sustainable local production systems based on the valorization of heritage.
V. Networks of local development agencies that interconnect top-down projects with bottom-up projects.

VI. South–south, south–north cultural relations that densify the overlapping wefts of north–south networks: self-representations versus representations of the center (Magnaghi, 2000).

Therefore, in the expression of large-scale events with overwhelming global effects, attempts should be made to protect local communities by activating a range of policies, actions, processes and projects that enable:

- Strengthen the internal relations of each territorial system by constructing new social fabrics to express each territory's peculiarities and capacities within a framework of sustainable development.
- Develop and build networks between the local and the supralocal in the medium and long term. The new intralocal networks should modify the hierarchical system of metropolises and global cities toward a complexification and multiplication of regional systems.

Therefore, strengthening intraregional relationships and building new intra-regional networks will facilitate the construction of new intra-regional systems. A system that enables the building of new relationships in a way that fosters new processes of solidarity exchange and participation. Mutual respect for the global economic network will create a new green flow in the Olympic city after the Olympics (della Sala, 2022b).

2.1.6 Local, territorial system

Using the SLoT model Dematteis (2005) developed, this model can describe possible social interaction relationships for territory, governance, and sustainable development. By introducing the theoretical model of SLoT, we consider different perspectives of regional development that may emerge in the post-Olympic region. We hope to provide a contribution that allows us to think about constructing local territorial systems not influenced by the global context of the mega-event recognition model of territorial systems developed by Dematteis (2005). It consists of the following elements:

1. *The local network*: consists of all the relationships and interactions between all existing subjects that can be developed in a local area to establish a common objective of regional development. The term "local" refers to the geographical scale of the Project, allowing interaction beyond the physical proximity of the

places and communities that make up the local area. Communication, exchange, knowledge, history, heritage and customs of the local area enable the construction of medium- to long-term relationship systems in the target area. The SLoT model can be identified and developed by local actors promoting joint development projects without compromising the autonomous development of local character-istics. Regional transformation, reorganization, requalification, and development must be based on a shared vision for the region to exploit the synergies of place.

2. *The local milieu*: Identifying a set of permanent locations based on the socio-cultural and morphological characteristics identified in a particular geographical area, based on the heritage and history of each location. The territorial capital of each place is shaped by a set of processes, goals, and resources that prioritize the subjective potential of each place. The expression of territorial space becomes the expression of the characteristics of each region, which, thanks to all the activities of the local community, can improve the local environment and transform the area according to the needs of the local community.

3. *Local network relations*: form the whole system of local ecosystems within local networks through shared values and goals of critical actors in the region. The transformation and redefinition of local networks are seen as an intangible element for leveraging shared values over time.

4. *Interactive relations between local and regional networks*: These are identified in communication processes between local and supralocal levels (regional, national, European, and global). The relationship between different levels of intervention represents a table of dialogue in which relationships with the local environment can be achieved through mega-events without endangering local interactions and the development of sustainable regional development networks over time.

As we have observed, the SLoT model is structured by the organization and hierarchy of the system in the medium and long term, as well as the local com-munity's identity (Governa, 1999). For this reason, the organization of regional systems in mega-events must consider the region's various peculiarities and the various local development policies that must be known at the supralocal level and established at the national level (Poynter, 2010). As we saw in the case of Turin in 2006, organizing governance at the local level was a fundamental element for leveraging the Olympic Project across contextual areas. However, regional development strategies must be implemented in the post-Olympic period through collaborative planning and organization over time. In this sense, this mega-event is an impetus for implementing and developing new strategies that can serve as a model for regional development for the future of Olympic host regions after the

Olympics. Only through projects supported by local communities can we positively impact the image and perception of communities involved in the Olympic area. The SLoT model can provide a set of processes and goals that must be continuously stimulated to establish a territorial system that develops based on the principles of sustainability, participation and social cohesion (della Sala, 2022a). The concept of heritage and Olympic heritage is closely linked to regional strategic planning, which considers the host region's particularities. However, the demolition, redevelopment, reuse, or abandonment of Olympic venues could permanently jeopardize residents' perceptions of the region, the organizers, and the local government system. The dissolution of the organizing committee and the temporary organizations necessary to carry out construction work and tasks related to significant event activities may lead to a vacuum and a decline in support from local residents, so the local public poses substantial risks to challenges. Constructing one or more specific structures to realize the new post-Olympic goals is the only way to reduce the chances of sustainable territorial development being abandoned and failing over time. Therefore, by analyzing the results of a qualitative study on the Turin 2006 case study, we observe the different responses of respondents regarding the post-Olympic legacy and the long-term exploitation of the Olympic legacy. The Turin case study allows us to analyze in detail the different dynamics that emerged in the post-Olympic period regarding the organization and implementation of long-term plans. Turin 2006 was chosen as a case study due to the scale and spatial dimension of the event. In recent years, it has become increasingly important to comply with the Sustainable Development Goals of the United Nations 2030 Agenda through follow-up activities and monitoring of subsequent results. Therefore, the following section deals with assessing the impact of the Olympic Games using the technical documents of the IOC, which is recognized as the responsible body for the management of Olympic operations in Olympic cities.

2.2 Spatial models of the Olympic Villages

2.2.1 Urban analysis of the Olympic Villages

"A miniature city, replete with modern conveniences and facilities, had magically emerged high in the hills, within sight of the great Olympic Stadium, on top of the modern Mount Olympus, below which lay the modern plains of Elis."
(COJO, 1932, p. 235)

Similar measures have been implemented in Olympic interventions, but the Olympic Project can only be analyzed by considering our cities' urban history. The development of architectural ideas and different formal languages allows us to think about developing an Olympic village within the region. In the analysis of the Olympic Village according to varying levels of urban dimensions, carried out by Muñoz (1996), particular attention is paid to four fundamental aspects:

i.   Aspects related to the evolution of the architectural idea, the different housing types and the different formal languages used.
ii. Aspects related to the evolution of city plans, from choosing the urban concept model to the basis of the operations adopted.
iii. Aspects related to the conception of the Olympic Village as an urban instrument, from the production of the city's projects to the insertion of the urban context in the post-Olympic period.
iv. Moreover, the change in the economic circuit and the different types of management require a specific section (Muñoz, 1996).

Thus, in Muñoz's study (1996), we can observe the first classification of the different urban models adopted by the candidate cities to construct the Summer Olympic Village: "Garden City, Satellite City, Urban Centres and metropolises" (Muñoz, 1996). The following classification will help you identify the general pattern of summer spending thus far. As stated in the study's introduction, one of the objectives of this study was to update the contribution of Muñoz (1996) to advance the classification of urban models adopted so far and to analyze the issue for the winter edition. Therefore, Winter Olympic Villages can be classified according to the four-city model: satellite cities, mountain centers, metropolises, and clusters, as explained in Section 5.4. By analyzing the different spatial models developed by candidate cities, this study shows how the concept of Olympic accommodation evolved over time and how the Olympic Village developed differently in the two editions of the Olympic Games. You can think deeply about an Olympic village, initially conceived by Coubertin in 1924. Coubertin wanted to promote the creation of a sports city that could foster cultural exchange between residents. Since that historical moment, different models of the Olympic Village have been observed in the summer edition, respecting the typical housing shapes and typologies of each historical moment. Furthermore, according to the classification proposed by Wimmer (1976), three stages are observed depending on the solution chosen for constructing the Olympic Village.

1. The first corresponds to single-family houses or *bungalows* arranged similarly to the housing estates or colonial houses seen in Europe or the United States.
2. The second corresponds to the creation of the community except Melbourne 56 and the integration of wooden modules.
3. The third corresponds to the construction of large complexes on a single module developed in height and identical, in some cases, even with different designs.

Muñoz (1996) then analyses the evolution of the form and situation of the Olympic Village and presents the following models and stages observed in the summer edition.

1. Olympic Village and urban planning. The utopian content of Olympic urban planning.
2. The garden city and the suburban world. The "inaugural" villages.
3. The satellite city and the city machine. The people of the 1960s.
4. The central city and the accumulation of leisure. The people of the 1970s.
5. The metropolitan city and the central "non-place." The people of the last two decades.

Therefore, as explained in the next section, the Olympic Village has had to adapt to various transformations and modifications throughout its history to be incorporated into the framework of long-term urban development. However, some structural changes were necessary to accommodate the new leisure and lifestyle needs of recent years. Although the city-village model has been entirely replaced by the regional-metropolitan model, this model continues to define different types of spatial models, services, and administrative responsibilities involved in the Olympic Project. I'm making it complicated. The evolution of the Olympic Village over time reflects the evolution of national lifestyles, and athlete demands over time. Olympic Villages is an outcome of the Olympic period within a contextual area that requires permanent physical structures to fit and accommodate the specific housing needs of each venue. The following section analyses the different spatial models used to date for constructing the Olympic Village in the host region. The following sections instead analyze the different urban phases of the proposed Olympic Village up to the Beijing 2022 Games.

2.2.2 Spatial models of the Olympic Villages

Over time, different spatial models for the location of the Olympic Village in the host city have been observed. Moreover, since 1924, with the introduction of the winter edition, the organization of the Olympic Village has changed and acquired other values and functions over time. However, the development of Olympic events after 1924 led to rethinking the event model and athlete accommodation.

Figure 6: Spatial dimension of the Olympic Villages

Spatial dimension of Olympic Villages

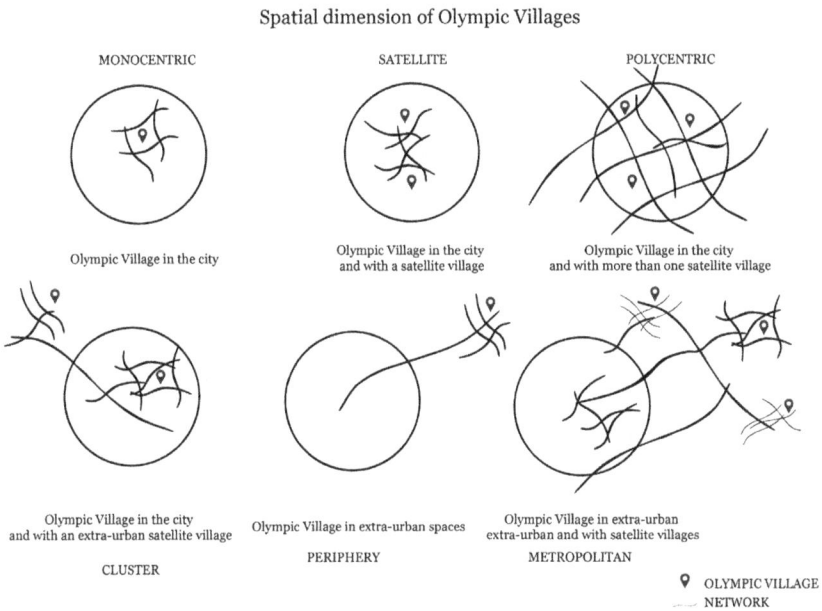

MONOCENTRIC

Olympic Village in the city

SATELLITE

Olympic Village in the city
and with a satellite village

POLYCENTRIC

Olympic Village in the city
and with more than one satellite village

Olympic Village in the city
and with an extra-urban satellite village

CLUSTER

Olympic Village in extra-urban spaces

PERIPHERY

Olympic Village in extra-urban
extra-urban and with satellite villages

METROPOLITAN

♀ OLYMPIC VILLAGE
⸺ NETWORK

Source: Own implementation

The first Olympic Games were organized according to a spatial model centered on the main stadium. Since its inauguration in Los Angeles in 1932, the event has adopted a new peripheral spatial format, and the Olympic Village has become an essential element of Olympic urban planning in the host region. The 1932 project is considered the first interim sports district built and is still used today. The Los Angeles project inspired the construction of future residential buildings. Therefore, in the report of the 1936 Berlin Games, the organizing committee emphasized the importance of developing the Olympic Village in the same philosophy and form as the model observed at the previous Games. The 1936 Berlin edition was the first to take inspiration from earlier editions and develop a model that could be reproduced over time. However, the first permanent accommodation will be the Berlin Olympic Village. From this historic moment, Olympic host cities begin proposing and developing urban planning projects incorporating surrounding sports facilities and services.

Figure 7: Location of the Berlin Olympic Village 1932

Source: Own implementation

On the other hand, the first Olympic Village in the winter version was based on using hotels in mountain resorts. The first permanent model of the winter edition only appeared in the 1952 Oslo edition. For the 1952 edition, the organizing committee developed three new Olympic quarters in the center that could be used as permanent housing for the community. In addition, after World War II, the obligation to provide housing in central states required host countries to develop large-scale projects that could meet the needs of their citizens. Furthermore, establishing three Olympic Villages within the territory will change the spatial dimensions of the Olympic Games over time. Starting with the Rome Games, the Olympic Games will play a vital role in redesigning and rebuilding Europe's largest city. The need for urban expansion in the 1960s and 1970s, changes in infrastructure and the renewal of urban centers will be the determining factors for the construction of future Olympic Villages.

Figure 8: Location of the Rome 1960 Olympic Village

Source: Own implementation

Furthermore, it is fundamental to highlight how the 1960 version of Rome promotes spatial transformation through Olympic events and serves as a model of urban transformation for all future candidate cities. In 1960, it was first observed how major sporting events could be integrated into the long-term strategy of a host city. From this historic moment onward, the Olympic Games became a catalyst for a more complex process, evolving and changing to suit the city's needs.

The interdependence between Olympic events and cities is developing through new formats and elements attached to Olympic events. Additionally, since 1991, the IOC has introduced notable changes to the Winter Olympics in case countries cannot provide all Olympic facilities within their territory due to geographic restrictions. In this way, the spatial dimension of the Winter Olympics will expand significantly and develop into a kind of cluster of different locations connected by transnational infrastructure systems. Although the IOC does not specify physical, economic, social, or environmental criteria for awarding a host city, Table 6 shows that the summer event remains the world's major metropolitan event.

Table 6: Population of the editions of the Summer Olympics

Edition	Population of the city
Berlin 1936	4.242.501
Helsinki 1952	381.000
Melbourne 1956	5.000.000
Roma 1960	2.455.581
Tokyo 1964	11.829.000
Mexico 1968	19.400.000
Munich 1972	2.316.000
Montreal 1976	2.950.000
Mosca 1980	13.200.000
Los Angeles 1984	3.400.000
Seoul 1988	10.100.000
Barcelona 1992	1.643.000
Atlanta 1996	394.000
Sydney 2000	3.610.000
Atene 2004	772.072
Beijing 2008	19.612.368
London 2012	8.174.000
Rio 2016	13.047.000
Tokyo 2020	37.435.191
Media	8.419.038
Max	37.435.191
Min	381.000

Source: Own implementation

Winter editions have historically been those developed in mountain communities benefiting from Olympic events and taking advantage of winter sports tourism. Since Turin 2006, the winter edition has been transformed into a metropolitan edition that includes regional aspects of the Olympic venue. Therefore, the winter edition is now given to large cities that want to benefit from Olympic events and promote their regions. Table 7 shows that the winter edition cities have an average population of at least 1.4 million. On the other hand, summer cities are large cities with an average of 8.5 million inhabitants. Olympic cities vary in size depending on the event, so each venue requires completely different training sessions.

Figure 9: Olympic space in Turin 2006

(Source: Own implementation)

The Olympic Games, therefore, require a high concentration of effort and resources within a limited time frame, which places high demands on service infrastructure and the availability of temporary accommodation. Tables 6 and 7 show that most Olympic venues are located in the world's most influential metropolises. The analysis of the development of the Olympic city based on the form of urban housing is an opportunity to consider the possibilities of the development of modern cities over this century. As explained in the next section, the Olympic Village has undergone various transformations and restructurings of the urban landscape, establishing itself as a tangible legacy of the Olympic legacy in the host city.

Figure 10: Olympic space in Beijing 2022

(Source: Own implementation)

Table 7: Population of the editions of the Winter Olympic Games

Edition	Population of the city
Oslo 1952	447.000
Squaw Valley 1960	4.000
Innsbruck 1964	100.000
Grenoble 1968	180.000
Sapporo 1972	1.000.000
Innsbruck 1976	117.000
Lake Placid 1980	5.000
Sarajevo 1984	448.000
Calgary 1988	640.000
Albertville 1992	20.000
Lillehammer 1994	23.000
Nagano 1998	361.000
Salt Lake 2002	174.348
Turin 2006	900.000
Vancouver 2010	603.400

Edition	Population of the city
Sochi 2014	364.000
Pyeongchang 1918	43.600
Beijing 2022	19.638.000
Media	1.392.686
Max	19.638.000
Min	4.000

Source: Own implementation

2.2.3 Evolution of the location of the Olympic Villages

Before analyzing the different development stages and spatial patterns of the Olympic Village, this study aims to observe the changes in the distance between the two main structures, namely the Olympic Village and the Olympic Stadium, in the summer and winter versions. We are proposing. Furthermore, to observe the evolution of the spatial pattern outlined above, the distances between the Olympic Village and the administrative centers of the summer and winter host cities were analyzed in Tables 8 and 9. The following parameters allow you to account for changes in the location of the Olympic Village over time in the two editions. Considering the location of the Olympic Village makes it possible to analyze the spatial patterns observed over time and to develop new hypotheses about the evolution of the Olympic Village as an urban and central city element of Olympic events.

Table 8: Distance of the Olympic Village from the stadium and the Summer Olympics administrative center

Edition	Distance from the main stadium	Distance from the administrative center of the city
Paris 1924	950 m	17.2 km
Los Angeles 1932	8.2 km	17.5 km
Berlin 1936	21.1 km	31 km
Helsinki 1952	2.4 km	6.9 km

(*Continued*)

Edition	Distance from the main stadium	Distance from the administrative center of the city
Melbourne 1956	14.0 km	15.3 km
Rome 1960	3.1 km	6.0 km
Tokyo 1964	3.1 km	3.4 km
Mexico 1968	4.2 km	21.5 km
Munich 1972	850 m	8.2 km
Montreal 1976	1.1 km	5.5 km
Moscow 1980	17.85 km (average)	18.5 km (average)
Los Angeles 1984	1.7 km	8.2 km
Seoul 1988	6.5 km	18.5 km
Barcelona 1992	7.1 km	3.0 km
Atlanta 1996	7.8 km	5.6 km
Sydney 2000	2.6 km	18.9 km
Athens 2004	15.6 km	21.0 km
Beijing 2008	900 m	16.0 km
London 2012	2.5 km	10.1 km
Rio 2016	28.6 km	28.2 km
Tokyo 2020	9.9 km	16.3 km
Media	7.63 km	14.13 km
Max	28.6 km	31 km
Min	0.85 km	3 km

Looking at summer spending based on the distance between the Olympic Village and the competition venue, we find that the average distance to the Olympic Stadium is 7.63 km. The average distance between the host city's administrative center and the Olympic Village is 14.13 km. Meanwhile, in the winter version, we see that the average distance between the Olympic Village and the Olympic Stadium is 16.74 km. The average distance between the Olympic Village and the administrative center is 22.31 km.

Figure 11: Location of the Tokyo 2020 Olympic Village

Source: Own implementation

An analysis of the Olympic Village's location shows that the summer version of the Olympic Village has evolved over time through a spatial model that increasingly resembles the central structure of the host city. The only exceptions in recent competitions are Athens 2004 and Rio 2016. A peripheral model for organizing events was developed for these conventions, as described in the next section. Additionally, the distance between the Olympic Village and the administrative center continues to evolve, with the 2022 Winter Games in Beijing increasing the maximum average distance between the city's administrative center and the mountain sports venue Olympic Village to 115.63 km.

Table 9: Distance of the Olympic Village from the stadium and the Winter Olympics administrative center

Edition	Distance from the main stadium	Distance from the administrative center of the city
Oslo 1952	2.77 km (average)	4.87 km (average)
Squaw Valley 1960	0.8 km	13 km

(Continued)

Edition	Distance from the main stadium	Distance from the administrative center of the city
Innsbruck 1964	5.8 km	5.0 km
Grenoble 1968	600 m	4.0 km
Sapporo 1972	1.7 km	9.1 km
Innsbruck 1976	5.6 km	6.4 km
Lake Placid 1980	10.1 km	10.4 km
Sarajevo 1984	8.6 km	8.2 km
Calgary 1988	1.3 km	8.6 km
Albertville 1992	36.3 km	35.1 km
Lillehammer 1994	4.3 km	3.4 km
Nagano 1998	3.8 km	9.3 km
Salt Lake 2002	1.6 km	9.6 km
Turin 2006	62.17 km (average)	65.43 km (average)
Vancouver 2010	1.2 km	1.5 km
Sochi 2014	40.13 km (average)	64.33 km (average)
Pyeongchang 1918	13.4 km (average)	27.8 km (average)
Beijing 2022	101.17 km (average)	115.63 km (average)
Media	16.74 km	22.31 km
Max	101.17 km	115.63 km
Min	0.6 km	1.5 km

Source: Own implementation

In addition, some winter editions, such as Oslo, Turin, Sochi, Pyeongchang, and Beijing, have different Olympic Villages associated with the Olympic competition venues. Table 10 shows the specific distances of each Olympic Village in several permanent housing organizations.

Table 10: Distance of Olympic Village subvenues from the
stadium and the Winter Olympic Games administrative center

Edition	Distance from the main stadium	Distance from the administrative center of the city
Oslo 1952		
Ulleval	2.2 km	4.3 km
Sogn	4.3 km	6.6 km
Illa	1.8 km	3.7 km
Turin 2006		
Main Village	2.2 km	5.9 km
Bardonecchia	94.1 km	89.4 km
Sestriere	90.2 km	101 km
Sochi 2014		
Rosa Khutor	58.1 km	76.6 km
Main Village	1.4 km	34.2 km
Sloboda	60.9 km	82.2 km
Pyeongchang 2018		
Village 1	7.2 km	23.1 km
Gangneung	19.6 km	32.5 km
Beijing 2022		
Main Village	2.0 km	17.1 km
Yanqing	72.5 km	90.8 km
Zhangjiakou	229 km	239 km

Source: Own implementation

The latest edition of the Beijing 2022 Winter Games allows us to observe new spatial aspects of the event, reaching a distance of 239 km from the city's administrative center to the mountainous Olympic Village in some cases. In conclusion, we see that the scale of the winter edition is changing to a regional organization, requiring new resources for infrastructure works to temporarily connect Olympic subvenues. This way, host cities have become prime locations for promoting more extensive and complex regions. The next dimension of the Winter Olympics will be in a transnational space, requiring new resources and new models of regional organization to comply with IOC standards.

Figure 12: Spatial organization in Oslo 1952

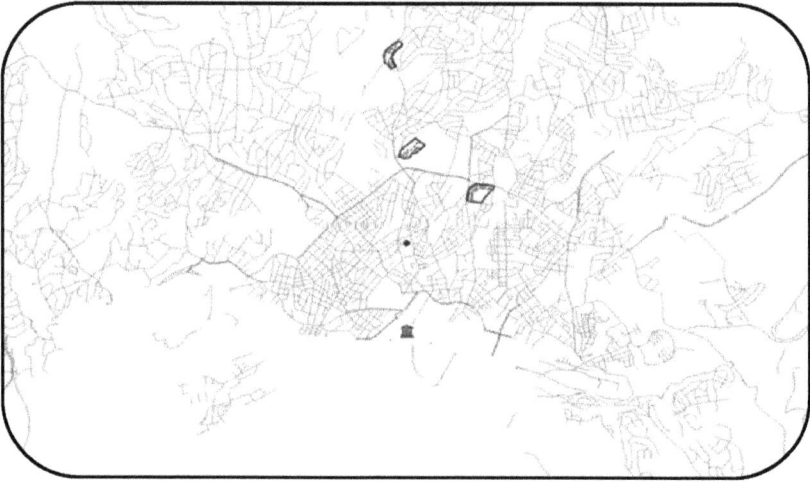

Source: Own implementation

2.2.4 Use and development of the Olympic Village area

As identified in the previous section, the area of the Olympic Village includes not only the provision of accommodation facilities but also sports facilities, public parks, amphitheaters, services and other essential facilities necessary for the post-Olympic use of the area. Also includes elements. Event period. Area selection is, therefore, a fundamental aspect of area allocation and post-Olympic village utilization. Looking at Tables 11 and 12, it is possible to identify the different uses of this region in the post-Olympic phase, which helps to think about the transformation of urban, mountainous or metropolitan spaces. Considering the pre-Olympic Games use, a common language is observed between the two editions in selecting available areas to become public property.

Regarding the use of the site after the event, there is a possibility that the Olympic Village will be turned into a park during the summer, and offices will be integrated into a mixed-use space. However, in the winter edition, sports facilities and the Olympic Village are the only common elements between the various experiences. After considering the different uses of the area, the following section considers the dimensions and location of the Olympic Village in both editions at different stages of the development of the model.

Table 11: Use of the area of the Summer Olympic Village before and after the Olympic Games

City	Previous use of selected areas	Use of areas chosen after the Games
Paris 1924	Lands	
Los Angeles 1932	Lands	
Berlin 1936	Land. Forests	Olympic Village, Olympic Park, sports facilities
Helsinki 1952	Lands	Olympic Village, sports facilities
Melbourne 1956	Lands	Olympic Village, sports facilities
Rome 1960	Stadium, land, barracks	Olympic Village, sports facilities
Tokyo 1964	Military area	Public park
Mexico 1968	Lands	Olympic Village, sports facilities
Munich 1972	Land, forest	Olympic Park, Olympic Village, transport, sports facilities
Montreal 1976	Lands	Olympic Park, Olympic Village
Moscow 1980	Lands	Olympic Villages
Los Angeles 1984	University area	New student accommodation

(*Continued*)

City	Previous use of selected areas	Use of areas chosen after the Games
Seoul 1988	Contaminated, unhealthy sites	Olympic Park, sports facilities, Olympic Village, healthy spaces
Barcelona 1992	Brownfields, land	Olympic Village, residential area, services, sports facilities, harbor
Atlanta 1996	Residential area in the city center	Office space, new student accommodation, sports facilities
Sydney 2000	Land, abandoned spaces	Olympic Park, residential area, park, Olympic Village
Athens 2004	Military and Industrial Area	Sports facilities, port, Olympic Village
Beijing 2008	Underdeveloped area	Olympic Village, park, sports facilities
London 2012	Industrial area	Olympic Village, offices, Olympic Park
Rio 2016	Land, barracks	Olympic Park, Olympic Villages
Tokyo 2020	Land and residential space in the city center	Olympic Villages

Source: Own implementation

Table 12: Use of the area of the Winter Olympic Village before and after the Olympic Games

City	Previous use of selected areas	Use of selected areas after the Games
Oslo 1952	Earth	Olympic Village, sports facilities
Squaw Valley 1960	Land, hotels	Sports facilities, hotels
Innsbruck 1964	Earth	Olympic Village, sports facilities

City	Previous use of selected areas	Use of selected areas after the Games
Grenoble 1968	Earth	Olympic Village, sports facilities
Sapporo 1972	Land	Olympic Village, sports facilities
Innsbruck 1976	Land	Olympic Village
Lake Placid 1980	Military area	Prison
Sarajevo 1984	Lands	Sports facilities, hotels
Calgary 1988	University area	New student accommodation
Albertville 1992	Hotels	New tourist accommodation, sports facilities
Lillehammer 1994	Land, forest	Sports facilities
Nagano 1998	Lands	Olympic Village, sports facilities
Salt Lake 2002	Military area	New student accommodation
Turin 2006	Brownfields	Tourist accommodation, Olympic Village, sports facilities
Vancouver 2010	University area	Olympic Village
Sochi 2014	Land, forest	Olympic Village
Pyeongchang 1918	Lands	Sports facilities, Olympic Villages
Beijing 2022	Lands	Olympic Villages, sports facilities

Source: Own implementation

CHAPTER 3

Transformation of Olympic Accommodation from Paris 1924 to Beijing 2022

3.1 The different stages in the evolution of the Summer Olympic Village in the urban fabric of the metropolis

Figure 13: Evolution of the Summer Olympic Village

PARIS 1924   ROMA 1960   BARCELONA 1992   LONDON 2012

LOS ANGELES 1932   LOS ANGELES 1984   SIDNEY 2000   PARIS 1924/LOS ANGELES 1928

Source: Own implementation from OCOG, 1924, 1932, 1960, 1984, 1992, 2000, 2012, 2024, 2028

Phase 1: Temporary accommodation in military sites (1896-1920)

From the first Olympic Games in Athens in 1896 to Paris in 1924, the event also hosted the World's Fair and was held in locations of great international recognition. In the next phase, the number of athletes would be limited and housed in hotels, military facilities, ships and other places with temporary beds.

It was not until after the 1924 Paris Games that the Olympic Village became a fundamental element in developing the Olympic Games. The Olympic response in the second stage was carried out with temporary solutions using removable materials. The Paris Olympic Village was planned near the main stadium by constructing temporary wooden huts containing public services. The Paris version was the first to have some essential services, such as a post office, leisure area, and leading services, which would later become the elements forming the village's international area. The Los Angeles Olympic Village became a model for developing subsequent Olympic cities. The village's location in the surrounding area will provide an impetus for developing sports facilities elsewhere (Figure 14).

The Olympic Village location also facilitates temporary urbanization through low-cost, removable materials. Los Angeles Village was the first to include an amphitheater, hospital, church, and other essential facilities for Olympic athletes. In this way, the practice of the old Olympic Games was reestablished, in which the athletes were temporarily housed in the community of Elis (OCOG, 1932).

Figure 14: Spatial organization in Los Angeles 1932

Los Angeles 1932

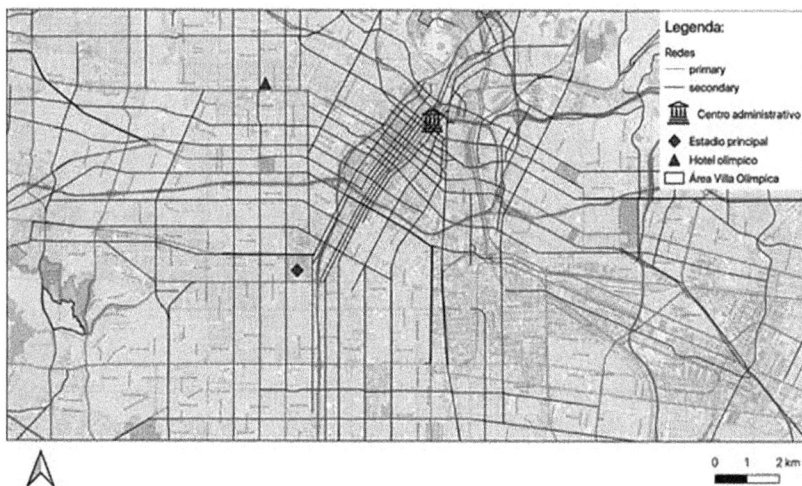

Source: Own implementation

The 1932 Village is based on the repetition of a prefabricated model around a morphology similar to the circus of ancient Rome. The 550 wooden huts will be the promoters of Olympic accommodation throughout the centuries.[1]

Phase 3: Construction of a sports district in peripheral areas (1936-1956)

The stimulating project of Los Angeles in 1932 served as an inspirational model for the Berlin Organizing Committee, which in 1936 realized the construction of a new sports quarter in a peripheral area of the city. The Berlin edition will become the first to offer a permanent solution for the Olympic event, which can be used as residential accommodation in the post-Olympic phase. This entire area includes sports facilities, reception, restaurant, meeting rooms, and services included in previous editions. The Berlin project will introduce a new concept for Olympic accommodation. In the future, this property will be promoted as a multifunctional event venue for future host cities. The Berlin model establishes the application of a satellite city or garden city model in the surrounding space and introduces a model of Olympic urbanism, characterized by a complex of sports facilities and an Olympic village. However, after the Olympics, it was used only as a military school and the facility remains abandoned with no specific purpose. Berlin events would inspire future projects in Helsinki in 1952 and Melbourne in 1956. In the next stage, the Olympic host city planned to build a new sports district in the surrounding area, focusing on building sports facilities close to Olympic accommodation.

Furthermore, the Helsinki project will be the first model for residential reuse in the post-Olympic phase. Melbourne will then propose building a new district in the abandoned area. In 1952, Helsinki became the first post-war Olympic village, bringing about changes in hospitality for athletes. The Organizing Committee proposed different housing for the participants of the rowing competitions, bringing forward multiple Olympic Villages for the athletes. From this historic moment on, participants in the sailing and rowing competitions will be housed in temporary structures close to the competition venue. The Helsinki Village housed some 4,800 people in 13 buildings, four stories high (COJO, 1952). The neighborhood included a restaurant, a cinema, saunas and toilets.

---

[1] In the Los Angeles 1932 edition, the candidate cities will be obliged to propose an Olympic site to celebrate the Olympic medals.

Meanwhile, for the 1956 Melbourne edition, the model adopted by the Organizing Committee was centered on a suburb (Heidelberg) 15.3 km from the administrative center of Melbourne. This suburb was built 14 km from the Olympic Stadium, and for the first time, men and women were housed in the same Olympic village. This project included the construction of 365 apartments, which were sold to residents in a post-event phase (COJO, 1956).

Figure 15: Spatial organization in Berlin 1936

Berlín 1936

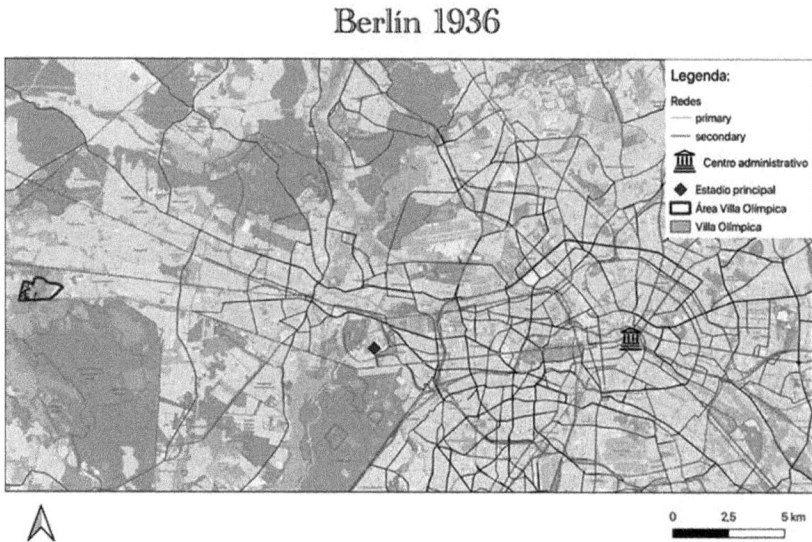

Source: Own implementation

Phase 4: Modern housing. Rationalism and functionalism (1960-1988)

Continuing the development of Olympic accommodation, the next stage, the 1960 Rome edition, would involve the promotion of a new scale of Olympic projects, which would influence the scale of new projects. The Rome Project is considered one of the most ambitious projects in history. One of the first sports city models developed by Enrico Del Debbio, Italy's leading rationalist architect of the 1930s, with the legacy of his *Foro Italico* park, built the Olympic Village and most of the Olympic facilities in an area of 0.30 km^2. The Olympic Village was designed under the guidelines of the rationalist style and in the post-event period, it will be converted into a neighborhood for state employees (COJO, 1960). Undoubtedly, the Rome edition inspired the promotion of the modernist style in future candidate cities. In 1964, Tokyo provided a significant transformation project that included infrastructural development as the main objective for the post-event phase (OCOG, 1964). Therefore, the Olympic Village was planned in a peripheral area of the city through temporary accommodation made of inexpensive and demountable materials.[2]

Subsequently, the Olympic Village area was transformed into one of the most famous parks in Japan, the *Yoyogi* Park.[3] The only exception to this phase, characterized by heavy investment in social housing to accommodate the world's largest city's population growth, was the Olympic Village, which was demolished after the Games. The Mexico 1968 edition, on the other hand, followed a planning philosophy that envisages the construction of satellite cities on the periphery of large cities and proposes solutions based on residential facilities in the post-event phase. The construction of new sports districts with apartments led to an unprecedented new philosophy of high-rise development. They built two villas in the Olympic Village area, one for an athlete and a journalist named "Miguel Hidalgo" and the other for a referee and Olympic volunteer named "Narciso Mendoza." The main village was built near the main stadium, consisting of 29 buildings, 10 floors from the sixth floor (COJO, 1968). The Mexico Olympic Village can be defined as a self-sufficient residential city that would house almost 10,000 people in the post-Olympic period.

Meanwhile, the Judges' and Volunteers' Village comprised 686 two-story and 90 four-story buildings (OCOG, 1968). Both Olympic Villages were intended to be sold to middle-class families in the post-Olympic period. In the Mexico edition, the International Olympic Committee (IOC) published guidelines for the design and planning of the Olympic Village for the first time. The consideration of the access, the main requirements, the average facilities and the instructions for the construction of the accommodation will promote a new type of centralized development of the Olympic Village. Then, in 1972, Munich developed a large sports park of 473,000 m² in the center, creating a new green area. This area was planned to become one of the largest sports parks in the world (COJO, 1972).

---

[2] Before the event, the area was owned by the US military. The location was expropriated, and ownership was transferred to the Japanese state.

[3] After the Olympic event, the park has become one of the symbolic spaces of the transformation of the city of Tokyo. Today, only one of the houses built for the Olympic event can be found in the park.

In the post-event phase, a large housing complex was converted into a dormitory for young couples, and buildings for university accommodation were added.

In contrast to previous complexes, Munich's Olympic Village will be used as an integrated element in the host city's central space, realizing a new philosophy of urban growth. Munich 1972 and Montreal 1976 would undoubtedly be two efforts to enhance urban centers through brutalist architecture. Both represent an urban phenomenon in which athletes' villages and sports facilities are incorporated into sports areas without expanding or expanding the metropolitan area. The Munich complex and the future Olympic Park were located 8.2 km from the city center. This large-scale complex included the realization of a complex that could accommodate more than 12,000 people. The concept of residential and international zones was first introduced in Munich. Therefore, the planning of Olympic accommodation in recent years has been aimed at the function of interventions, considering leisure and green spaces.

The Montreal version will then follow the same philosophy as Munich, building large accommodation complexes near sports venues and turning the area into a

Figure 16: Spatial organization in Munich 1972

Munich 1972

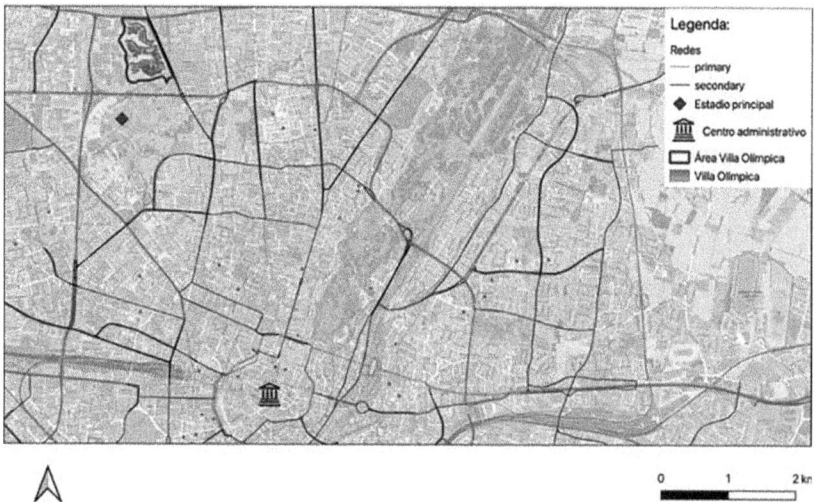

Source: Own implementation

huge sports center for future events. However, plans to build an Olympic village on the vast green space have sparked protests from some local residents. The Montreal edition will be a significant crisis for the Olympic movement, as future editions will need to be reconsidered so as not to jeopardize the development of the sport around the world. The Montreal Olympic Village comprises four 19-story blocks that integrate services and offices. After the event, the property was sold to the family (COJO, 1976). The 1980 Moscow edition was part of a 20-year (1971-1990) project for Moscow's reconstruction and metropolitan development. This plan called for reorganizing the urban structure and establishing new sports infrastructure in the city (OCOG, 1980).

Moreover, he integrated the development strategies of eight different areas in this plan, providing centers in these areas and forming satellite areas of the metropolitan area. The government proposed creating Olympic Villages in two areas included in the infrastructure reform of the Russian capital. Therefore, constructing two different Olympic villages would be an opportunity to expand the Olympic buildings in the area. The Olympic Village consisted of 34 apartment blocks of 16-18 stories in the Soviet brutalist style. In the post-event phase, all accommodation was aimed at young families (OCOG, 1980). The Los Angeles edition is considered the first civilian edition of the event and the first in which university dormitories were used to house Olympic athletes. This also influenced the use of existing structures and university dormitories to promote knowledge through university services. The University of Southern California, the University of California, Los Angeles, and the University of California, Santa Barbara, could accommodate more than 12,000 participants and provide all the services necessary to comply with Olympic regulations (COJO, 1984). Four years later, the 1988 Seoul performance followed the same philosophy as other performances on this stage. Plan a comprehensive renovation project and incorporate housing as a catalyst for residential construction. Villages were built on the outskirts of the city near sports facilities and the central stadium. The block structures provided to Seoul will be converted into permanent housing and made available to citizens in a post-event phase. Seoul Olympic Village was a large-scale housing project comprising 86 blocks of 26-story buildings with a total area of 1.19 km^2 (COJO, 1988). This housing project was included in the metropolis' strategic plan to improve services and health conditions for residents. This area was home to more than 14,000 people, but it was converted into youth accommodation after the event.

*Phase 5: The promotion of housing as a tool for a
new lifestyle (1992-2004)*

As mentioned previously, the industrial crisis of the late 1980s significantly impacted the development of the world's major industrial cities. With the candidacy of Barcelona in 1992, a new phase in the development of the Olympic Village began. The restoration and transformation of a vast abandoned and unused space in Barcelona's city center will significantly impact the design of Olympic accommodation. The transformation of post-industrial cities through mixed financing opens the door to new economic flows related to tourism and services (Venturi, 1994). The Olympic Village is at the heart of one of the city's primary goals: destroying borders and opening the city to the sea. The village enjoys a privileged location close to the promenade and Olympic Port. The Olympic Village is seen as a catalyst for transforming the entire industrial area through its Barcelona housing project.

Furthermore, its central location in the village allows us to observe how housing promotes new lifestyles in the host city. The Olympic Village, located in the

Figure 17: Spatial organization in Barcelona 1992

Barcelona 1992

Source: Own implementation

Poblenou district, a former industrial area, restored the connection between the city and the sea, continued the Cerda urban pattern, and introduced new uses for space (COJO, 1992). The Olympic Village comprises 18 residential blocks ranging from two to nine stories. The project involved the creation of large-scale specific spaces for commercial services, hotels and offices. The Barcelona Olympic Village is an exciting project for constructing accommodation with mixed financing in an area at risk of speculation in the post-event phase. Implementing the Barcelona Strategy will ensure a new push for Olympic accommodation and promote a new international image for the host city. One Olympic cycle later, the Atlanta 96 edition proposed a temporary solution through the use of temporary structures for the pre-organization of university dormitories and services. Atlanta's organizational model was inspired by Los Angeles. In 1984, the Olympic Village was established on the Georgia Tech campus due to its proximity to sports facilities.

The use of existing infrastructure was complemented by the construction of two new buildings, and the availability of university accommodation in the city increased after the Olympics (COJO, 1996). Sydney 2000 is now considered the first project to incorporate sustainable solutions for constructing and maintaining an Olympic Village. Sydney's plans call for a new sports precinct to be built on a derelict area near the Olympic Park, which will be developed to promote sport through a large sports precinct (Davidson, 2012). Sydney's Olympic Village was planned by constructing 870 apartments, converting them into residential buildings after the event, creating new neighborhoods, and fostering the expansion of Australia's metropolis (Blunden, 2012). The area of the community is 510,861 m^2.

Furthermore, using sustainable materials, providing solar panels, and recycling water paved the way for adopting new sustainable housing models in other futuristic cities (Spooner et al., 2000). However, the Sydney Olympic Village project has reached its peak regarding the number of new Olympic accommodation facilities. For the next Olympic Games in Athens 2004, an Olympic village was built in a 1.09 km^2 suburb, where most of the sports facilities were housed. Due to the similarities, the Olympic Village of Athens can be identified as a satellite city project located 21 km from the city's administrative center. The next project was to create new living spaces for the post-Olympic period. The Olympic Village consists of 366 four-story blocks (COJO, 2004). After the Olympics, this plan was abandoned due to the economic crisis, and various immigrants still live there. The initiative marks a new moment of crisis for Olympic accommodation and will lead to a rethink of Olympic spending and the scale of projects. Thus, the Athens project became one of the worst outcomes in the history of Olympic villages.

Phase 6: Sustainability and heritage as a stimulus for metropolitan development (2008-2028)

In the next stage, the Beijing version will bring new changes to the future of Olympic accommodation. Choosing green spaces and using sustainable materials and environmentally friendly solutions places greater emphasis on environmental protection and sustainable development (Smith, 2007). The Beijing project was driven by the 1990 Asian Games and incorporated into an area in the northern part of the city that the city planned to turn into a large sports park (COJO, 2008). Therefore, the Olympic House was constructed as public housing after the Olympics. The Beijing project will be the catalyst for a new model of housing construction in global cities. Subsequently, the 2012 London project is another fundamental step in developing a new metropolitan architectural model on vacant land with high development potential (Poynter, 2012). The East London area was included in projects to reorganize infrastructure and visions of urban expansion[4] (Smith, 2014). However, the London 2012 Games project will be a defining moment for privately financed housing development in areas at high risk for post-Olympic real estate speculation. The London Olympic Village will be a turning point in post-Olympic planning and the importance of its heritage to the city and its citizens. The city can create a sports park in the heart of Britain's largest city by redefining derelict spaces and providing new environmental protection measures. Additionally, including services and offices in the Olympic Village will encourage new typologies of mixed housing and encourage housing diversification to increase profitability in the post-Olympic phase.

The 2016 Rio de Janeiro Games brought about a new crisis in the history of Olympic housing. The housing project was organized by defining a new neighborhood that could be configured as a satellite city. Before becoming the new sports district, the entire area was occupied by shacks and unconventional buildings, which forced the inhabitants further inland. The Rio Olympic Village was planned to be 28.2 km from the city center. The project is integrated into the organization of infrastructure reforms and new rapid transport services and will bring new conclusions to connectivity between the Olympic regions. The Olympic Village comprises 31 residential blocks of 17 stories (COJO, 2016).

---

[4] Like the Olympic Park, the site required the removal of toxic waste and poisoned soils before construction and was part of the regeneration of the Greenwich Peninsula (Evans, 2017).

Figure 18: Spatial organization in London 2012

Londres 2012

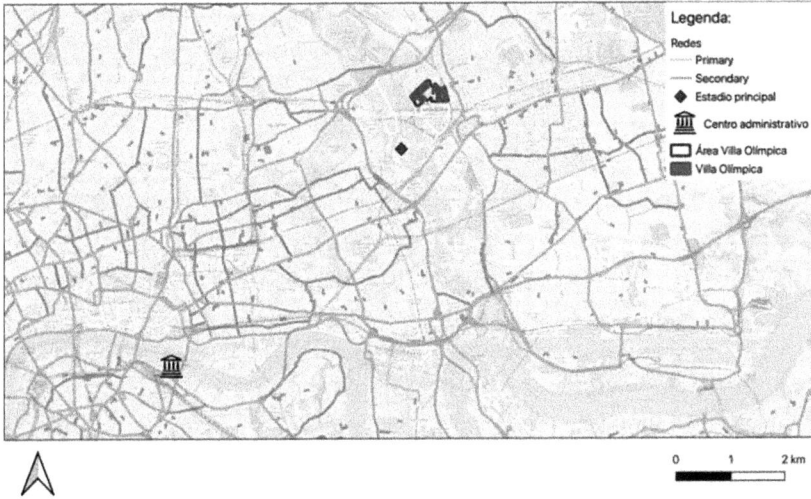

Source: Own implementation

Figure 19: Spatial organization in Tokyo 2020

Tokio 2020

Source: Own implementation

Urbanization projects converted into housing for citizens. However, the Olympic Village in Rio and the Olympic Village in Athens can be seen as two models for satellite cities that were abandoned and sometimes populated by citizens after the Olympics. Subsequently, Tokyo 2020 proposed a development model similar to the London 2012 project. This location was chosen due to its strategic importance for the integration of the area, which will be used as a venue for international events. Post-event accommodation was secured by building new apartments in the city center under a private agreement. The "Olympic Village" project envisaged the construction of two skyscrapers for offices and apartments (COJO, 2020). The following projects confirm the importance of the Olympic Village as a tool for the redevelopment of vacant land in the metropolitan area and as a catalyst for a new economy in the center. The division of Paris in 2024 and Los Angeles in 2028 allows us to observe a new model and formal language of the Olympic Village, constituted by temporality and the presence of sports facilities. The Olympic Village was an opportunity to develop new housing in the heart of the world's largest metropolis.

Further projects include a Paris–Los Angeles version of the Olympic Village, the only existing work of Olympic city design. Using existing and temporary facilities will lead to rethinking Olympic urban planning and housing construction in host cities. In conclusion, the Olympic Village of the next decade of the 21st century clearly indicates the main directions of postmodern urbanism, including sustainability, safety, experience, heritage, and landscape aspects. Similarly, the experience of the Olympic Village at this stage reflects the reality of the most cost-effective urban development (see Table 13).

Table 13: Stages of the Olympic Villages at the Summer Olympics

Phase I	1896–1920	Temporary accommodation	Prospects for the development of an Olympic Village
			Use of hotels and military spaces
Phase II	1924–1932	Peripheral areas Removable housings	Prospects for the development of a permanent Olympic Village
			Specific area for holding the event
			Development of a temporary location for Olympic accommodation

Phase III	1936–1956	Establishment of a sports district Permanent housing	Creation of a sports quarter in the peripheral areas of the cities Sports facilities and services The foundations are laid for developing residential accommodation in the post-Olympic phase.
Phase IV	1960–1988	Expansion of the Olympic Village Residential development tool	Increase in the number of Olympic athletes. Public sector funding for the construction of new accommodations Increasing the size of the Olympic Village area
Phase V	1992–2004	Olympic Village in the city Stimulus for the transformation of abandoned areas	Olympic Village as part of the re-valuation of industrial areas Mixed economy for the construction of the residences The Olympic Village is a tool for the promotion of a new lifestyle.
Phase VI	2008–2028	Transformation of the Olympic Village Global cities	Metropolitan development in empty spaces. Tool for the redefinition and reorganization of the economy of the Olympic area. Greater emphasis on the protection of the environment and the sustainable development Olympic legacy assumes great importance in planning for post-Olympic phase Inclusion of services and offices Mixed housing solutions for social inclusion in cities

Source: Own implementation

3.1.1 Spatial models of the Summer Olympic Villages

The following projects reflect significant changes in the host city's urban structure for the Summer Olympics. Historically, Summer Olympic Villages have
been integrated into urban intervention policies through different urban models
tailored to the needs of each host city. Each Olympic Village has different configurations and constraints that reflect each city's housing philosophy. In general,
the rationalist model of block development is one of the most frequently used
models for the strategic development of Olympic villages. On the other hand,
decentralized models are those observed in cities where large-scale infrastructure changes are made or required to connect different areas within the urban
area. Finally, since London 2012, the inner-city planning model has become the
most commonly used model in large cities seeking to transform their centers.
Strategically located areas to operate new services and infrastructure. Finally,
in the summer edition, the peripheral cluster development model was used only
to address the coordination requirements identified in Chapter 2, Section 2.1.

Analyzing the Olympic Village in the context of the evolution of the Olympic City helps to observe the development and sensitivity of housing issues in
modern metropolises. Today, the Olympic city is a more complex geographical
concept that must meet new requirements regarding air quality, water reuse, waste

Figure 20: Spatial models of the Olympic Village at the Summer Olympics

○ OLYMPIC VILLAGE
⌒ NETWORK

MONOCENTRIC

Munich 72; Montreal 76; Atlanta 96; London 12;
Tokyo 20; Paris 24 ; Los Angeles 28

POLYCENTRIC

Moscow 80; Beijing 08

CLUSTER

Melbourne 56; Roma 60;
Barcelona 92

PERIPHERY

Paris 24; Los Angeles 32;Berlin 36;
Mexico 68; Seoul 88; Sydney 00; Athens 04; Rio 16

SATELLITES

Helsinki 52; Tokyo 64

Source: Own implementation

collection, public space and welfare. The Olympic City must, therefore, be seen as an open and dynamic space where new theories of sustainable development are reinterpreted and implemented for the community's future. We observed that there are no construction plans or reference models for the Olympic Village. However, some models may be a reference for urbanizing future Olympic sites and venues. Figure 24 shows the spatial model observed in the summer edition. Therefore, in the next section, we will look at what model was used to introduce Olympic Villages in the host cities of the Winter Games.

3.2   The different stages of the development of the Winter Village on the regional territory

Figure 21: Evolution of the Winter Olympic Village

Source: Own implementation from COJO, 1924, 1952, 1968, 1988, 1992, 1994, 2006, 2022

Phase 1: Promotion of mountain tourism in resorts (1924-1948)

Since Chamonix hosted the first Winter Olympics in 1924, the event has been held in mountainous locations with ski resorts, sports pavilions, and accommodation options. As noted in Table 10 in Chapter 2, until Oslo in 1952, the Winter Olympics were planned in locations focused on winter sports tourism. The selected mountain locations either had accommodation options or new projects were planned aimed at developing winter tourism in mountain resorts.[5] From a development perspective, Oslo was considered the first winter city to build a permanent Olympic village in 1952 (Delorme, 2014).

---

[5] For example, the Olympic Village in Lake Placid was included in a New York State tourism promotion project.

The 1952 Oslo project was designed through a polycentric spatial organization that incorporated three Olympic Villages into the urban fabric of the Norwegian capital. Since 1952, the Winter Olympic Village has become a spatial transformation model similar to that observed in the summer version. Olympic Villages were organized in three different districts (Illa, Sogn, and Ulleval), which were included in the urban redevelopment plan. Each Olympic district must be self-sufficient and serve as a new living space in the post-Games phase. The Olympic Village was organized into areas containing most primary and secondary services. The building was organized into 18 blocks ranging in height from two to eight stories (COJO, 1952). In the post-Olympic era, structures were organized through mixed solutions. The growing interest in promoting winter sports will provide new tools for cities to incorporate Olympic events into urban transformation.[6] Then, in the

Figure 22: Spatial organization in Oslo 1952

Oslo 1952

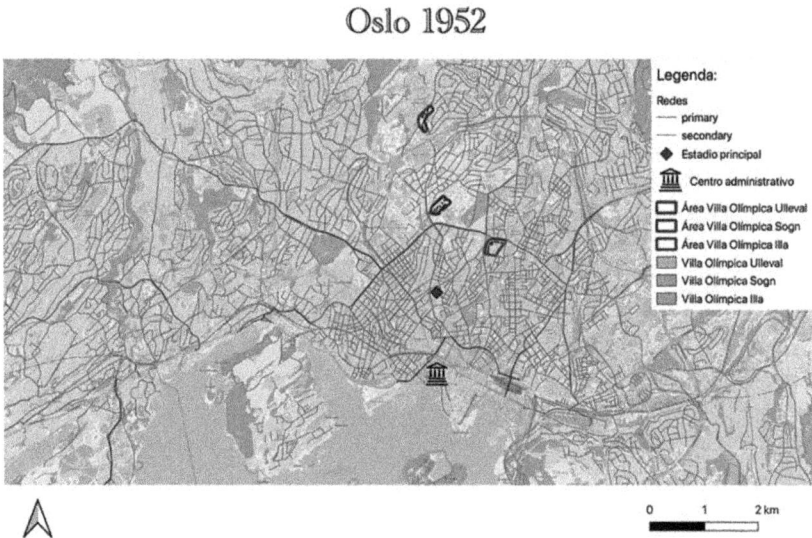

Source: Own implementation

---

[6] With a resident population of 447,200, the city was by far the most significant center to have hosted the Games to that date. The larger population created new opportunities for the type of facilities offered, as viability and future use after the Games were more than assured. Essex, S. (2017). *The Winter Olympics-Driving urban change, 1924–2022, in Olympic cities, City agendas, planning and the World's Games.* Routledge.

1964 Innsbruck edition, it was proposed to build an Olympic village in the area included in the central canton housing plan. He designed the village by building four 10-story blocks (COJO, 1964). The project was intended to become a large residential area in the post-event phase. For this reason, we are seeing an increase in public funding for new housing construction triggered by the Olympic bid.

Phase 3: Mixed housing in a regional development dimension (1968-1988)

As the scale and interest in winter sports grew, cities began to promote a new spatial model in their Olympic venues, which was expanded to the entire region during the organization of Grenoble in 1968. The growing demand for infrastructure will enable Grenoble to realize new regional transformation projects with support from the central government to increase tourism and trade in the mountain region.[7] The project in Grenoble proposes an accommodation solution in the city center close to the main stadium and is planned to have a demountable structure in the post-event phase. The structure and architecture of the Olympic Village were designed in a rationalist style that respected Le Corbusier's idea of building a new functional city. Meanwhile, Olympic accommodation should be used through mixed management, which benefits the university, the public and tourists. The village was divided into 11 blocks of fourth to fifth floors. The construction of new highways, roads, airports and railway lines will determine new models for hosting Olympic events.

The Olympic Village was included in a priority urbanization area identified in the General Plan as an area of new interest for regional development. Therefore, in the next stage, this event will become a regional development tool to promote infrastructure interventions, as was done in the summer edition several years ago. Like Grenoble, Sapporo also embarked on a project to repair and redefine its urban and regional infrastructure in 1972 (Kagaya, 1991). Sapporo became the first city with a population of over 1 million to host the Olympics. The Olympic Village is included in the housing development plan, providing block-shaped buildings that could be converted into residential spaces at a post-Olympic stage. In the next stage, we will observe how the housing emergency influences the

---

[7.] The Grenoble project was financed by the central government and the French central bank in a framework of international trade development.

Figure 23: Spatial organization in Grenoble 1968

Grenoble 1968

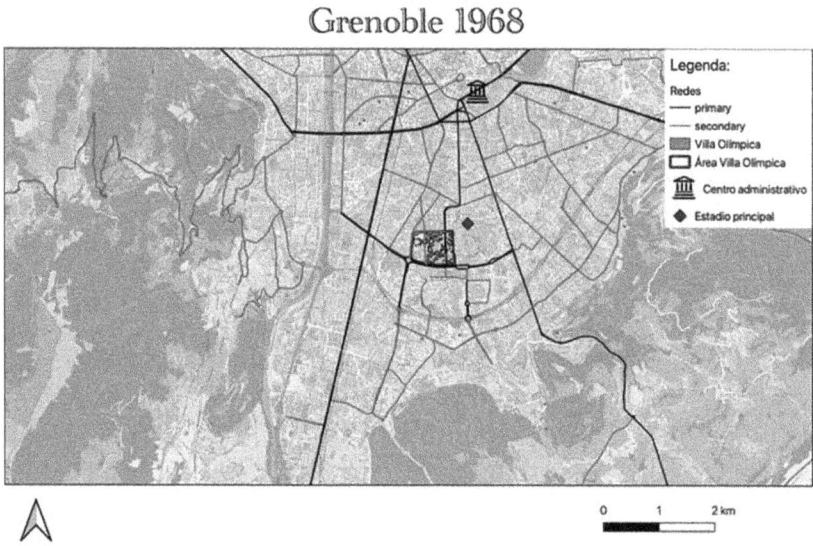

Figure 23: Spatial organization in Grenoble 1968

Source: Own implementation

design and construction of housing projects and expands its scale within the fabric of the open city. Only a few hotels catering to alpine athletes will be built in mountainous villages during that time. The Sapporo Olympic Village will champion a new construction model never achieved before in its winter version. The complex was realized by constructing 20 residential blocks ranging in height from 5 to 11 floors (COJO, 1972). Sapporo was the first city, until Grenoble, to not have the sports facilities essential to hosting Olympic events. Subsequently, at the 1976 Innsbruck Games, it was proposed to build a new Olympic Village in an area adjacent to the area built at the 1964 Games (OCOG, 1976). Knowing that the accommodation was being used by the community, the organizing committee needed to provide a new accommodation solution that implied the same philosophy of reuse for the post-Olympic period. Therefore, after the Olympic Games, the area was to be transformed into a new residential area for the population, facilitating the expansion of the area built for the 1964 Games. By the 1988 Calgary Games, the number of athletes had increased, and Olympic host cities began to promote new solutions for Olympic accommodation projects. In the Winter issue, Calgary is recognized as the first city to offer a university-style accommodation solution (Olds, 1998).

Furthermore, the organizing committee focused the project on the realization of new sports facilities for university students and the promotion of winter sports (COJO, 1988). The accommodation solution in Calgary greatly motivated future editions to provide a new model for transforming the Winter Olympics. The third phase will see a significant increase in the size of the Olympic space. In addition, the increased number of competitions and athletes will bring new sports facilities and solutions to several Olympic Villages.

Phase 4: Tourism development tool (1992–2002)

Albertville in 1992 is considered the first project to propose multiple accommodation solutions in various mountain resorts, and the main Olympic village of the area is included in the tourism development of the entire region. However, in 1992, Albertville proposed a polycentric spatial model that incorporated and strengthened the region's position as an international tourism center (Terret, 2008). Significant investment in this event has made it possible to build new accommodation facilities and hotels across the Olympic venues and update the entire mountain infrastructure system to reposition locations within it. By offering eight hotel structures tailored to the needs of the Olympic event, new spatial dimensions that did not exist before are now possible. After Albertville, the IOC was concerned about the size of the Games and the distribution of athletes to different mountain resorts. However, given the increasing number of athletes, it will be difficult for the host city to propose an Olympic village. Since Albertville, the Olympic event has become a new tool for reconstructing new regions and repositioning the town in the winter tourism market.[8]

Already in Lillehammer in 1994, the organizers had raised the topic of temporary accommodation for athletes. Furthermore, the organizing committee introduced the theme of sustainability and sustainable development by providing 185 demountable wooden huts (COJO, 1994). The solution chosen by Lillehammer inspired the entire Olympic movement and the cities of the future. The Olympic Village in Lillehammer was demolished in the post-Games stage. Therefore, sustainability and environmental care have been a critical element

---

[8.] The number of overnight stays increased from 100,000 in 1989 to 700,000 in 1995. Thus, in 1996, Brides' financial situation aligned with expectations. The municipality's budget increased from 15 million francs in 1992 to 25 million francs in 1996 (Sordet, 1996).

Figure 24: Spatial organization in Albertville 1992

Albertville 1992

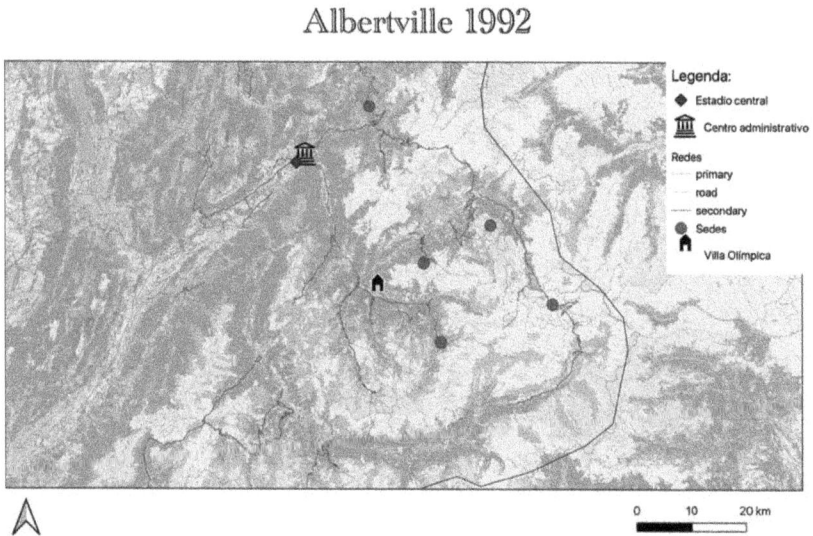

Figure 24: Spatial organization in Albertville 1992

Source: Own implementation

of the winter edition since Lillehammer. However, significant infrastructural changes and increased scale of events affected candidate cities' environment and regional development (Spilling, 1996). Lillehammer allowed the IOC to add sustainability as a third pillar of the Olympic movement. The next edition, Nagano 1998, proposed the construction of a new district and adjacent sports facilities. This edition was included in a series of regional transformations to incorporate the city into a new regional economy. The construction of a railway connecting Nagano and Tokyo will significantly change the economy of Nagano City. The Nagano Olympic Village was planned to be converted into private housing on the city's outskirts after the Olympics. The village was realized by constructing 23 residential blocks ranging in height from two to four stories (COJO, 1998). Then, in 2002, Salt Lake proposed a university-like accommodation solution similar to Calgary's 1988 version. Additionally, the organizers have developed new environmental protection measures, including a new sustainable development process for the event (OCOG, 2002). The Salt Lake Project met its carbon reduction goals to reduce pollution, and the event was recognized as one of the most sustainable ever.

*Phase 5: Multiple Olympic Villages in a regionalization
context (2006-2022)*

Then, in the fifth phase, the 2006 Turin Games changed the spatial aspects of
the Olympic project and event again. The Turin version implements sustainable
development practices by applying a strategic assessment of environmental
development throughout the Olympic process. The organizers proposed a new
spatial model that included large cities as venues for ceremonies, ice sports competitions and the main Olympic village while offering a spatial configuration in
two mountain tourist destinations: Bardonecchia and Sestriere. The three Olympic
Villages' location and the Olympic event's spatial dimension aim to transform
the region permanently, encourage increased winter tourism, and provide the city
with opportunities to develop new markets. The Olympic Village was planned
in an abandoned area included in the city of Turin's development plan and was
intended to become a mixed area of services, housing, shops, and offices after
the Olympics. However, Turin's Olympic Village suffered from many structural
problems and was occupied by people seeking political asylum in 2012, so it
was never thoroughly mixed. In the meantime, Olympic villages in mountain
resorts should be converted into hotel accommodations and holiday apartments.
The realization of the Olympic Village of Bardonecchia was integrated into the
regional development plan by funding the renovation and redesign work of the
1930s building.

On the other hand, the Sestriere Olympic Village was built by a private
company, which was contracted to build the resort and obligated to make it
accessible to the organizing committee during the Olympic Games. Turin's
transformation symbolized the rebirth and transformation of the new metropolitan process after the Industrial Revolution. This strategy aimed to extend
the benefits of Olympic investments beyond the city, i.e., the entire region,
thanks to the possibility of improving ski facilities and structures and developing the tourist season (Dansero, 2003). Therefore, in the fourth phase, the
dimension of the winter event will change to a metropolitan event, prompting
the restructuring of regional infrastructure.

In 2010, Vancouver introduced a new blended financing model by introducing
a new post-Olympic planning model that served as a tool to promote long-term
Olympic investment (VanWynsberghe et al., 2012). The City of Vancouver and the
organizing committee had planned to build an Olympic village in the area as part

Figure 25: Spatial organization in Turin 2006

Turin 2006

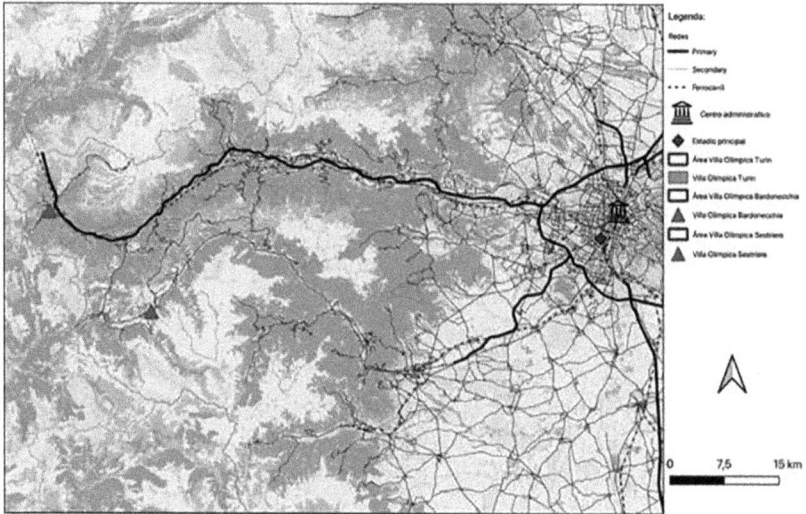

Source: Own implementation

of an urban renewal project. The Olympic Village was realized on a completed brownfield site thanks to private participation and was able to provide new living spaces for the post-Olympic period. The new district consists of 37 buildings ranging from 5 to 10 stories. In the post-Olympic period, it was redesigned and transformed into a central space in the Vancouver metropolis (COJO, 2010). However, the Vancouver Olympic Village would face additional issues related to Olympic housing speculation in the post-Olympic period (Scherer, 2011). Development goals for mixed and market-rate housing were changed to provide only 10% of the planned 30%. In the post-Olympic period, evictions increased in the city due to rising rent prices (Essex, 2017).

The 2014 Sochi Games proposed a spatial configuration, an essential step in expanding the new Olympic event to regions with subtropical climates (Scott, 2015). The purpose of this event was to develop a new territorial system by constructing new tourist attractions and planning several Olympic villages connected by a railway system. Since Sochi, the scale of the event has continued to grow and will become a powerful force for change in regional systems. This event will undoubtedly raise new questions about respect and protection of the environment. Organizers proposed a solution based on three Olympic Villages. The main village is near the ice rink and ceremony site, and there are two further Olympic villages in the mountains. Ninety-nine new buildings were constructed from two to seven stories (OCOG, 2014). Olympic villages in urban areas will be converted into housing after the Olympics, while Olympic villages in the mountains will be converted into hotels and resorts after the Games to promote local tourism. However, the post-Olympic version was widely criticized due to the vast financial expenditure and distance between Olympic venues. Sochi still needs to raise questions about its post-Olympic development. During the Pyeongchang 2022 and Beijing 2022 Games, the Olympic Village will promote sports tourism in the mountainous region. Pyeongchang offered a metropolitan cluster model with subvenues and two Olympic villages for residential accommodation in the post-Olympic period. However, apartment complexes in mountainous areas are still abandoned.

Meanwhile, the 2022 Beijing Games will see a large Chinese city become the first city in the world to host both the Summer and Winter Games. The Games were an essential stage in the metropolitan and regional aspects of the Winter

Figure 26: Spatial organization in Beijing 2022

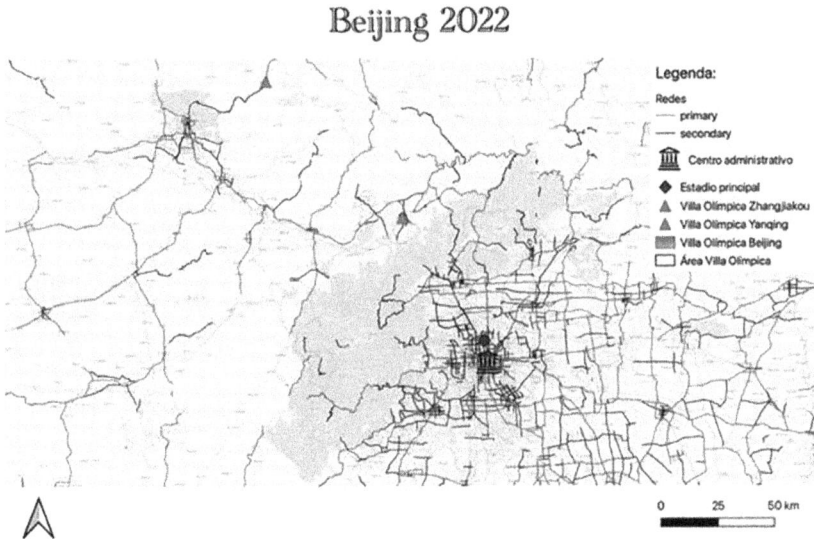

Source: Own implementation

Olympics. This spatial model is strongly inspired by the scale of the 2006 Turin Games through the organization of three Olympic Villages within the region. The central Olympic Village will be built adjacent to the Summer Olympic Village and offered as housing through public tender during the post-Olympic period. On the other hand, after the Olympics, an athletic village was built in a mountain village as a tourist accommodation facility.

Phase 6: Tool for infrastructural development of tourism sites.
Multiple cities, multiple regions (2026-Future)

The average distance between major cities and Olympic venues will be 115.63 km, facilitating new forms of Olympic development ahead of the joint bid of Milan and Cortina d'Ampezzo in 2026 and the allocation of Barcelona and the Pyrenees in 2030. Beijing will begin a new era of short-term bidding, but the metropolis will only use it as a promotional tool to award events and leverage tourism and service benefits. Metropolitan Olympic villages will, therefore, become a fundamental element of housing construction plans in future world metropolises and are integrated into the new urban dynamics of consumer society. Additionally, the 2026 Milano Cortina Games will involve three regions in north-eastern Italy by organizing two capital cities and 13 subvenues. Such aspects will lead to new developments in winter events and new tools for managing the economy of almost a fifth of the country. Furthermore, the development of new infrastructure poses new challenges for candidate cities. The following notable fact that Barcelona and the Pyrenees are in the running for the 2030 Games allows us to recognize the unique extraterritorial aspects that the Winter Olympics can achieve (see Table 14).

Table 14 Stages of the Olympic Villages at the Winter Olympics

Phase I	1924–1948	Mountain locations Temporary accommodation	Prospects for the creation of an Olympic Village Existing sports facilities Use of hotels and resorts
Phase II	1952–1964	Cities with more than 100,000 inhabitants	Construction of the Olympic Village Different areas for the celebration of the event

		Permanent accommodation	Developing a public policy for Olympic accommodation Growing interest in winter sports
Phase III	1968–1988	Regional expansion Residential accommodation	Encouragement for the creation of new sports facilities Development of the infrastructural system for the transfer of athletes. The foundations are laid for developing residential accommodation in the post-Olympic phase. New transformation model
Phase IV	1992–2002	Increase in Olympic space Tourism development tool	Increase in competitions and athletes Construction of multiple Olympic Villages New housing solutions (universities, demountable housing) Olympic space is organized in multiple locations. Respect for the environment
Phase V	2006–2022	Olympic Village in the city and Olympic Villages at competition venues Stimulus for the transformation of the regional system Metropolis	Main Olympic Village in the metropolitan city Mixed economy for the construction of residences in the mountain places The Olympic Village as a tool for the promotion of sports tourism in mountain areas Increased emphasis on environmental protection and sustainable development Legacy begins to enter into post-Olympic planning

(*Continued*)

			Regional development
Phase VI	2026–Future	Multiple Olympic cities Multiple regions	Tool for the reorganization of the economy of the Olympic area Creation of new mixed accommodation solutions Development of new infrastructure for the transport of Olympic athletes

Source: Own implementation

3.2.1 Spatial models of the Winter Olympic Villages

The next stage represents the evolution of the host city's significant urban and territorial changes. Historically, Winter Olympic Villages have been integrated into territorial development policies and have become essential in reconfiguring regional strategies. Generally speaking, the athlete accommodation model remains essential for competitions in mountainous areas. However, the mountain Olympic village model is evolving through the concept of tourism development in Olympic sites. The "candidate city" housing model is now establishing itself as a critical element in the organization of several Olympic villages. The decentralized model is one of the most widely used models for the strategic development of Olympic Villages in cities. However, recent experience allows us to observe how Olympic housing projects have been integrated into the central fabric of cities.

On the other hand, the peripheral *cluster* model is considered one of the most used models to provide various adaptations in expanding territorial dimensions. Analyzing the Olympic Village in the context of regional transformation helps to monitor the development of aspects of the winter event in the context of the regional expansion of the host city. The Olympic winter city has become a global metropolis that can provide new infrastructure for short-term connections between mountainous regions and large cities. Today, cities need to rethink the new dimensions achieved and solutions in dynamic and open spaces that can be modified in a participatory way. Although no model or reference scheme can be identified when evaluating the Olympic Village, a trend of regional expansion of the world's largest metropolises can be observed. However, climate, temperature, and landscape restrictions are unsuitable for a winter event.

Figure 27: Spatial models of the
Olympic Village at the Winter Olympics

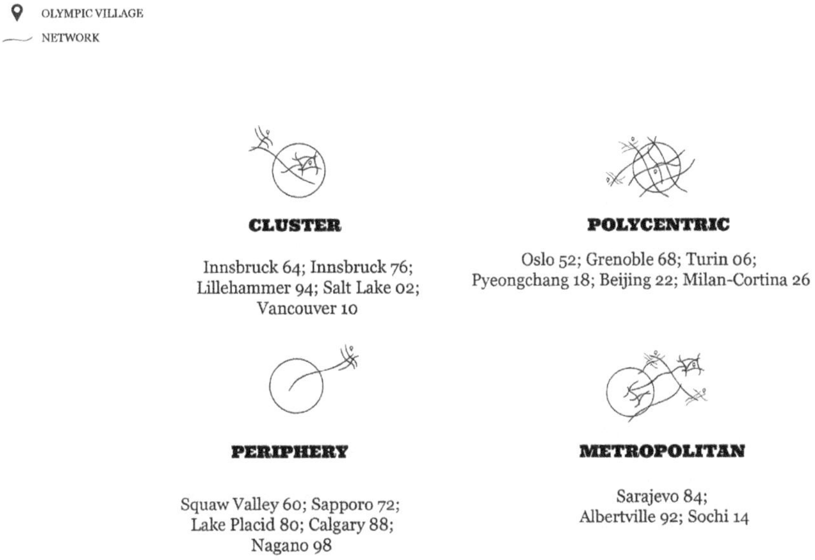

📍 OLYMPIC VILLAGE
⌒ NETWORK

CLUSTER

Innsbruck 64; Innsbruck 76;
Lillehammer 94; Salt Lake 02;
Vancouver 10

POLYCENTRIC

Oslo 52; Grenoble 68; Turin 06;
Pyeongchang 18; Beijing 22; Milan-Cortina 26

PERIPHERY

Squaw Valley 60; Sapporo 72;
Lake Placid 80; Calgary 88;
Nagano 98

METROPOLITAN

Sarajevo 84;
Albertville 92; Sochi 14

Source: Own implementation

Additionally, the 2014 Sochi Games showed that hosting the Winter Games in locations with subtropical climates and no historical value as sports venues is possible. The following diagram shows different regional models for host cities. Next, we will classify the Olympic villages in terms of their territory.

3.2.2 Considerations on the urban strategies of the Olympic Village

The evolution and concept of Olympic urbanism, typified by the Olympic Village in the 20th century, allows us to observe the evolution of different urban, regional, and metropolitan strategies that disproportionately increased the spatial dimension and character of the original event. After World War II, Olympic Villages became essential in promoting permanent housing integration into host areas. However, the spatial dimensions of the two editions and the features of the Olympic Village have evolved and continue to grow with the housing needs of the host city in mind. Therefore, The Olympic Village functions not only as a temporary accommodation facility but also as an independent element that is permanently integrated into the area within the various urban strategies of the individual host cities (see Table 15). As we saw in the previous section, the last two versions of the Olympic Village became private residences after the Olympics. Building temporary shelters or accommodations for tourists is not the committee's first choice. Undoubtedly, since the experiences of Barcelona (1992), Turin (2006), and London (2012), the Olympic Village must be included in the strategic plans of various programs to rebuild and redefine urban functions. It is an essential urban element (see Table 16). Therefore, the cartographic representation is used to classify Olympic Villages according to their characteristics and post-Olympic use development.

Table 15: Examples of classification according to the character of each Olympic Village

Summer Olympic Villages		Winter Olympic Villages	
Permanent	Temporary	Permanent	Temporary
1. Berlin 1936	1. Paris 1924	1. Oslo 1952	1. Lake Placid 1980 (prison)
2. Helsinki 1952	2. Los Angeles 1932	2. Squaw Valley 1960	2. Calgary 1988 (university)
3. Melbourne 1956	3. Tokyo 1964	3. Innsbruck 1964	3. Albertville 1992
4. Rome 1960	4. Los Angeles 1984 (university)	4. Grenoble 1968	4. Lillehammer 1994
5. Mexico 1968	5. Atlanta 1996 (university)	5. Sapporo 1972	5. Salt Lake 2002 (university)
6. Monaco 1972		6. Innsbruck 1976	
7. Montreal 1976		7. Sarajevo 1984	
8. Moscow 1980		8. Nagano 1998	
9. Seoul 1988		9. Turin 2006	
10. Barcelona 1992		10. Vancouver 2010	

Summer Olympic Villages		Winter Olympic Villages	
Permanent	*Temporary*	*Permanent*	*Temporary*
11. Sydney 2000		11. Sochi 2014	
12. Athens 2004		12. PyeongChang 2018	
13. Beijing 2008		13. Beijing 2022	
14. London 2012			
15. Rio 2016			
16. Tokyo 2020			

Source: Own implementation

Figure 28: Classification of Winter Olympic Villages according to character

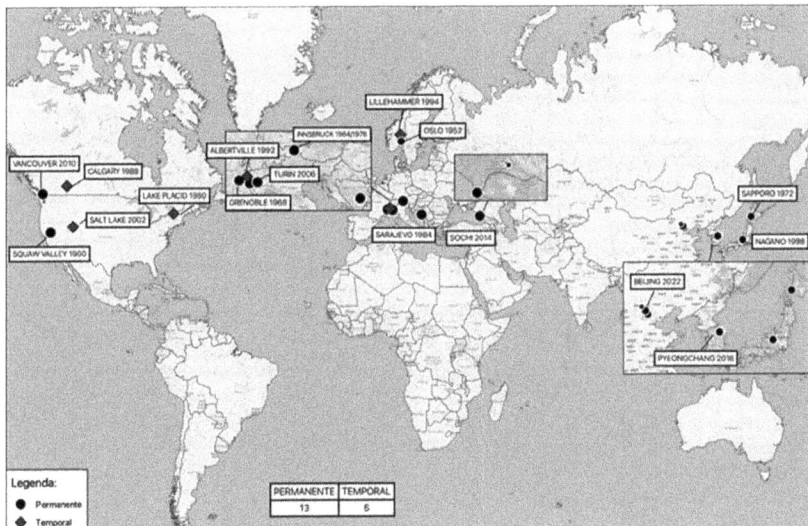

Source: Own implementation

Figure 29: Classification of Summer Olympic Villages
according to character

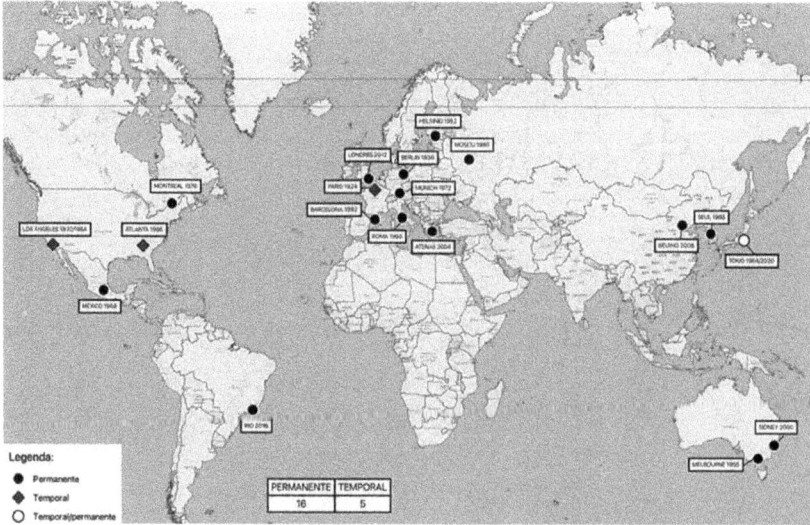

Source: Own implementation

Table 16: Examples of classification according to the
ex-post evolution of the games

Summer Olympic Villages		Winter Olympic Villages	
Reuse	*Abandoned*	*Reuse*	*Abandoned*
1. Helsinki 1952	1. Berlin 1936	1. Oslo 1952	1. Sarajevo 1984
2. Melbourne 1956	2. Athens 2004	2. Squaw Valley 1960	2. Torino 2006 (inner city)
3. Rome 1960	3. Rio 2016	3. Innsbruck 1964	
4. Mexico 1968		4. Grenoble 1968	
5. Monaco 1972		5. Sapporo 1972	
6. Montreal 1976		6. Innsbruck 1976	
7. Moscow 1980		7. Lake Placid 1980 (prison)	

Summer Olympic Villages		Winter Olympic Villages	
Reuse	Abandoned	Reuse	Abandoned
8. Los Angeles 1984		8. Calgary 1988 (University)	
9. Seoul 1988		9. Albertville 1992	
10. Barcelona 1992		10. Lillehammer 1994	
11. Atlanta 1996		11. Nagano 1998	
12. Sydney 2000		12. Salt Lake 2002 (University)	
13. Beijing 2008		13. Torino 2006	
14. London 2012		14. Vancouver 2010	
15. Tokyo 2020		15. Sochi 2014	

Source: Own implementation

Figure 30: Classification of Winter Olympic Villages according to post-Olympic evolution

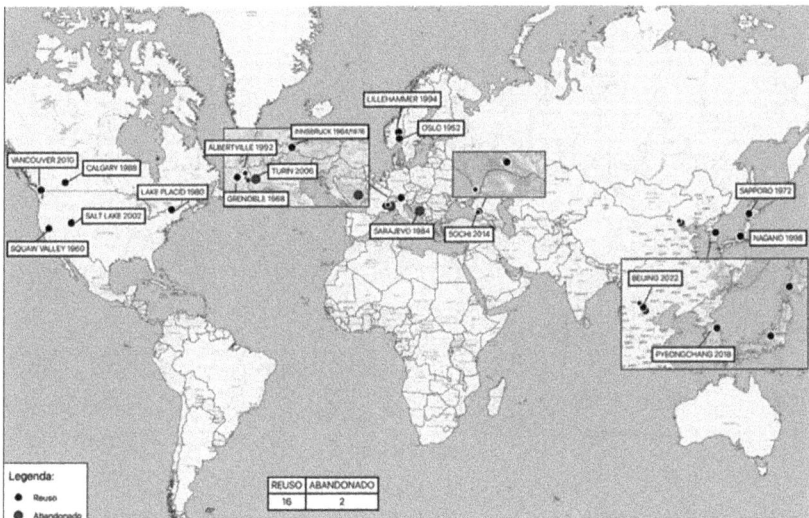

Source: Own implementation

Figure 31: Ranking of Summer Olympic Villages according to
post-Olympic evolution

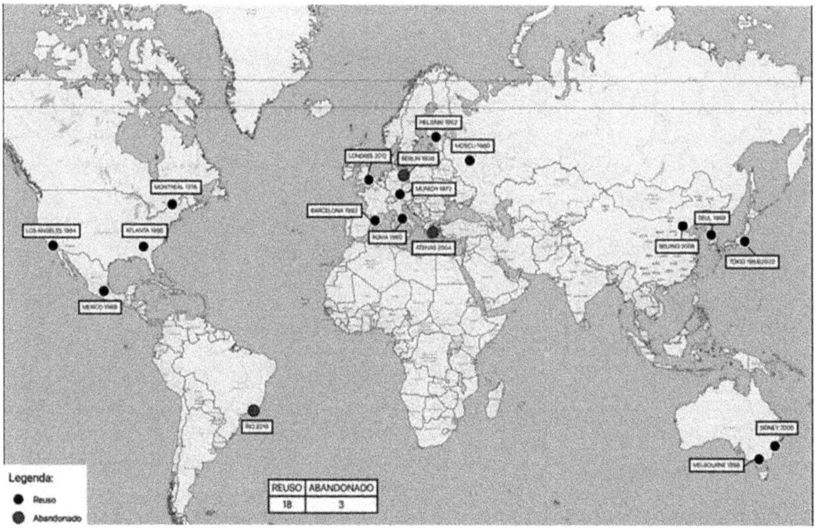

Source: Own implementation

CHAPTER 4

Two Centuries of Olympic Villages

4.1 The evolution of Olympic Village models developed throughout Olympic history

The following section allows us to examine some comparative parameters to deepen the quantitative analysis of the Olympic Village and its development in the host cities. A brief description of the Olympic editions accompanies the graphical representations.

About the variables considered, the following list has been used to provide an optimal characterization of each of the Olympic Villages:

- The population of the city.
- The capacity of the Olympic Village (number of inhabitants).
- A number of buildings.
- Height of buildings.
- Typology of buildings.
- Urban density.
- Occupied area.
- Residential area.
- International area (public spaces).
- Distance from the main stadium.
- Distance from the administrative center of the city.
- Ownership of the area before the Olympic Games.
- Post-Olympic use.
- Heritage value (financing).
- Current value.

The variables chosen will provide some considerations on the future evolution of Olympic Village spatial patterns in the host cities.

4.1.1 The evolution and validity of an urban model

Before going deeper into the individual Summer Olympic Villages, it is specified that the following analysis was carried out to specifically analyze the Olympic Villages through their spatial dimension and characteristics. Therefore, the Olympic Villages analyzed will be the following:

1. Paris 1924 2. Los Angeles 1932 3. Berlin 1936	13. Seoul 1988
4. Helsinki 1952	14. Barcelona 1992
5. Melbourne 1956	15. Atlanta 1996
6. Rome 1960 7. Tokyo 1964	16. Sydney 2000
8. Mexico 1968	17. Athens 2004
9. Munich 1972	18. Beijing 2008
10. Montreal 1976	19. London 2012
11. Moscow 1980	20. Rio 2016
12. Los Angeles 1984	21. Tokyo 2020

4.1.2 Paris 1924

The Paris Olympic Village is recognized as the first housing model at the Olympic Games by proposing a temporary solution using wooden huts that were dismantled during the post-event period. The Olympic Village was planned close to the main stadium. It included the first shared services, such as the post office, a telegraph and telephone service, a laundry, a newspaper kiosk and a hairdressing salon.[1] The structure had running water and communal dining facilities for the participants.

---

[1] Comité olympique français. (1924). *Les jeux de la VIIIe Olympiade Paris 1924: rapport officiel* (pp. 51, 60–61, 799–800). Librairie de France.

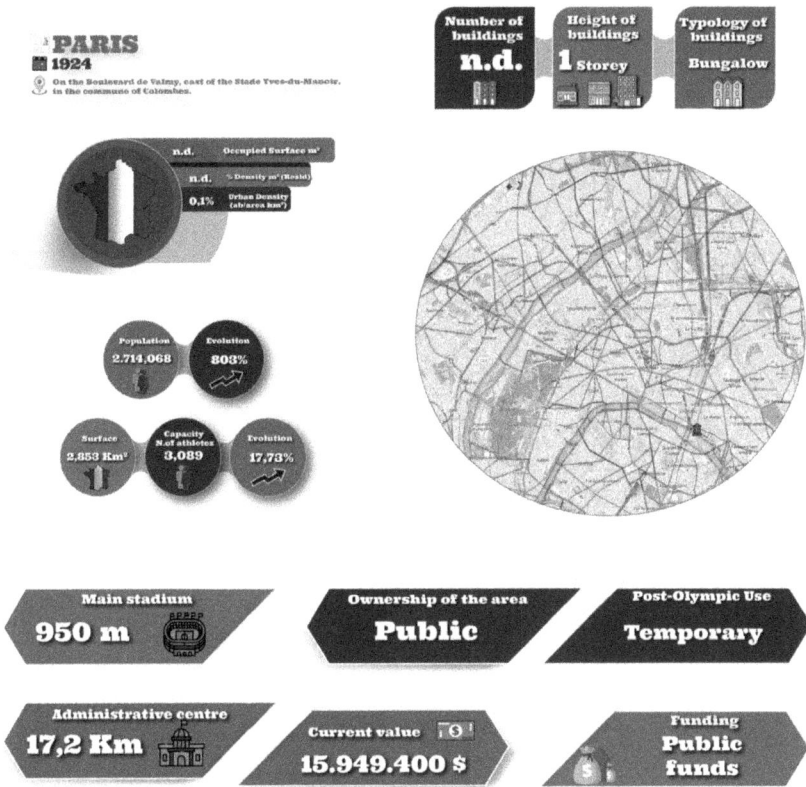

4.1.3 Los Angeles 1932

The Los Angeles Olympic Village concept was strongly inspired by the materials and temporality of the wooden structures seen in the first Olympic Village but with an entirely new spatial conception. The Olympic Village was planned on a peripheral site that was a catalyst for the expansion of the Los Angeles metropolis. The Village included a hospital, a fire station, a security service, a post office, a telephone network, and an open-air theater for 2,000 people.[2] During the post-Olympic period, the Village was dismantled. The Los Angeles edition inspired the creation of a new Olympic Quarter in addition to the Olympic Plaza, the current site of the medal ceremony.

---

[2] The Xth Olympiad Committee of the Games of Los Angeles. (1933). *The Games of the Xth Olympiad Los Angeles 1932: Official report* (pp. 157, 187–190, 235–296).

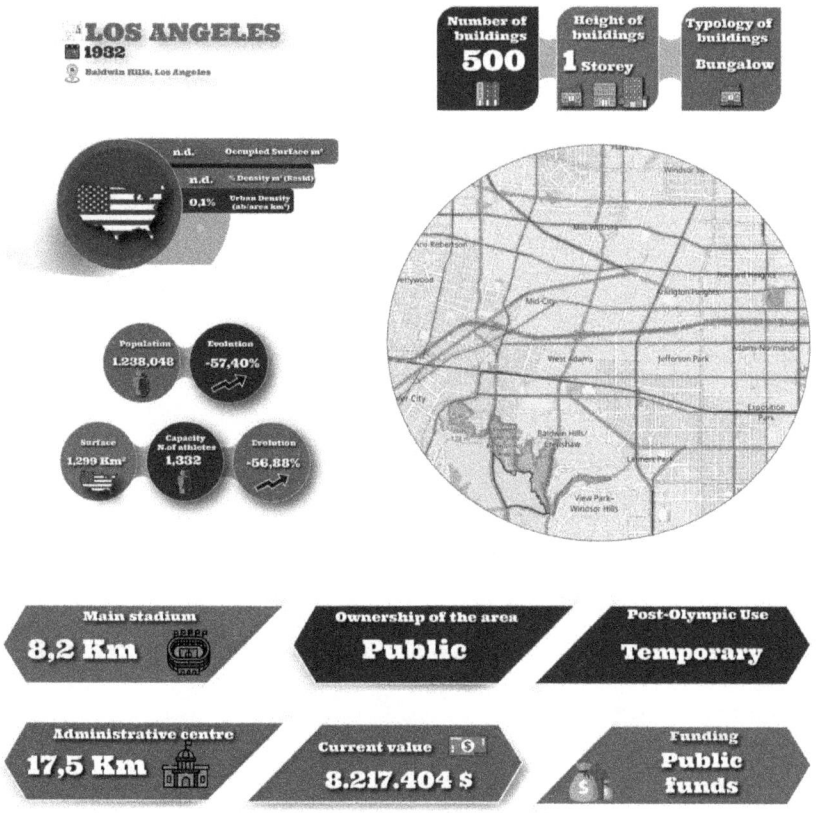

LOS ANGELES
1932
Baldwin Hills, Los Angeles

Number of buildings
500

Height of buildings
1 Storey

Typology of buildings
Bungalow

n.d.   Occupied Surface m²
n.d.   % Density m² (Resid)
0,1%   Urban Density (ab/area km²)

Population   Evolution
1.238,048   -57,40%

Surface   Capacity N.of athletes   Evolution
1,299 Km²   1,332   -56,88%

Main stadium
8,2 Km

Ownership of the area
Public

Post-Olympic Use
Temporary

Administrative centre
17,5 Km

Current value
8.217.404 $

Funding
Public funds

4.1.4 Berlin 1936

The Berlin Olympic Village was built on the experience of Los Angeles in 1932, representing an excellent success for the American Organizing Committee. The planning and construction of the Olympic Village had great political relevance for the promotion of the ideals of Nazi Germany and the exaltation of the philosophies of the German sports school. The concept of the Berlin Olympic Village can be seen through the ideological concepts of the socialists of the second half of the 19th century. A new sports quarter was created on 55 ha with all training facilities, a sports hall, religious services, a railway station, a post office, etc. The Olympic Village was intended as a satellite city of 5,000 inhabitants to be reused as military accommodation in the post-Olympic period. Today, however, the Olympic Village is abandoned and converted into an open-air museum. Two more temporary Olympic Villages were planned in Kiel and Granau 3 to house the athletes of the sailing and rowing events.

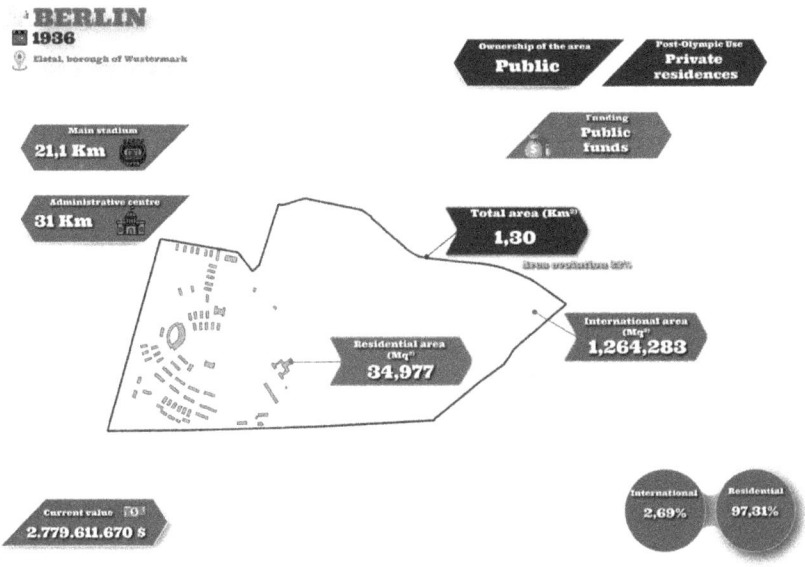

BERLIN
1936
Elstal, borough of Wustermark

Ownership of the area — **Public**

Post-Olympic Use — **Private residences**

Main stadium — **21,1 Km**

Funding — **Public funds**

Administrative centre — **31 Km**

Total area (Km²) — **1,30**

Residential area (Mq²) — **34,977**

International area (Mq²) — **1,264,283**

Current value — **2.779.611.670 $**

International — **2,69%**

Residential — **97,31%**

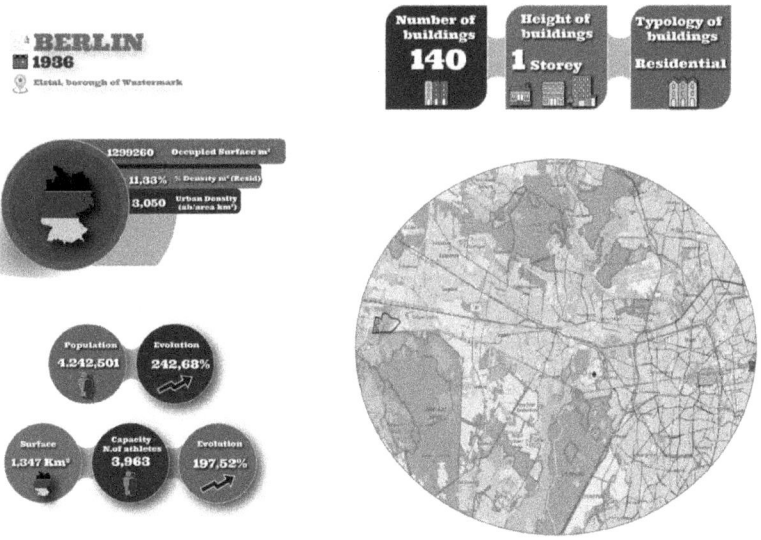

BERLIN
1936
Elstal, borough of Wustermark

Occupied Surface m² — **1299260**

% Density m² (Resid) — **11,33%**

Urban Density (ab/area km²) — **3,050**

Number of buildings — **140**

Height of buildings — **1 Storey**

Typology of buildings — **Residential**

Population — **4.242,501**

Evolution — **242,68%**

Surface — **1,347 Km²**

Capacity N.of athletes — **3,963**

Evolution — **197,52%**

4.1.5 Helsinki 1952

The 1952 Helsinki Olympic Village concept was strongly linked to population growth and demands for new accommodation. Therefore, the planning of the Olympic Village was related to the construction of a new residential neighborhood.

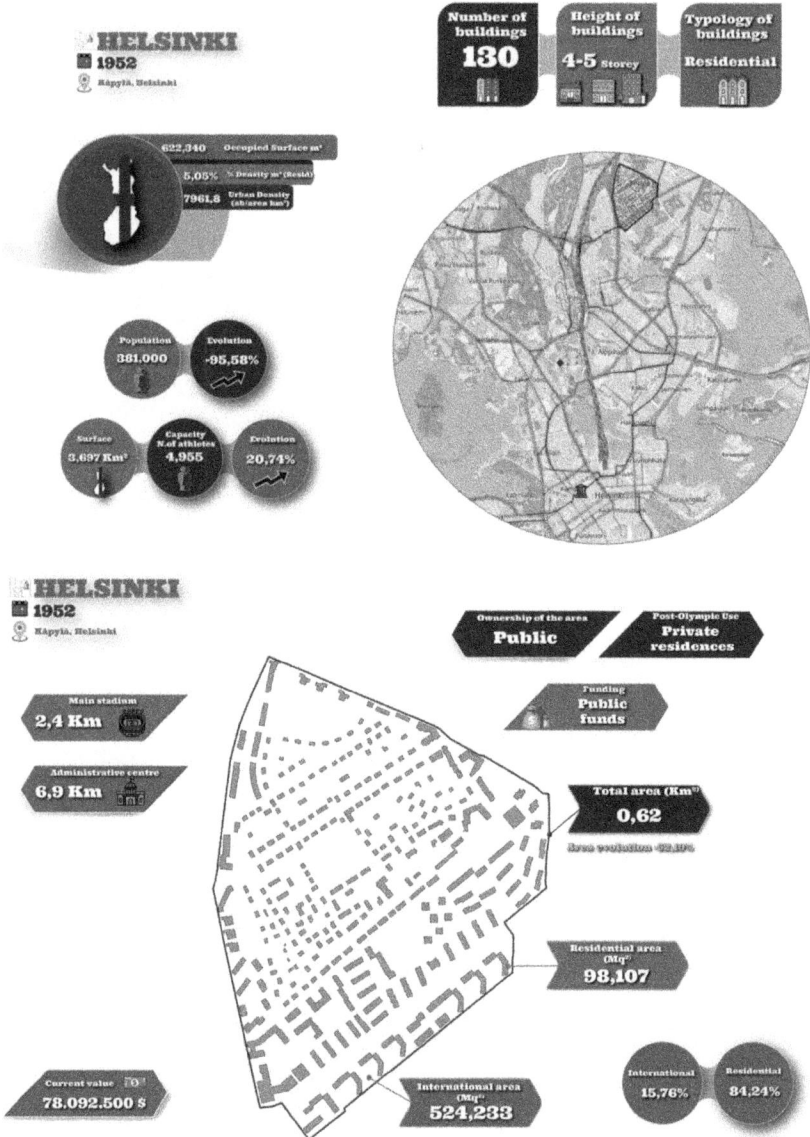

The Village was close to the Olympic stadium, sports facilities, hospital, cinema, bank, and all other services in general. In the post-Olympic period, the neighborhood became a residential area for 5,000 people.[3] However, some hotels and military residences were used to house the women's teams and the teams of the former USSR. The Helsinki Olympic Village inspired the creation of a new residential neighborhood in the central area of a medium-sized metropolis.

4.1.6 Melbourne/Stockholm 1956

The construction of the Melbourne Olympic Village followed the same philosophy observed in Helsinki. A new Olympic quarter with its master plan responded to the accommodation needs of the citizens in the city of Heidelberg. Thanks to public funds, other temporary and permanent annexes could be built. The Village included different types of houses and buildings for the post-Olympic conversion. In addition, the general plan foresaw some services such as a medical center, training areas, a canteen, a post office, restaurants, shops, and other functional facilities to enhance the experience of the Olympic athletes. The Melbourne edition foresaw using another temporary Olympic Village in Ballarat for the sailing

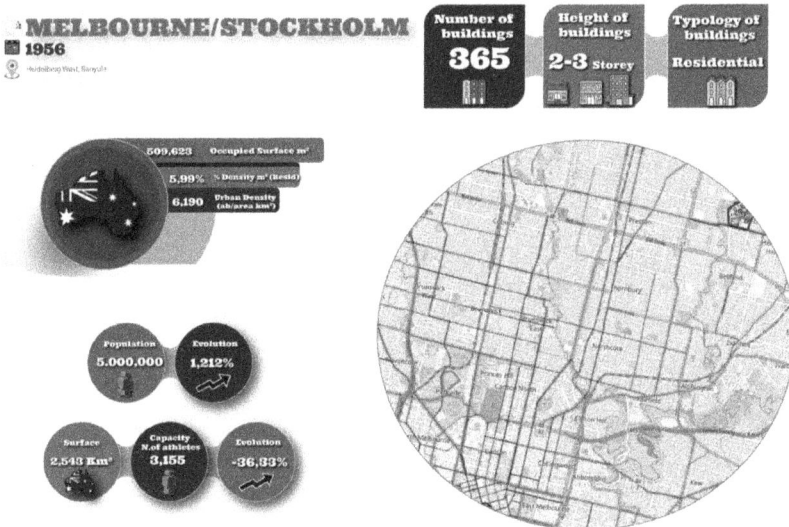

[3] Organising Committee for the Helsinki Games. (1952). "New Olympic Village under construction." *Official News-Service: XV Olympiad*, 6, 3; Kolkka, Sulo. (Ed.). (1955). *The official report of the Organising Committee for the Games of the XV Olympiad* (pp. 84–102). W. Söderström.

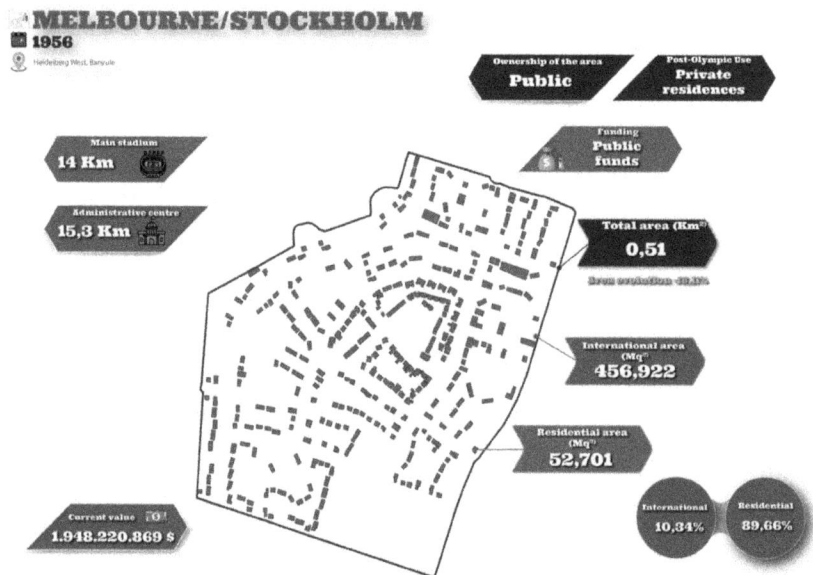

MELBOURNE/STOCKHOLM
1956
Heidelberg West, Bansule

Ownership of the area	Post-Olympic Use
Public	**Private residences**

Main stadium **14 Km**

Administrative centre **15,3 Km**

Funding **Public funds**

Total area (Km²) **0,51**

International area (Mq²) **456,922**

Residential area (Mq²) **52,701**

Current value **1.948.220.869 $**

International **10,34%**   Residential **89,66%**

competitions and Stockholm for the horse competitions.[4] The Melbourne Olympic Village still exists and continues to function as residential accommodation. In addition, between 2005 and 2013, the suburb was included in an urban renewal program supported by the Australian government.

4.1.7 Rome 1960

The construction of the 1960 Rome Olympic Village was included in the general plan to expand the metropolitan city through a rationalist philosophy of Italian architecture. The Olympic Quarter was intended to be converted into residential accommodation in the post-Olympic period and still exists today. The concept of the Olympic Village included some sports facilities, services, functional areas and proximity to the Foro Italico, the main venue of the Rome event.[5] The edition enjoyed two other temporary Olympic Villages, one in Naples for the sailing competitions and one in Castel Gandolfo for the rowing competitions. The Rome Olympic Village catalyzed a new development process in a neighborhood with 10,000 inhabitants.

[4.] Organising Committee for the Games of the XVI Olympiad. (1958). *The official report of the Organizing Committee for the Games of the XVI Olympiad Melbourne 1956* (pp. 121–137).

[5.] Organising Committee for the Games of the XVII Olympiad. (1963). *The Games of the XVII Olympiad Rome, 1960: The official report of the Organising Committee* (Vol. 1, pp. 89–93, 164–167, 223–295).

ROMA
1960
Villaggio Olimpico, Roma

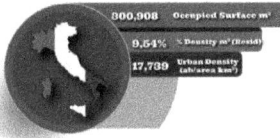

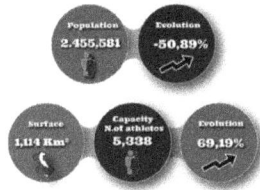

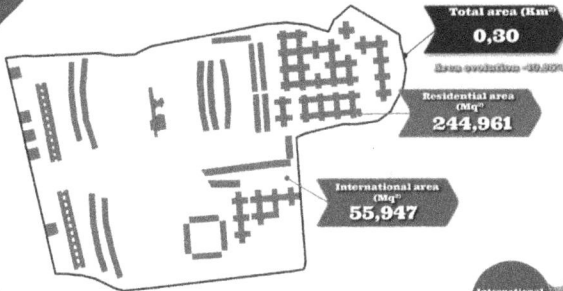

Number of buildings	Height of buildings	Typology of buildings
33	2-5 Storey	Residential

800,908 Occupied Surface m²
9,54% % Density m² (Resid)
17,739 Urban Density (ab/area km²)

Population 2.455,581
Evolution -50,89%

Surface 1,114 Km²
Capacity N.of athletes 5,938
Evolution 69,19%

ROMA
1960
Villaggio Olimpico, Roma

Ownership of the area: **Public**
Post-Olympic Use: **Private residences**

Main stadium 3,1 Km
Administrative centre 6 Km

Funding: **Public funds**

Total area (Km²) 0,30
Area evolution -49,50%
Residential area (Mq²) 244,961
International area (Mq²) 55,947

Current value 124.621.000 $

International 18,59%
Residential 81,41%

4.1.8 Tokyo 1964

The 1964 edition of Tokyo proposed a temporary accommodation solution in the form of wooden rooms that could be dismantled in the post-Olympic period and reclaimed the natural space where the US Army was stationed. The Tokyo

Olympic Village was built as a temporary solution already seen in Los Angeles and involved fewer problems for post-Olympic conversion. The Olympic Village included all the services, offices, shops, two swimming pools, and sports facilities that still exist today.[6] Yoyogi Park became famous in the post-Olympic

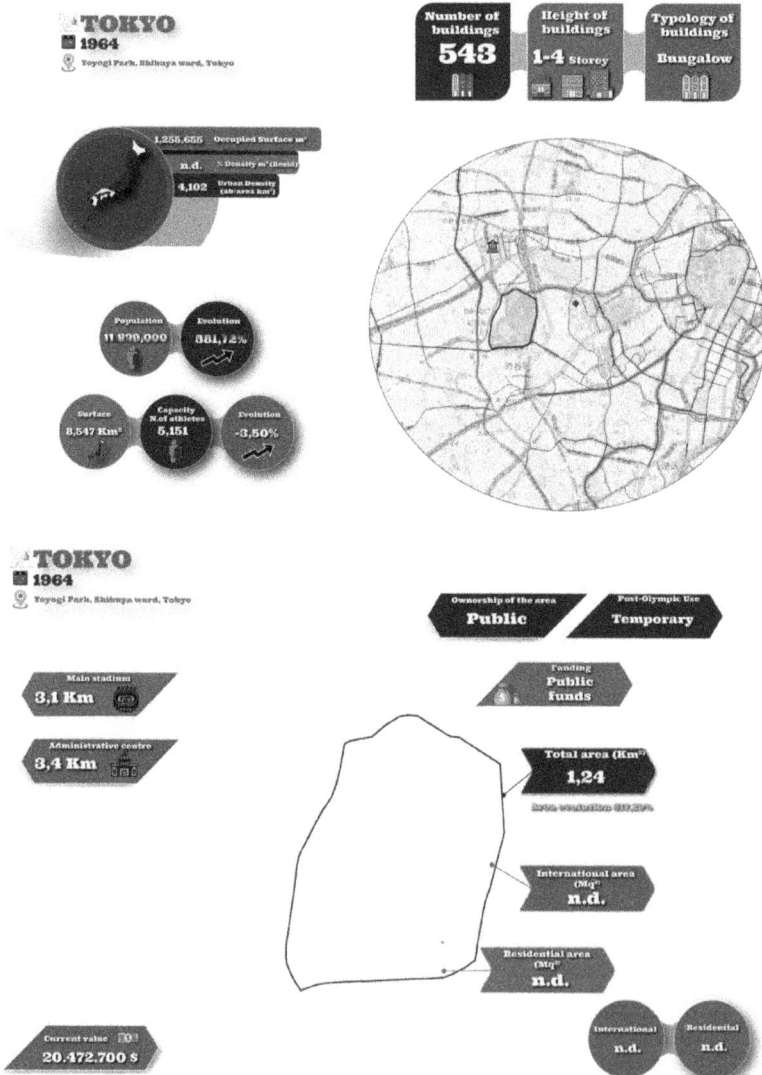

6. The Organising Committee for the Games of the XVIII Olympiad. (1966). *The games of the XVIII Olympiad, Tokyo 1964: The official report of the Organising Committee* (Vol. 1, pp. 281–352).

period because of the cherry blossom. The issue comprised different temporary accommodation solutions in other locations connected by bus lines. The temporary structures were mainly existing hotels. Today, the heritage of the Tokyo Olympic Village can only be seen in a small memorial house in the middle of Yoyogi Park.

4.1.9 Mexico City 1968

The construction of the Mexico City Olympic Village was planned near the Olympic stadium in an area of 11 ha with 27 blocks of buildings constituting a new neighborhood of 10,000 inhabitants as in Rome. However, the block buildings did not respect the in-line development philosophy observed in Rome. The Village included medical clinics, a press center, recreational and training facilities, a theater, an international club, and a public auditorium.[7] Participants in the sailing and football competitions were accommodated in hotels. The Olympic Village was intended to transform a new residential area, one of the largest neighborhoods in the southern part of the metropolis.

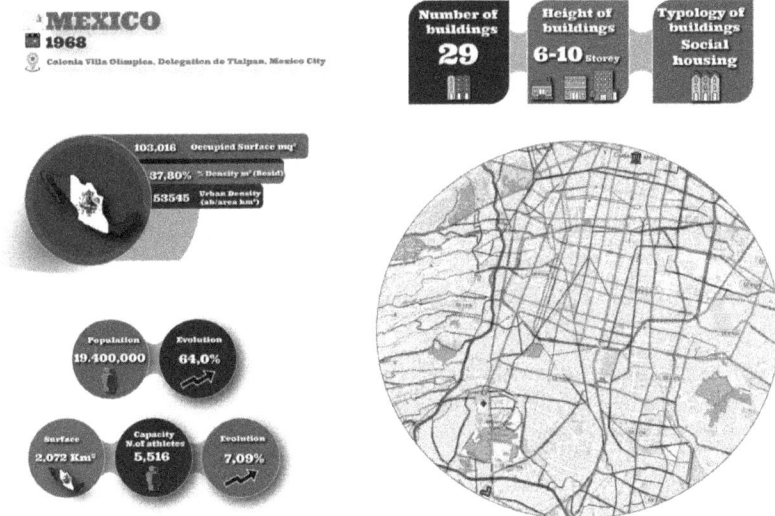

[7.] Organising Committee of the Games of the XIX Olympiad. (1969). *Mexico 68* (Vol. 2, pp. 246–265; Vol. 4, pp. 627–630).

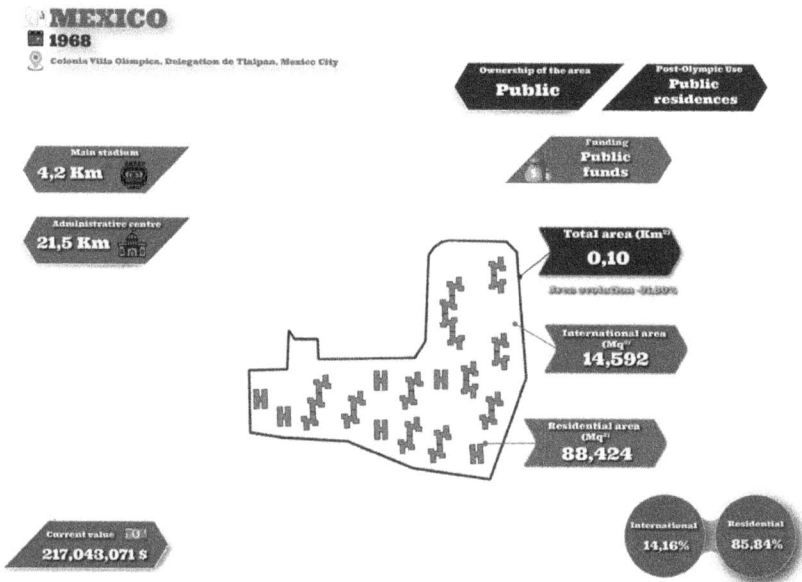

MEXICO
1968
Colonia Villa Olimpica, Delegation de Tlalpan, Mexico City

Ownership of the area
Public

Post-Olympic Use
Public residences

Main stadium
4,2 Km

Funding
Public funds

Administrative centre
21,5 Km

Total area (Km²)
0,10

Area evolution -91,90%

International area (Mq²)
14,592

Residential area (Mq²)
88,424

Current value
217,043,071 $

International
14,16%

Residential
85,84%

4.1.10 Munich 1972

The Munich Olympic Village was built near the Olympic Park in a green area that could accommodate more than 12,000 people. The buildings comprised different construction typologies and were divided into three distinct areas: one for men, one for women, and a central area. The main area of the Village is concentrated in the primary services, the leisure center, shops, restaurants, banks, a medical center, a laundry, and others. Green areas and forests surrounded the Olympic Quarter. In addition, the construction of the Olympic Village was included in the infrastructural works to provide new means of transport between the sports facilities and the city center.[8] The Village in the post-Olympic period became a residential neighborhood that still exists today. The temporary accommodation in Kiel for the sailing competitions was converted into university accommodation. The Munich Olympic Village inspired the construction of a new sports district near the center of the German metropolis.

---

[8] Prosport. (1974). *Die Spiele: The official report of the Organizing Committee for the Games of the XXth Olympiad Munich 1972* (Vol. 1, pp. 124–141, 150; Vol. 2, pp. 98, 100–111); Bath, Henning. (Ed.). (n.d.). *Village olympique—Olympic Village—Olympisches Dorf* (pp. 7, 25). Organising Committee for the Games of the XXth Olympiad Munich.

MUNICH
1972
Milbertshofen-Am Hart district / Am Riesenfeld, Munich

Number of buildings	Height of buildings	Typology of buildings
534	**2-20** Storey	**Residential**

473,006 — Occupied Surface m²
6,64% — % Density m² (Resid)
15082 — Urban Density (ab/area km²)

Population — 2.136,000
Evolution — -88,06%

Surface — 5,991 Km²
Capacity N.of athletes — 7,134
Evolution — 29,33%

MUNICH
1972
Milbertshofen-Am Hart district / Am Riesenfeld, Munich

Ownership of the area — **Public**
Post-Olympic Use — **Private residences**

Main stadium — **850 m**
Administrative centre — **8,2 Km**

Funding — **Public funds**

Total area (Km²) — **0,47**
Area evolution 659,57%

Residential area (Mq²) — **365,580**

International area (Mq²) — **107,426**

Current value — **115.636.128 $**

International — 22,71%
Residential — 77,29%

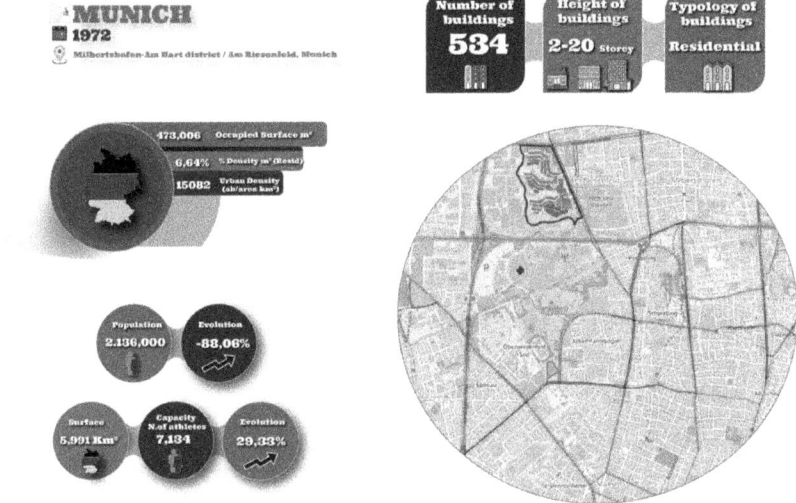

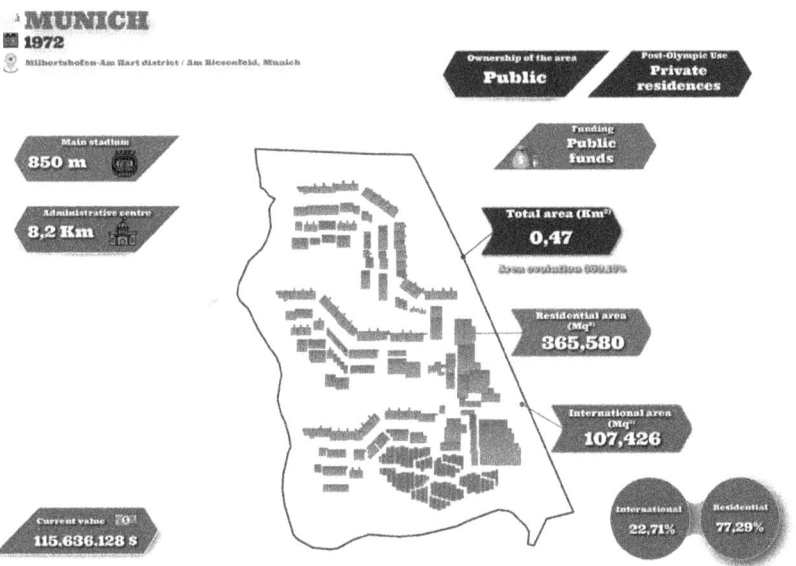

4.1.11 Montreal 1976

The Montreal Olympic Village project was strongly inspired by previous projects to create a new sports district through pyramidal block structures inspired by Le Corbusier's rationalist philosophy. The Olympic Village benefited from some temporary structures and offered all the services to the Olympic athletes. The division of public and private activities was a crucial aspect in the realization of the Olympic Village. The area included sports facilities, restaurants, leisure areas, medical services, a market, a religious center, shops, press and conference

MONTREAL
1976
Rue Sherbrooke Est, Rosemont-La Petite-Patrie, Montreal

Number of buildings	Height of buildings	Typology of buildings
4	**19** Storey	Residential

631,305 Occupied Surface m²
27,22% % Density m² (Resid)
18363 Urban Density (ab/area km²)

Population 2.950.000
Evolution 27,37%

Surface 1.546 Km²
Capacity N.of athletes 6.084
Evolution -14,72%

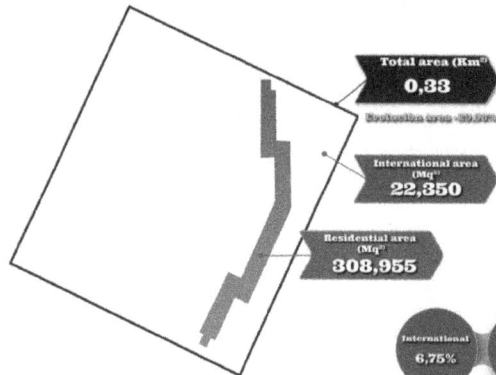

MONTREAL
1976
Rue Sherbrooke Est, Rosemont-La Petite-Patrie, Montreal

Ownership of the area **Public**
Post-Olympic Use **Private residences**

Main stadium **1,1 Km**

Funding **Public funds**

Administrative centre **5,5 Km**

Total area (Km²) **0,33**

International area (Mq²) **22.350**

Residential area (Mq²) **308.955**

Current value **392.546.023 $**

International 6,75%
Residential 93,25%

rooms.[9] The Montreal Olympic Village inspired the construction of accommodation that would become residences in the post-Olympic period. Today, the Olympic Village continues to function as a residential neighborhood. Two temporary Olympic Villages were erected and converted into student accommodation in the post-Olympic period for the sailing and equestrian competitions.

4.1.12 Moscow 1980

The 1980 Moscow Olympic Games provided two Olympic Villages organized as satellite cities. The central Olympic Village was connected to the Olympic Stadium through a network of infrastructure that allowed movement between the Olympic Villages and the sports venues. The accommodation was built using blocks identical to Soviet buildings within a completely natural area with a large amount of vegetation and included the sports facilities, a polyclinic, a cultural center and most of the training facilities.[10] The Olympic Village space in the post-Olympic period became a new residential area that still exists today.

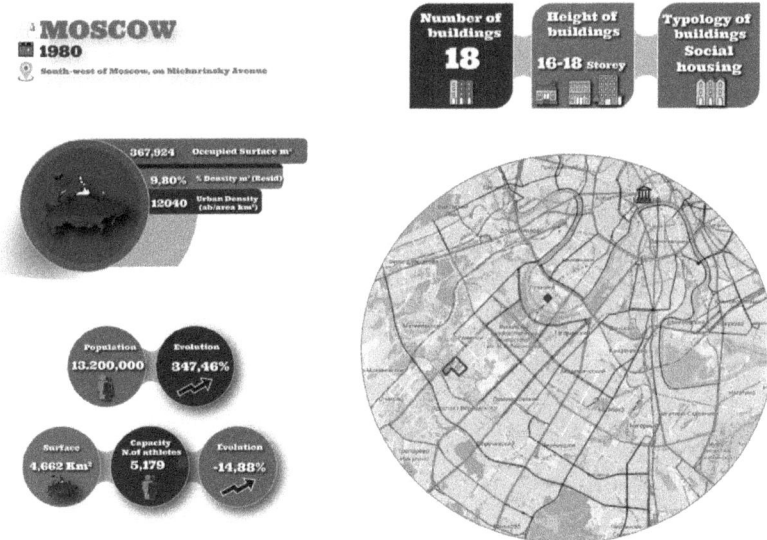

[9.] COJO 76. (1978). *Montreal 1976: Games of the XXI Olympiad Montreal 1976: Official report* (Vol. 1, pp. 258–279; Vol. 2, pp. 196–201, 222–225); OCOG. (1976). *Guide to Olympic Village* (pp. 8, 38, 82).

[10.] OCOG-80. (1981). *Official report of the Organising Committee of the Games of the XXII Olympiad, Moscow 1980* (Vol. 1, pp. 158, 190, 234; Vol. 2, pp. 132–135, 307–332).

MOSCOW
1980
South-west of Moscow, on Michurinsky Avenue

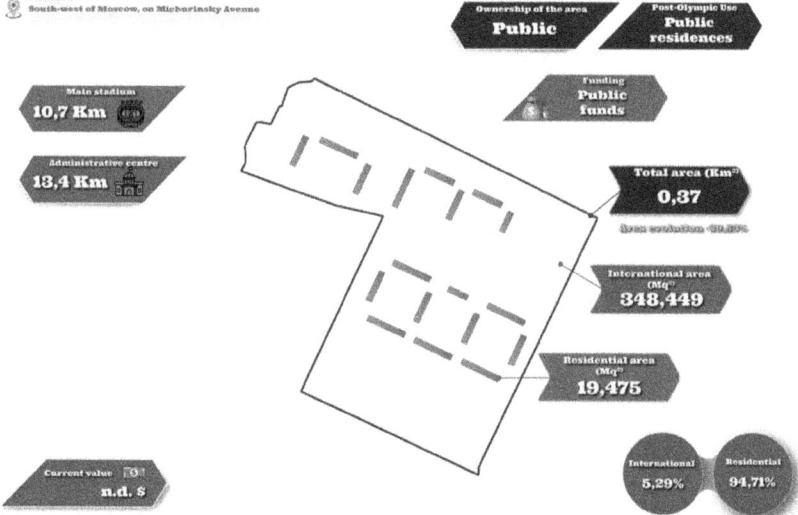

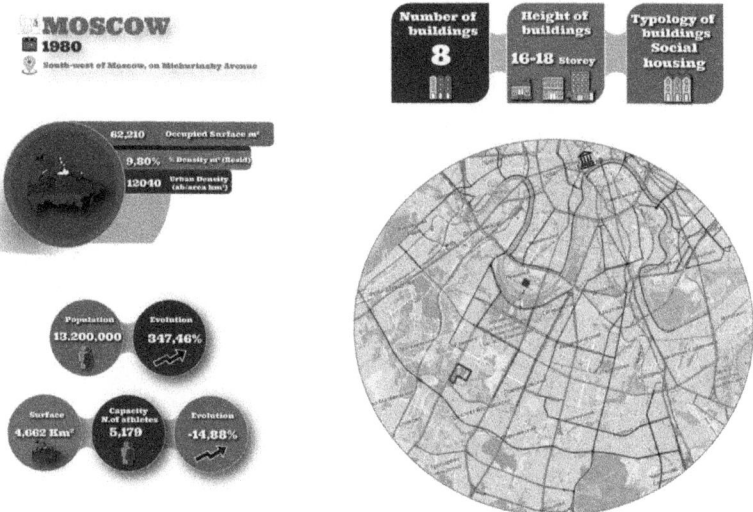

Ownership of the area Public

Post-Olympic Use Public residences

Funding Public funds

Main stadium 10,7 Km

Administrative centre 13,4 Km

Total area (Km²) 0,37

Area evolution -99,60%

International area (Mq²) 348,449

Residential area (Mq²) 19,475

Current value n.d. $

International 5,29%
Residential 94,71%

MOSCOW
1980
South-west of Moscow, on Michurinsky Avenue

62,210 Occupied Surface m²
9,80% % Density m² (Resid)
12040 Urban Density (ab/area km²)

Population 13.200.000
Evolution 347,46%

Surface 4,662 Km²
Capacity N.of athletes 5,179
Evolution -14,88%

Number of buildings 8

Height of buildings 16-18 Storey

Typology of buildings Social housing

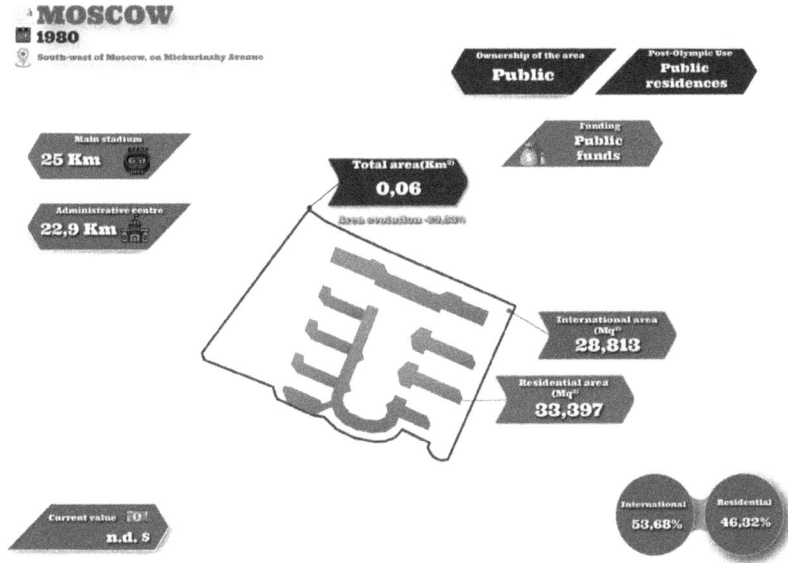

MOSCOW
1980
South-west of Moscow, on Michurinsky Avenue

Ownership of the area
Public

Post-Olympic Use
Public residences

Main stadium
25 Km

Total area(Km²)
0,06

Funding
Public funds

Administrative centre
22,9 Km

Area evolution -99,83%

International area (Mq²)
28,813

Residential area (Mq²)
33,397

Current value
n.d. $

International **53,68%**   Residential **46,32%**

4.1.13 Los Angeles 1984

The Los Angeles edition was the first edition to be financed mainly by private funds and through temporary or existing structures. The Los Angeles Organizers provided an accommodation structure by using the California residence halls and other temporary structures added for some services. In addition, the existing sports facilities at the university provided a large training park close to the accommodation. The university town included all the catering, leisure, medical, religious, and other services.[11] The athletes used the University of Santa Barbara accommodation for the sailing competitions. The temporary facilities were dismantled in the post-Olympic period, and the accommodation was returned to the university students for the start of the academic year. The solution adopted by Los Angeles signed a change in the concept of Olympic accommodation in the host city.

[11] Organizing Committee of Los Angeles Olympic. (1984). *Athlete's Village Guide: Games of the XXIIIrd Olympiad Los Angeles 1984* (pp. 32–37); Organizing Committee of Los Angeles Olympic. (1985). *Official report of the Games of the XXIIIrd Olympiad Los Angeles 1984* (Vol. 1, pp. 161–185, 368–388).

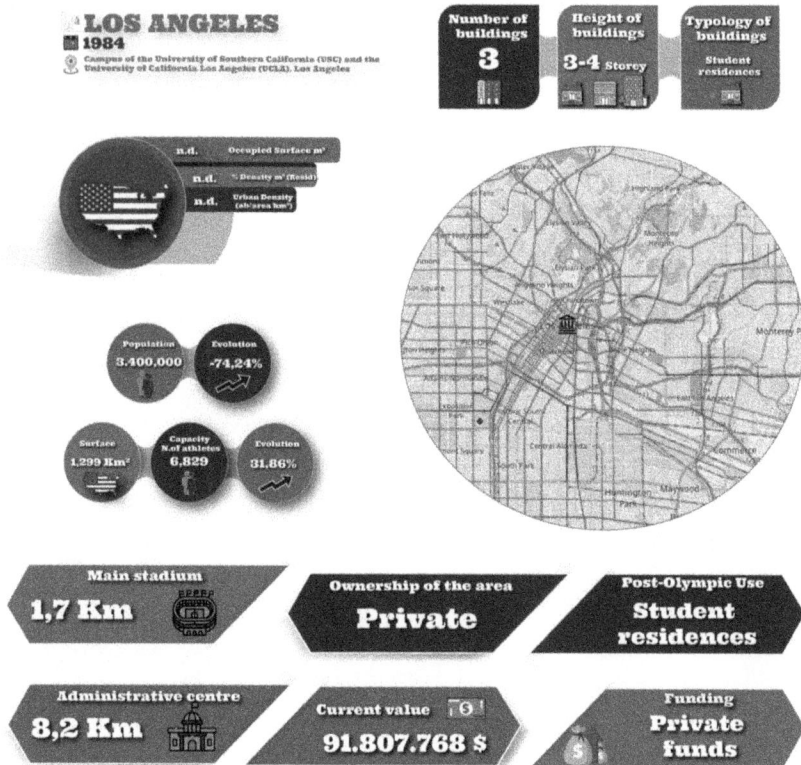

LOS ANGELES
1984
Campus of the University of Southern California (USC) and the University of California Los Angeles (UCLA). Los Angeles

Number of buildings	Height of buildings	Typology of buildings
3	3-4 Storey	Student residences

Population 3.400.000 — Evolution -74,24%

Surface 1.299 Km² — Capacity N.of athletes 6.829 — Evolution 31,86%

Main stadium 1,7 Km — Ownership of the area **Private** — Post-Olympic Use **Student residences**

Administrative centre 8,2 Km — Current value 91.807.768 $ — Funding **Private funds**

4.1.14 Seoul 1988

The Seoul Olympic Village was planned within a residential area with sports facilities, toilets, restaurants, a gymnasium, a theater, shops, entertainment venues, a religious center, and more.[12] The Seoul Olympic Village was in a strategic planning program for accommodation in the Korean capital and was intended to be reused as residences in the post-Olympic period. The Olympic Village area reached 15,000 inhabitants on 50 ha for the first time. Seoul marked a significant transformation in expanding services and accommodation for Olympic athletes.

[12.] Seoul Olympic Organizing Committee. (1989). *Official report: Games of the XXIVth Olympiad Seoul 1988, Seoul* (Vol. 1, pp. 527–570); Seoul Olympic Organizing Committee. (n.d.). *Guide du Village olympique* (pp. 3, 9).

SEOUL
1988
Oryan-dong quarter, in the Songpa-gu district, Seoul

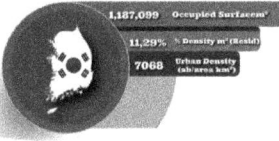

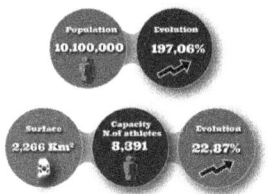

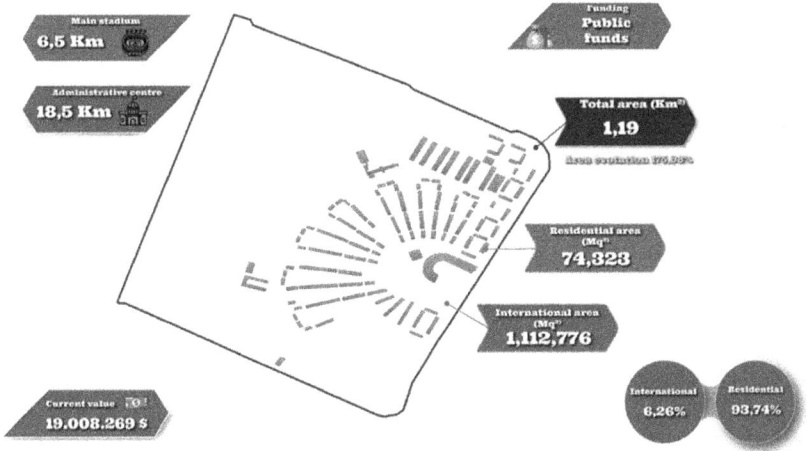

Number of buildings
86

Height of buildings
25 Storey

Typology of buildings
Social housing

1,187,099 Occupied Surfaces'
11,29% % Density m² (Resid)
7068 Urban Density (ab/area km²)

Population
10.100,000

Evolution
197,06%

Surface
2,266 Km²

Capacity N.of athletes
8,391

Evolution
22,87%

SEOUL
1988
Oryan-dong quarter, in the Songpa-gu district, Seoul

Ownership of the area
Public

Post-Olympic Use
Public residences

Main stadium
6,5 Km

Administrative centre
18,5 Km

Funding
Public funds

Total area (Km²)
1,19

Area variation 170,96%

Residential area (Mq²)
74,323

International area (Mq²)
1,112,776

Current value
19,008.269 $

International
6,26%

Residential
93,74%

4.1.15 Barcelona 1992

The construction of the Barcelona Olympic Village was strongly linked to urban transformation projects and the reuse of space. In addition, the recent opening of the city to the sea and the proximity of the Olympic Village to the marina allowed the accommodation structures to become a long-term exploitation model for the host cities. The new Olympic quarter was planned in a central area of the city to be converted into residential accommodation in the post-Olympic period. The Olympic Village area included all services, a shopping mall, sports facilities, games clubs, discotheques, post offices, banks and other services scattered throughout the area that could accommodate more than 15,000 athletes.[13] The organizing

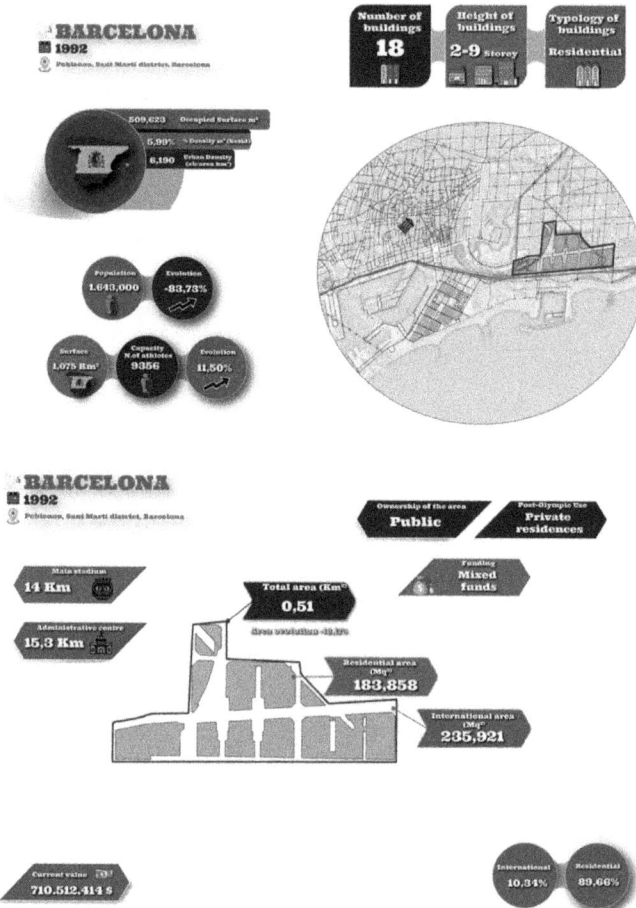

[13]. COOB'92. (1990). *Preliminary guide to the Olympic Village, March 1990'* (pp. 5–9, 26–27); COOB'92. (1992). *Official report of the Games of the XXV Olympiad Barcelona 1992'* (Vol. 3, pp. 183–201; Vol. 4, pp. 329–345); COOB'92. (1992, February 24). "Olympic Village apartments handed over to COOB'92". *BCN'92 Newsletter,'* n.p.

committee aimed to turn a derelict industrial area into a waterfront neighborhood for citizens who had never enjoyed the waterfront before. The Barcelona project will be inspirational for other future accommodation projects through public–private financing. Today, however, the Olympic Quarter has been transformed into an exclusive place exploited by the gentrification of the city's metropolitan area.

4.1.16 Atlanta 1996

The Atlanta edition was inspired by the Los Angeles edition for the organization of temporary accommodation for the Olympic athletes. The University of Georgia campus was used temporarily by the 15,000 athletes participating in the summer edition, with several facilities that were adjusted to the needs of the Olympic event. In addition, the organizers built new flats for the students to benefit from in the post-Olympic period. Thus, the Olympic Village was a huge campus with sports facilities, toilets, restaurants, medical centers, and all the services needed by the Olympic athletes. In addition to the essential services, the Village offers a spa, a gymnasium, a test center, a technology zone, a laser area, and a World Wide Web pavilion.[14] Sailing, rowing, football, and canoeing competitions were

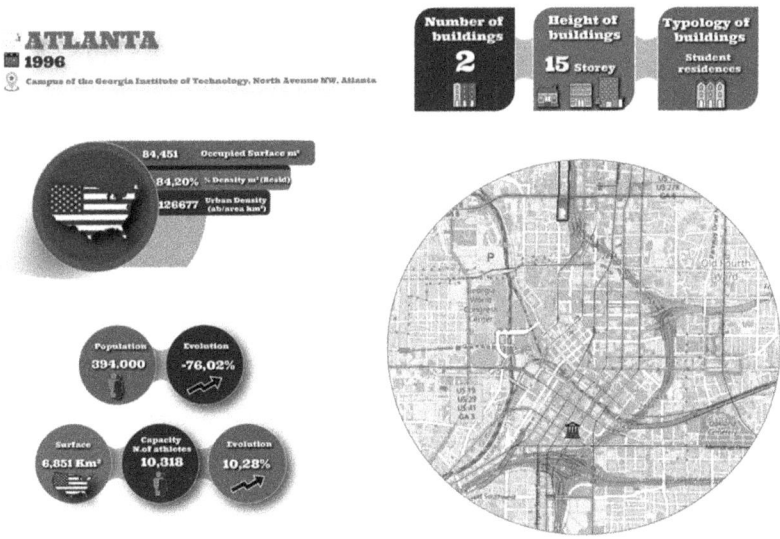

---

[14] Atlanta Committee for the Olympic Games (1996). *Atlanta Olympic Village Athletes guide* (pp. 17–20, 35–43); ACOG. (1997). *The official report of the Centennial Olympic Games* (Vol. 1, pp. 324–350.) Peachtree Publishers.

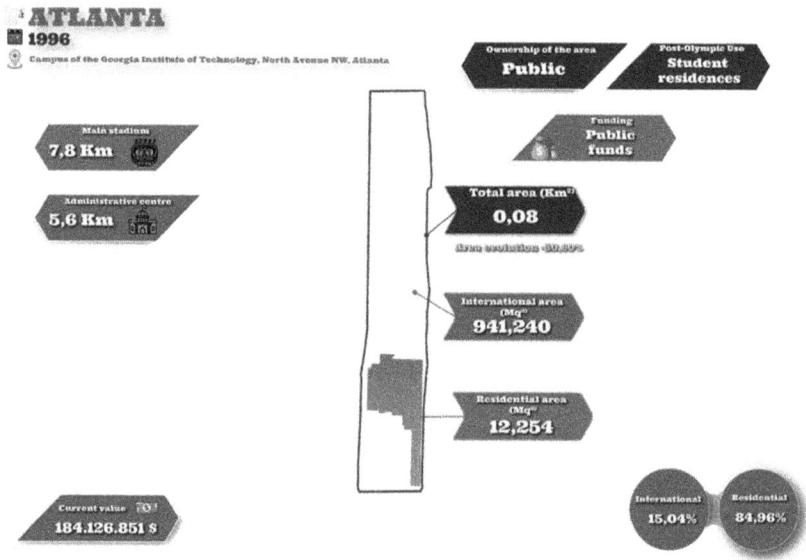

ATLANTA
1996
Campus of the Georgia Institute of Technology, North Avenue NW, Atlanta

Ownership of the area: **Public**
Post-Olympic Use: **Student residences**

Main stadium: **7,8 Km**
Administrative centre: **5,6 Km**

Funding: **Public funds**
Total area (Km²): **0,08**
International area (Mq²): **941,240**
Residential area (Mq²): **12,254**

Current value: **184.126.851 $**

International **15,04%**   Residential **84,96%**

held in other cities, and the organizers always used existing structures such as university campuses and hotels.

The campus was returned to the university and its students, and the Ring Fountain and Centennial Plaza remain in Atlanta today.

4.1.17 Sydney 2000

The Sydney Olympic Village project involved a significant area on the capital's outskirts that was neglected and placed in the middle of profound structural transformations. The Sydney Olympic Village was built concerning new environmental measures and the introduction of new technologies about renewable energies. The Olympic Village was on an area of 83 ha and could accommodate more than 15,000 athletes.[15] Athletes could use transport services to move around the neighborhood and between training facilities. In addition, the new neighborhood included all services and a wide range of restaurants in each block. More than 22 residential centers in the Village offered different essential services to

---

[15] Sydney Organizing Committee for the Olympic Games. (2001). *Official report of the XXVII Olympiad: Sydney 2000 Olympic Games, 15 September–1 October* (Vol. 1, pp. 68–70, 323–331).

SYDNEY
2000
Newington, Sydney

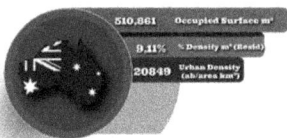

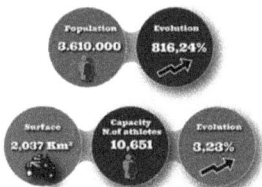

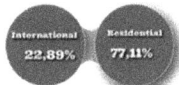

Number of buildings	Height of buildings	Typology of buildings
520	**4-5** Storey	**Residential**

510,861 Occupied Surface m²
9,11% % Density m² (Resid)
20849 Urban Density (ab/area km²)

Population **3.610.000**
Evolution **816,24%**

Surface **2,037 Km²**
Capacity N.of athletes **10,651**
Evolution **3,23%**

SYDNEY
2000
Newington, Sydney

Ownership of the area **Public**
Post-Olympic Use **Private residences**

Main stadium **2,6 Km**

Administrative centre **18,9 Km**

Funding **Mixed funds**

Total area (Km²) **0,51**
Area evolution 557,50%

International area (Mq²) **393,919**

Residential area (Mq²) **116,942**

Current value **186.983.779 $**

International **22,89%**
Residential **77,11%**

the athletes. The new flats and houses were sold or rented to citizens, and the neighborhood was named Newington, constituting a new residential area in the Australian metropolis.

4.1.18 Athens 2004

The construction of the Athens Olympic area was already included in other spatial and residential transformation projects of the central government. The Olympic Village was planned in a peripheral capital area that could accommodate more than 18,000 people in a new Olympic quarter. The Greek social housing association was responsible for constructing the new residential areas north of the Greek capital. The new urban centre enjoyed additional services such as sports facilities, a hospital, a gymnasium, a theater, shops, discotheques, a reception hall, and green spaces.[16] The distance between the Olympic Village and the sports facilities led to increased transport systems between the sports facilities and the Olympic Village. The construction of the new neighborhood was planned to accommodate families needing permanent accommodation. Still, in the post-Olympic period, the entire Village was occupied by immigrants and, to this day, has yet to achieve the objectives initially envisaged for developing the new satellite area.

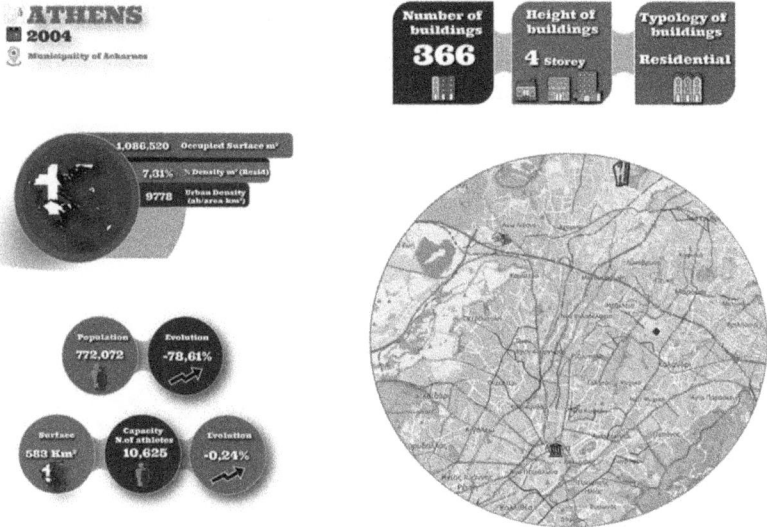

[16.] Athens 2004 Organising Committee for the Olympic Games. (2004). *Olympic Village guide* (pp. 21–23, 37–47); ATHOC. (2005). *Official report of the XXVIII Olympiad: Athens 2004* (Vol. 1, p. 161; Vol. 2, pp. 41–49).

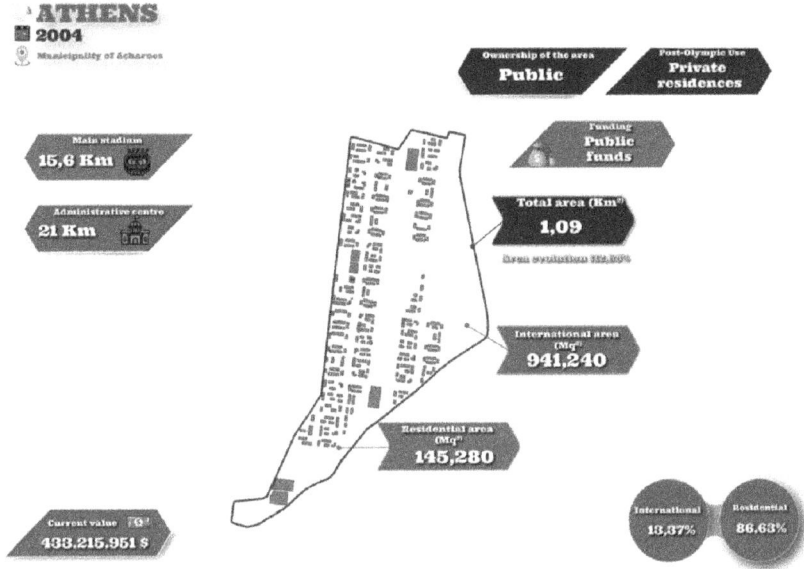

ATHENS
2004
Municipality of Acharnes

Ownership of the area — **Public**

Post-Olympic Use — **Private residences**

Main stadium — **15,6 Km**

Administrative centre — **21 Km**

Funding — **Public funds**

Total area (Km²) — **1,09**
Area evolution ???

International area (Mq²) — **941,240**

Residential area (Mq²) — **145,280**

Current value — **433,215,951 $**

International **13,37%** — Residential **86,63%**

4.1.19 Beijing 2008

The concept of the Beijing Olympic Village was that of developing a new neighborhood that could be incorporated into the area of Olympic venues and become a residential area for middle-class citizens. The project was planned by respecting the new environmental measures and incorporating the Olympic Forest Park in the northern area of the Village. In the center of the Olympic Village were the services and common spaces for the socialization of the athletes.[17] The north area of the Village housed the sports, cultural, and training facilities. Meanwhile, the southern area of the Village could accommodate more than 18,000 athletes. Buildings and residences were converted into flats and sold to private individuals. For the first time, the Beijing Games pointed out the exclusion problem and the expulsion of citizens from the Olympic area to the periphery. In the Olympic subvenue, hotels were used as temporary accommodations for Olympic athletes.

[17] Beijing Organizing Committee for the Games of the XXIX Olympiad. (2010). *Official report of the Beijing 2008 Olympic Games* (Vol. 2, pp. 211–225; Vol. 3, pp. 227–241); ""Projects"." Beijing Tianhong Yuanfang Architectural Design CO., LTD website.

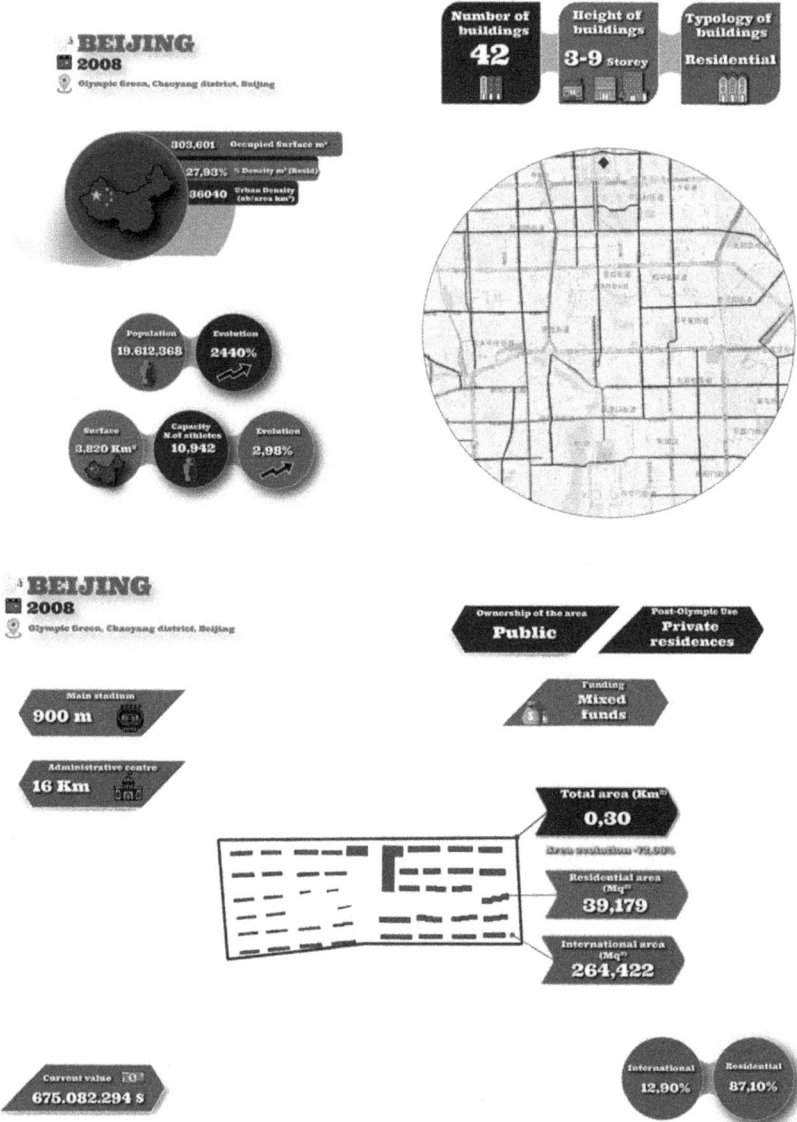

BEIJING
2008
Olympic Green, Chaoyang district, Beijing

Number of buildings	Height of buildings	Typology of buildings
42	3-9 storey	Residential

303.601 Occupied Surface m²
27,93% % Density m² (Resid)
36040 Urban Density (ab/area km²)

Population 19.612.368
Evolution 2440%

Surface 3.820 Km²
Capacity N.of athletes 10.942
Evolution 2,98%

BEIJING
2008
Olympic Green, Chaoyang district, Beijing

Ownership of the area **Public**
Post-Olympic Use **Private residences**

Main stadium 900 m
Funding **Mixed funds**

Administrative centre 16 Km

Total area (Km²) 0,30
Area evolution -73,00%

Residential area (Mq²) 39,179

International area (Mq²) 264,422

Current value [€]² 675.082.294 $

International 12,90%
Residential 87,10%

4.1.20 London 2012

The London Olympic Village project was part of a massive transformation of an industrial area in the eastern part of the metropolis. The Olympic Park and Olympic Village comprised an area of more than 10 ha that could accommodate more than 18,000 athletes. The Olympic Village was built to be converted into a mixed housing area, conceived with the utmost respect for the environment. However, the London project was the first example of applying principles that respected the concept of heritage and Olympic heritage. The proximity to the Olympic Park made it possible to reduce transport services between the training

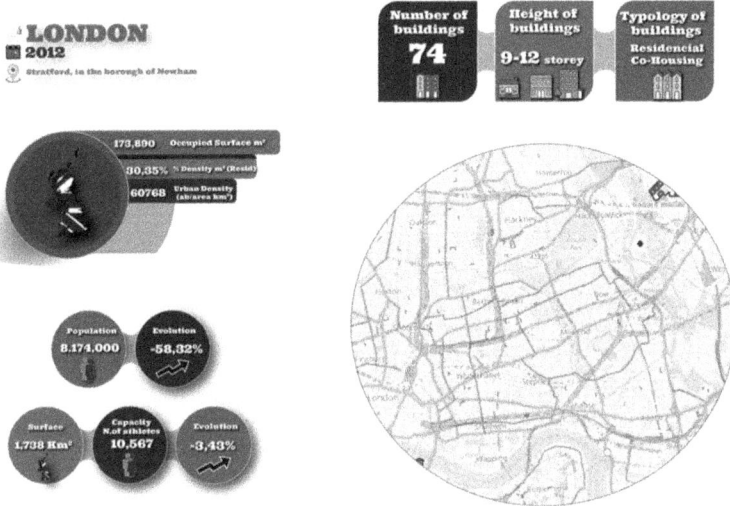

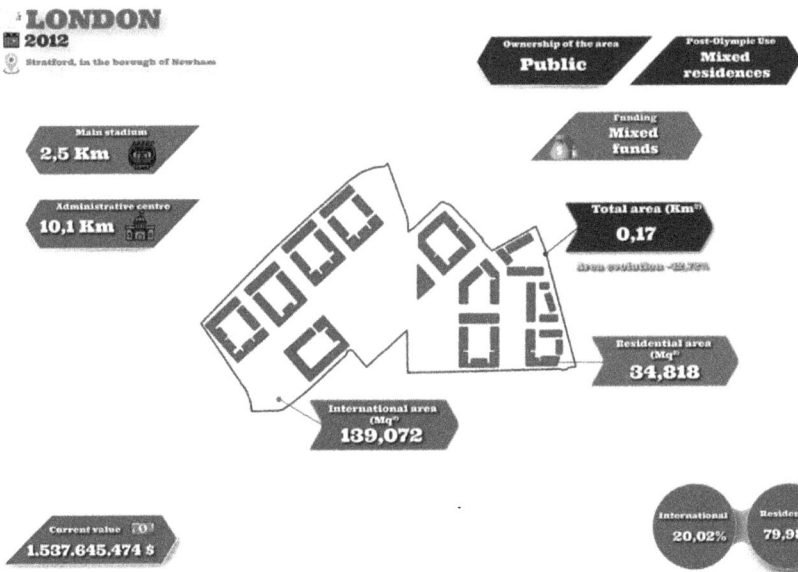

LONDON
2012
Stratford, in the borough of Newham

Number of buildings	Height of buildings	Typology of buildings
74	**9-12** storey	Residencial Co-Housing

173,890   Occupied Surface m²
30,35%   % Density m² (Resid.)
60768   Urban Density (ab/area km²)

Population	Evolution
8.174.000	-58,32%

Surface	Capacity N.of athletes	Evolution
1.738 Km²	10,567	-3,43%

LONDON
2012
Stratford, in the borough of Newham

Ownership of the area **Public**

Post-Olympic Use **Mixed residences**

Main stadium **2,5 Km**

Administrative centre **10,1 Km**

Funding **Mixed funds**

Total area (Km²) **0,17**

Area evolution -83,73%

Residential area (Mq²) **34,818**

International area (Mq²) **139,072**

Current value **1.537.645.474 $**

International	Residential
20,02%	79,98%

facilities and the Olympic Village. The area was planned to accommodate shopping centers, train stations, underground, cinemas, nightclubs, theaters, offices, consultancies, restaurants, bars, gymnasium, and other services. The London Olympic Village reached unprecedented dimensions. Athletes in the sailing and equestrian competitions were accommodated in hotels. The project was planned through a public–private partnership to exploit the entire area (East Village) and develop it into a new neighborhood, which would be very close to the city's administrative center. The London Olympic Village will be the first example of mixed accommodation and services built through the summer edition.

4.1.21 Rio de Janeiro 2016

A philosophy of urban expansion and infrastructural transformations in Rio de Janeiro strongly marked the Rio de Janeiro Olympic Village concept. Like the previous editions, the Rio edition had planned the Village close to the Olympic Park, where most venues were located. Services, roads, restaurants, transport, and green spaces were built in this area. The accommodation capacity of the Olympic Village was for more than 18,000 athletes, and it was planned to be converted into a residence during the post-Olympic period. The Rio Olympic Village project was very ambitious and still needs to find its function. The accommodation remains abandoned, and the Olympic area must be utilized more.

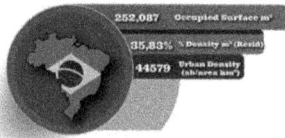

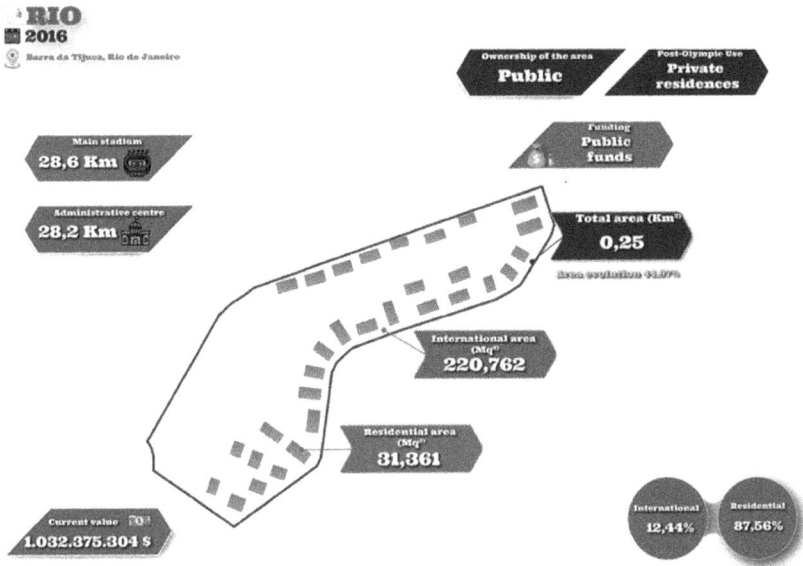

RIO
2016
Barra da Tijuca, Rio de Janeiro

Ownership of the area — **Public**

Post-Olympic Use — **Private residences**

Main stadium — **28,6 Km**

Funding — **Public funds**

Administrative centre — **28,2 Km**

Total area (Km²) — **0,25**

Area evolution 94,97%

International area (Mq²) — **220,762**

Residential area (Mq²) — **31,361**

Current value — **1.032.375.304 $**

International **12,44%** Residential **87,56%**

4.1.22 Tokyo 2020

The construction of the Tokyo Olympic Village was included in the Harumi waterfront district in the center of the Japanese capital. The Olympic Village area comprises a 133,906 m² site sold to the developers' consortium for residential development before the Olympic event. The project includes constructing 21 residential buildings between 14 and 18-stories, commercial premises and public parks. The capacity of the Olympic Village during the event was 17,000 people accommodated between the 2nd and 14th floors of each residential block. The Metropolitan Government aimed to establish a new community where different people could interact and live comfortably in a residential area after the Olympic event. In addition, after the Olympic event, work started constructing two 50-story residential skyscrapers. By 2024, the area will comprise 23 buildings with 5,650 flats.[18]

---

[18] Tokyo Metropolitan Government. (2016). *Tokyo Metropolitan Government, towards 2020: Building the legacy/coordination section, general coordination division, bureau of Olympic and Paralympic Games Tokyo 2020 preparation* (pp. 10–11).

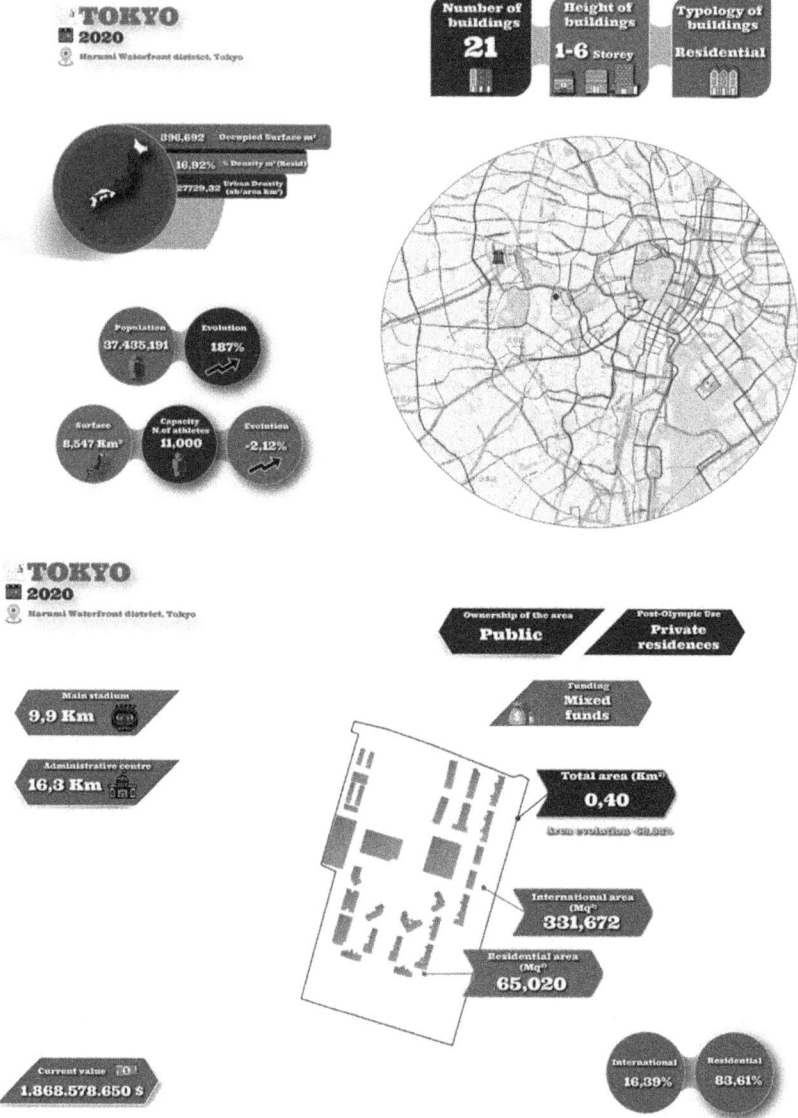

TOKYO
2020
Marumi Waterfront district, Tokyo

Number of buildings	Height of buildings	Typology of buildings
21	1-6 Storey	Residential

396.692 Occupied Surface m²
16,92% % Density m² (Resid)
27729,32 Urban Density (ab/area km²)

Population 37.435.191
Evolution 187%
Surface 8.547 Km²
Capacity N.of athletes 11,000
Evolution -2,12%

TOKYO
2020
Marumi Waterfront district, Tokyo

Ownership of the area **Public**
Post-Olympic Use **Private residences**

Main stadium 9,9 Km
Administrative centre 16,3 Km

Funding **Mixed funds**

Total area (Km²) 0,40
Area evolution -68,08%

International area (Mq²) 331,672

Residential area (Mq²) 65,020

Current value 1.868.578.650 $

International 16,39%
Residential 83,61%

4.1.23 Considerations of the Summer Olympic Villages

As we have seen in the proposed comparative analysis, the Olympic Village has evolved through different spatial models to solve housing problems in different historical stages. However, the projects in Helsinki, Rome, Mexico, Montreal,

Seoul, Barcelona, Sydney, Beijing, London, and Rio have encouraged host cities to propose permanent housing projects that meet the needs of each metropolitan context. Olympic Villages came in many different forms and had other ideas about housing. However, in recent years, the housing problem has become less severe than it was after World War II. In recent years, we have constantly observed different solutions involving services and other segments of the population that have the potential to unite and create new regions promoted by sports and cultural events. Finally, each analyzed element's minimum and maximum values are examined to develop a long-term ranking of Olympic Villages (Tables 17 and 18).

Table 17: Comparative analysis of Summer Olympic Villages

Main stadium			
Minimum		Maximum	
Munich 1952	850 m	Rio 2016	28.6 km
Administrative center			
Minimum		Maximum	
Barcelona 1992	3 km	Rio 2016	28.2 km
Number of buildings			
Minimum		Maximum	
Atlanta 1996	2	Sydney 2000	870
Urban density (inhabitants/area km^2)			
Minimum		Maximum	
Berlin 1936	3,050.20 km^2	Atlanta 1996	126,677.39 km^2
% Density m^2 (residential)			
Minimum		Maximum	
Helsinki 1952	5.50%	Atlanta 1996	84,20%
Occupied area (m^2)			
Minimum		Maximum	
Atlanta 1996	81.451 m^2	Berlin 1936	1.299,260 m^2

(*Continued*)

Total area (km²)			
Minimum		Maximum	
Atlanta 1996	0.08 km²	Berlin 1936	1.30 km²
International area			
Minimum		Maximum	
Barcelona 1992	56.20%	Berlin 1936	97.31%
Residential area			
Minimum		Maximum	
Berlin 1936	2.69%	Barcelona 1992	43.80%
Current value			
Minimum		Maximum	
Los Angeles 1932	$8,217,404.43	Berlin 1936	$2,779,611,670.00

Source: Own implementation

4.2 From a metropolitan perspective toward a regional strategy

Before going deeper into the individual Winter Olympic Villages, the following analysis was carried out to specifically analyze the Olympic Villages through their spatial dimension and characteristics. The next is a list of these:

1. Oslo 1952	10. Albertville 1992
2. Squaw valley 1960	11. Lillehammer 1994
3. Innsbruck 1964	12. Nagano 1998
4. Grenoble 1968	13. Salt Lake 2002
5. Sapporo 1972	14. Torino 2006
6. Innsbruck 1976	15. Vancouver 2010
7. Lake Placid 1980	16. Sochi 2014
8. Sarajevo 1984	17. Pyeongchang 2018
9. Calgary 1988	18. Beijing 2022

4.2.1 Oslo 1952

The Olympic Villages in Oslo are considered the first permanent constructions for athletes' accommodation in the winter edition. The organization of the athletes' accommodation was foreseen through an extensive accommodation program promoted by the central government in three new areas: Sogn, Ullevål, and Illa.

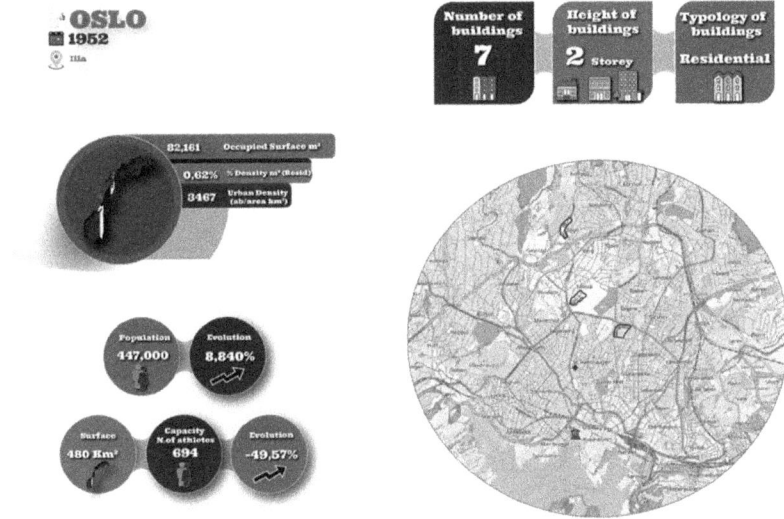

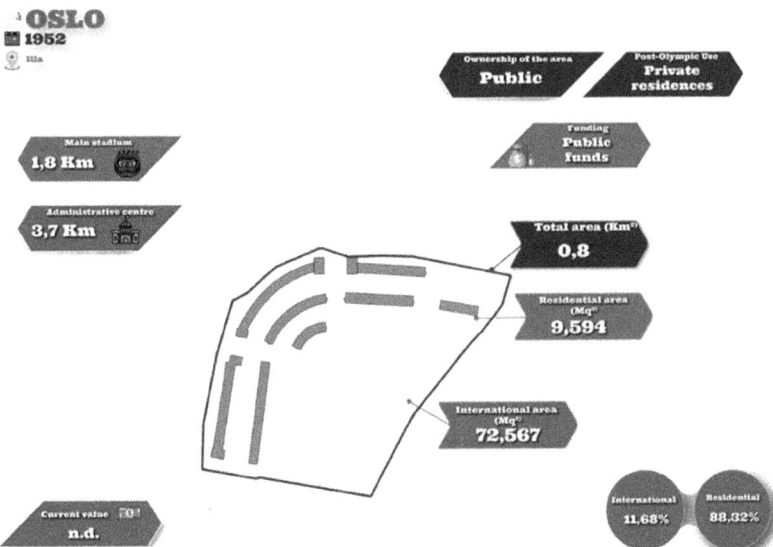

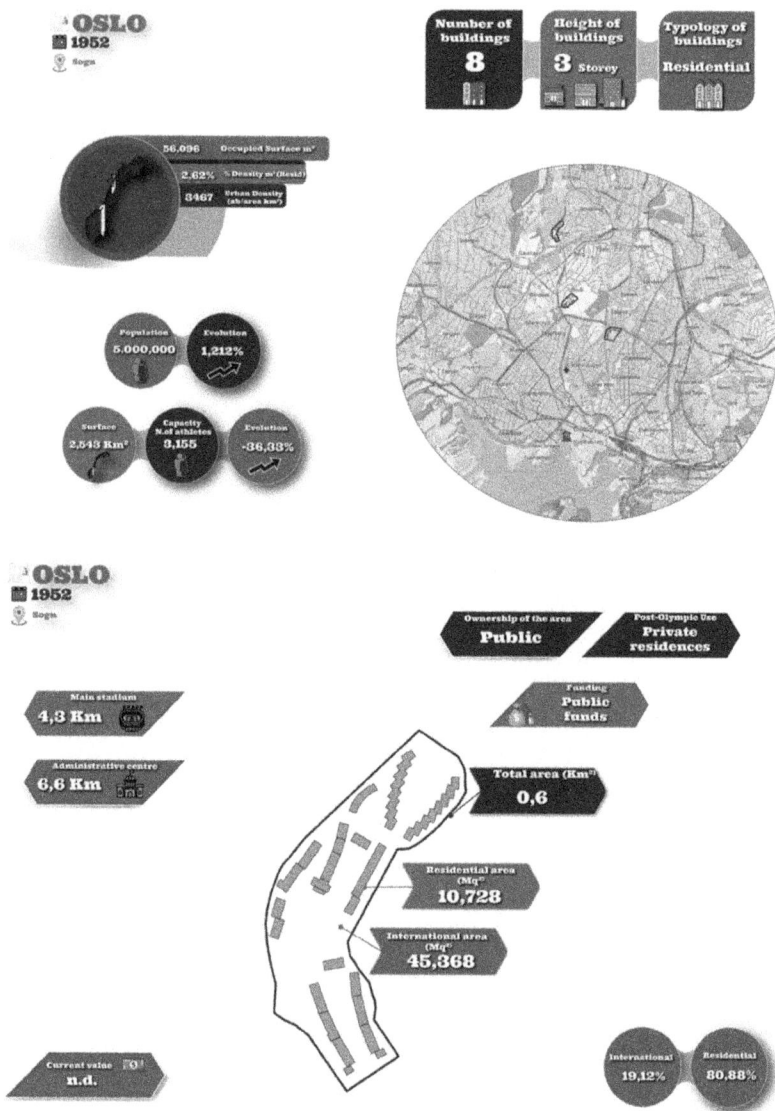

OSLO
1952
Soga

Number of buildings	Height of buildings	Typology of buildings
8	**3** Storey	**Residential**

56,096	Occupied Surface m²
2.62%	% Density m²(Resid)
3467	Urban Density (ab/area km²)

Population	Evolution
5.000.000	1,212%

Surface	Capacity N.of athletes	Evolution
2,543 Km²	9,155	-36,33%

OSLO
1952
Soga

Ownership of the area	Post-Olympic Use
Public	**Private residences**

Funding
Public funds

Main stadium
4,3 Km

Administrative centre
6,6 Km

Total area (Km²)
0,6

Residential area (Mq²)
10,728

International area (Mq²)
45,368

Current value
n.d.

International	Residential
19,12%	80,88%

The three regions became three self-sufficient Olympic quarters with the provision of all necessary services. Each neighborhood enjoyed postal services, kiosks, shops, banks, sports facilities, and so on.[19] The Olympic Villages were planned to become accommodation structures to meet different challenges.

[19] Organisasjonskomiteen. [ca 1953]. *VI Olympic Winter Games Oslo 1952* (pp. 23–25, 36, 41, 71, 80–88, n.p.).

OSLO
1952
Ullevål

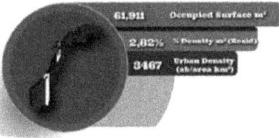

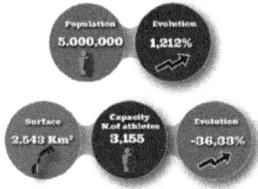

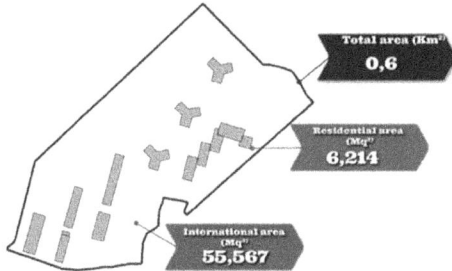

Number of buildings
6

Height of buildings
8 Storey

Typology of buildings
Residential

61,911 Occupied Surface m²
2,82% % Density m² (Resid)
3467 Urban Density (ab/area km²)

Population 5.000.000
Evolution 1,212%

Surface 2,543 Km²
Capacity N.of athletes 3,155
Evolution -36,33%

OSLO
1952
Ullevål

Ownership of the area
Public

Post-Olympic Use
Private residences

Main stadium 2,2 Km

Funding
Public funds

Administrative centre 4,3 Km

Total area (Km²) 0,6

Residential area (Mq²) 6,214

International area (Mq²) 55,567

Current value n.d.

International 89,96%
Residential 10,04%

Sogn became a student neighborhood, Ullevål a quarter for hospital staff, and Illa a quarter for senior citizens. The Oslo project is the first major permanent housing project to inspire future Olympic Village planning projects in the winter edition.

4.2.2 Squaw Valley 1960

The 1960 Squaw Valley edition was conceived as a large Olympic Park close to the tracks and sports facilities. The Olympic Village was established in a newly constructed area with the addition of other buildings for athlete services.

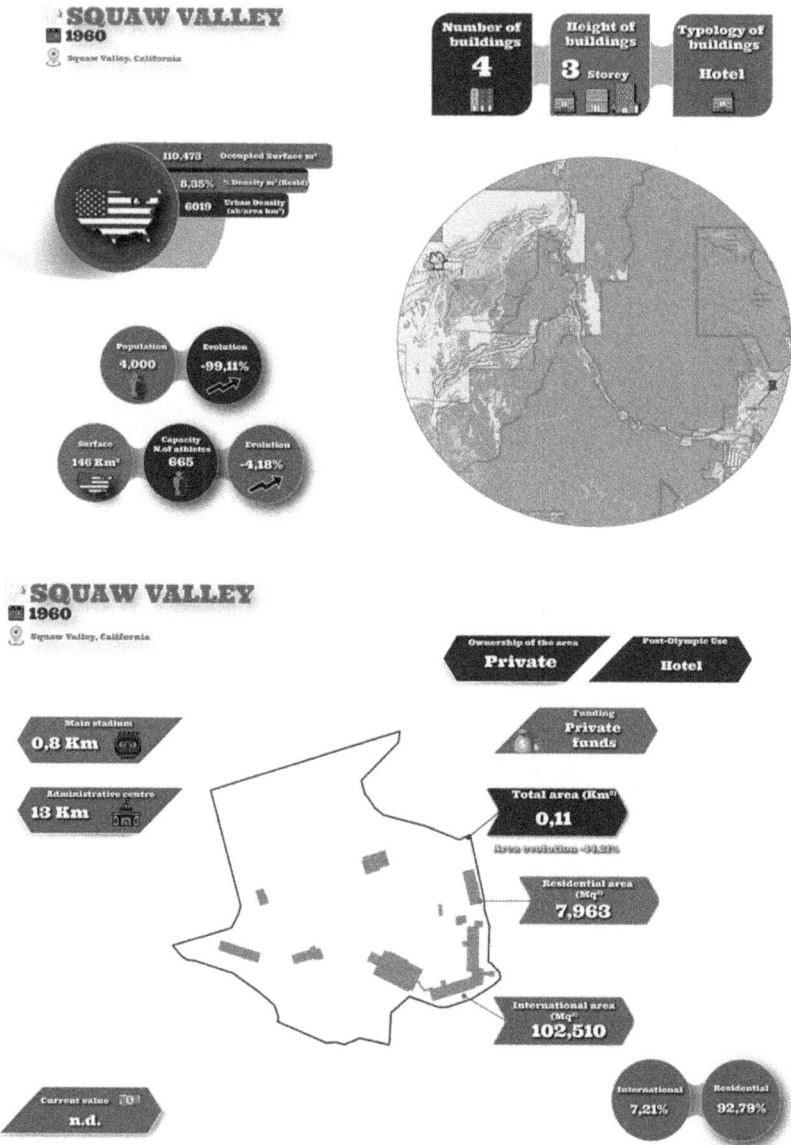

In the Olympic Valley, multipurpose spaces, training centers, auditoriums, leisure spaces, medical centers, storage for sports equipment, and more 20 were built. The Olympic Village was initially planned to be used as a hotel for winter tourism. However, in the early 1990s, it was remodeled and transformed into a conference and training center for the US Olympic team.

4.2.3 Innsbruck 1964

The planning of the Innsbruck Olympic Village was included in an overall transformation of an area of the city. The new quarter would accommodate more than 10,000 people in the post-Olympic period. However, the Olympic Village was reserved for 2,000 athletes and coaches. Of the four buildings used as the Olympic Village, three were for the men and one for the women. During the Olympic Games, the other buildings were transformed into service structures for the participants—restaurants, shops, leisure areas, storage, workshops, gymnasiums, and saunas. In the post-Olympic period, the buildings used as temporary accommodation were returned to the population and continue to be used as residences. The Olympic Quarter of Innsbruck will promote new accommodations in the 1976 edition.

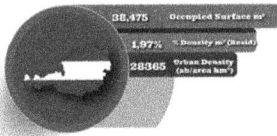

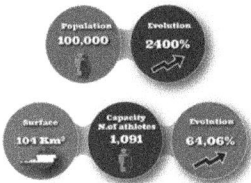

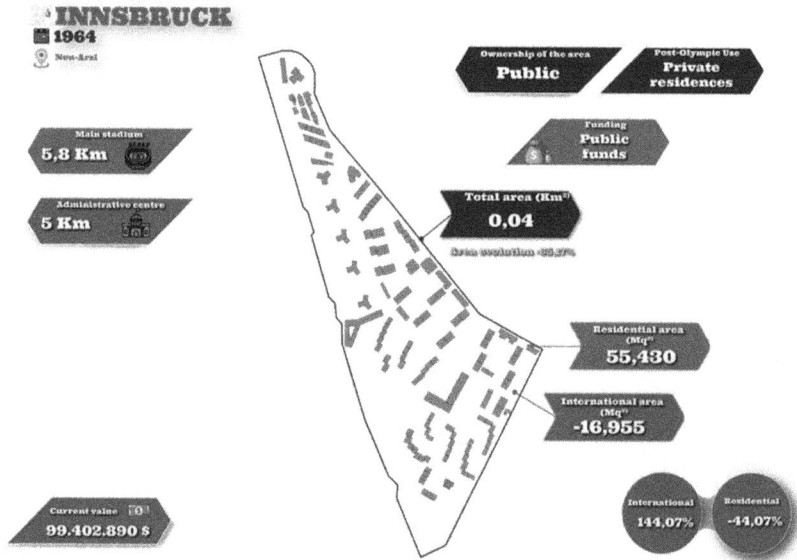

INNSBRUCK
1964
New-Area

Main stadium
5,8 Km

Administrative centre
5 Km

Current value
99.402.890 $

Ownership of the area
Public

Post-Olympic Use
Private residences

Funding
Public funds

Total area (Km²)
0,04

Area evolution -69,27%

Residential area (Mq²)
55,430

International area (Mq²)
-16,955

International
144,07%

Residential
-44,07%

4.2.4 Grenoble 1968

The Grenoble edition was planned to reconstruct and redefine new regional strategies, including new accommodation structures for citizens and the university. The Olympic Village project was a construction that could accommodate more than 2,000 people and catalyzed urban transformation processes in the surrounding districts. The Olympic Village was part of a more comprehensive development plan for the entire southern area of the city. The complex was divided into two parts, one dedicated to the Olympic Villages and one for the organizing committee and services.[20] The streets and squares allowed for the construction of a new neighborhood that would give the city a new image in the post-Olympic period. As initially planned, the Olympic Village became a residential area still called the Olympic Village today.

[20.] Organising Committee for the X Olympic Winter Games Grenoble. (1968, 1969). *Rapport officiel* (pp. 63–65, 69–70, 74, 112–113, 252).

GRENOBLE
1968
Grenoble

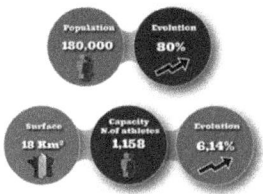

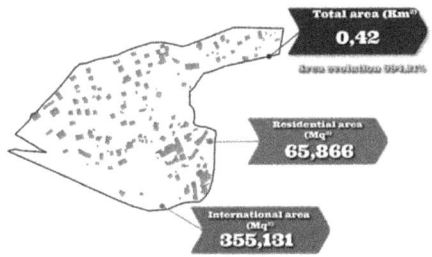

Number of buildings	Height of buildings	Typology of buildings
11	4-5 Storey	Residential

420,997 Occupied Surface m²
1,76% % Density m² (Resid)
2750 Urban Density (ab/area km²)

Population 180,000
Evolution 80%

Surface 18 Km²
Capacity N of athletes 1,158
Evolution 6,14%

GRENOBLE
1968
Grenoble

Ownership of the area: **Public**
Post-Olympic Use: **Private residences**

Main stadium 600 m
Administrative centre 4 Km

Funding: **Public funds**

Total area (Km²) **0,42**
Area evolution 994,87%

Residential area (Mq²) **65,866**

International area (Mq²) **355,131**

Current value 380.044.034 $

International 15,65%
Residential 84,35%

4.2.5 Sapporo 1972

For the first Winter Olympic Games in Asia, only one Olympic Village was planned, which was included in the various spatial transformations of the city of Sapporo. The sports facilities were close to the accommodation, and athletes could walk between the Olympic Village and the venues.[21] The new neighborhood was built in a peripheral area of the city to be converted into residences in the post-Olympic period. The Olympic Village was conceived through different blocks comprising all services. The international space had a central dining hall, shops, a workshop, a sauna, a gymnasium, an auditorium, a theater, a leisure space, and more. In the post-Olympic period, as initially planned, the neighborhood became a residential area.

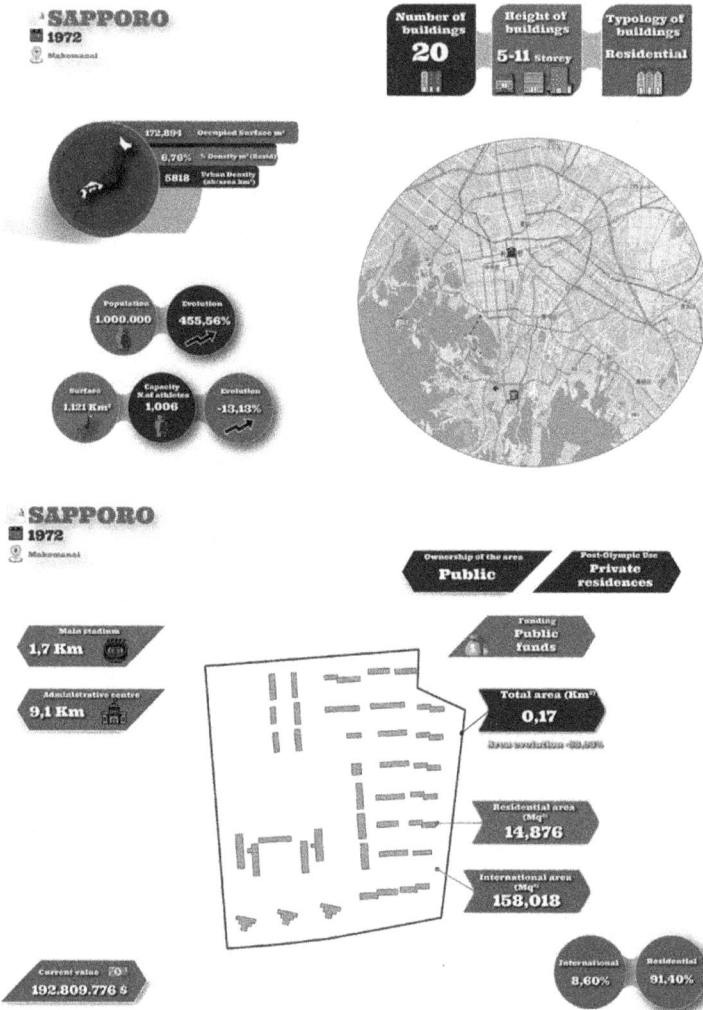

4.2.6 Innsbruck 1976

The Innsbruck Olympic Village was developed in the southern part of the district and was planned for the first Olympic Games in 1964. The Olympic Village was conceived to expand the neighborhood by constructing 35 new buildings. The residential area comprised sports training facilities, an indoor swimming pool, a reception area, restaurants, shops, a gymnasium, a school, and other services.[22] The new neighborhood was realized by constructing a master plan comprising a new hospital, a shopping center, and infrastructure. The entire area could accommodate more than 4,000 people in the post-Olympic period. The facilities and buildings of the 1964 Games were enlarged and restructured to meet the new requirements.

According to the organization, the facilities built for connecting and integrating the Olympic Games, the Village, the school, the swimming pool, and the bridge contributed significantly to the city's infrastructural development. The entire neighborhood was transformed into a new residential area in the post-Olympic period.

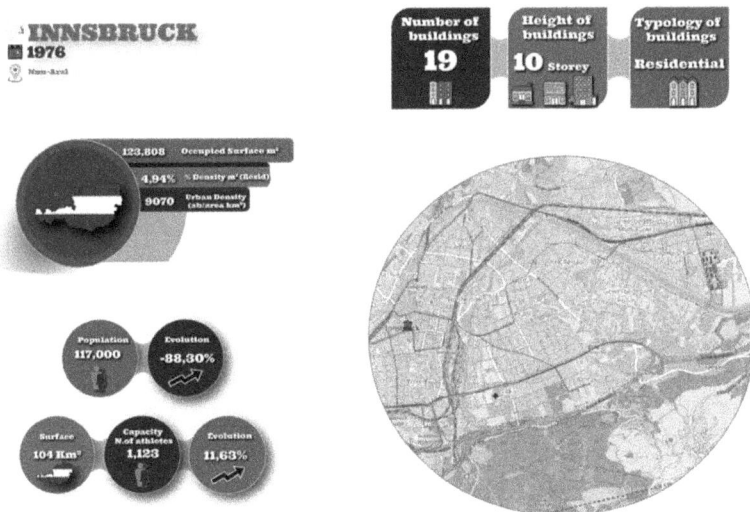

---

[22] Comité d'organisation des XIIes Games olympiques d'hiver. (1976). *Final report* "(pp. 182, 192–194, 274–278, 317, 333, 340, 396, n.p.).

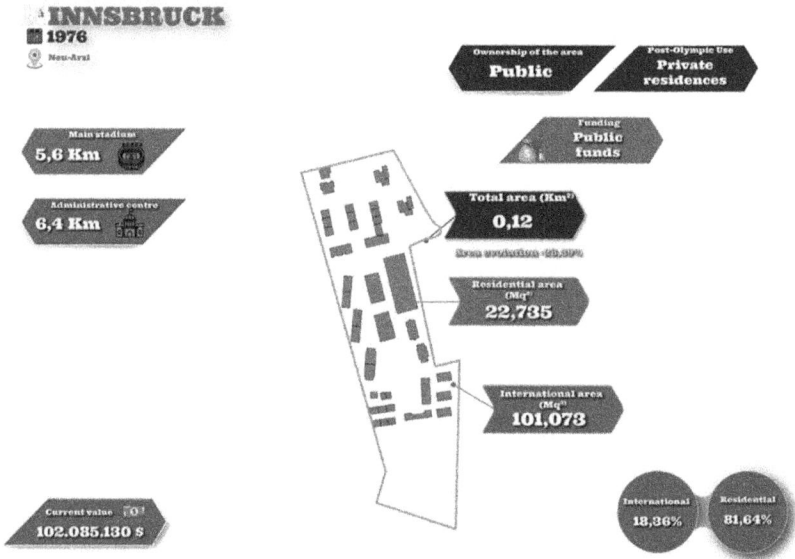

INNSBRUCK
1976
Neu-Arzl

Main stadium
5,6 Km

Administrative centre
6,4 Km

Current value
102.085.130 $

Ownership of the area
Public

Post-Olympic Use
Private residences

Funding
Public funds

Total area (Km²)
0,12

Area evolution -03.50%

Residential area (Mq²)
22,735

International area (Mq²)
101,073

International **18,36%**   Residential **81,64%**

4.2.7 Lake Placid 1980

The first plan for the Lake Placid Olympic Village proposed the construction of different buildings in the village's central area. After the election as Olympic city, the organizers decided to use a former Ray Brook Sanatorium between the towns of Lake Placid and Saranac Lake. The US Department of Justice assisted in the construction of the Olympic Village, which would be transformed into a prison in the post-Olympic period. The Olympic Village included different buildings and services such as a chapel, post office, library, theater, cafeterias, shops, restaurant, polyclinic, and rest areas. However, the Olympic Village could only accommodate 2,000 people, so other temporary accommodation was built to meet the organization's expectations. The sports facilities were connected through a private shuttle service. The Olympic Village at Lake Placid is the only example of Olympic accommodation converted into a prison.

LAKE PLACID
1980
Ray Brook

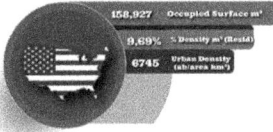

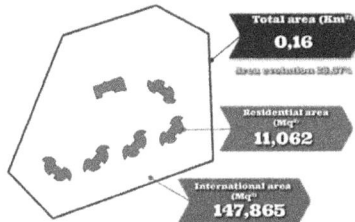

Number of buildings	Height of buildings	Typology of buildings
11	3-4 Storey	Residential

158,927 — Occupied Surface m²
9,69% — % Density m² (Resid)
6745 — Urban Density (ab/area km²)

Population 5,000 — Evolution -95,73%

Surface 3,98 Km² — Capacity N.of athletes 1,072 — Evolution -1,54%

LAKE PLACID
1980
Ray Brook

Ownership of the area — Public
Post-Olympic Use — Prison

Main stadium 10,1 Km

Funding — Private funds

Administrative centre 10,4 Km

Total area (Km²) 0,16
Area evolution 23,07%

Residential area (Mq²) 11,062

International area (Mq²) 147,865

Current value 72.264.762 $

International 6,96% — Residential 93,04%

4.2.8 Sarajevo 1984

The Sarajevo Olympic Village would originally have had to be built near Nedžarići Student Dormitory to be reused as student accommodation in the post-Olympic period. However, the residences needed to be more sufficient to house all the

Olympic athletes. So, instead of expanding the university accommodation, the committee provided a new Olympic Village in Mojmilo. The new area had a hospital, shops, restaurants, chapels, recreation center, discotheques, concert area, theaters, cinema, and more.[23] The training and competition facilities were

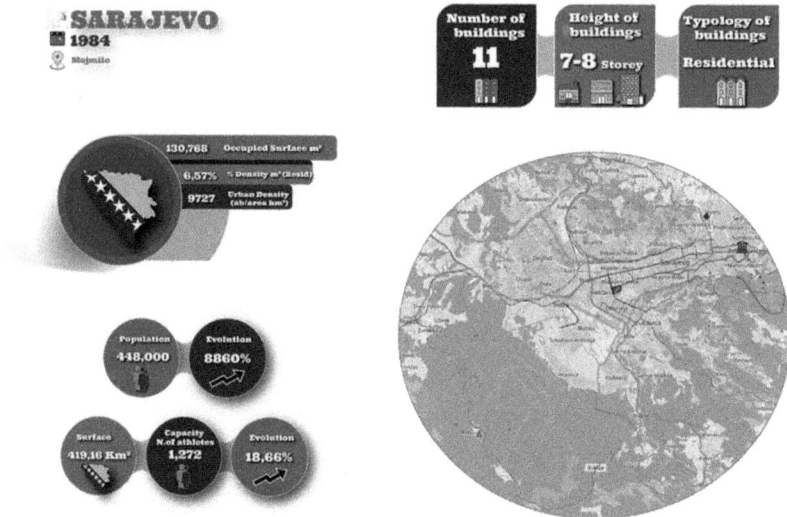

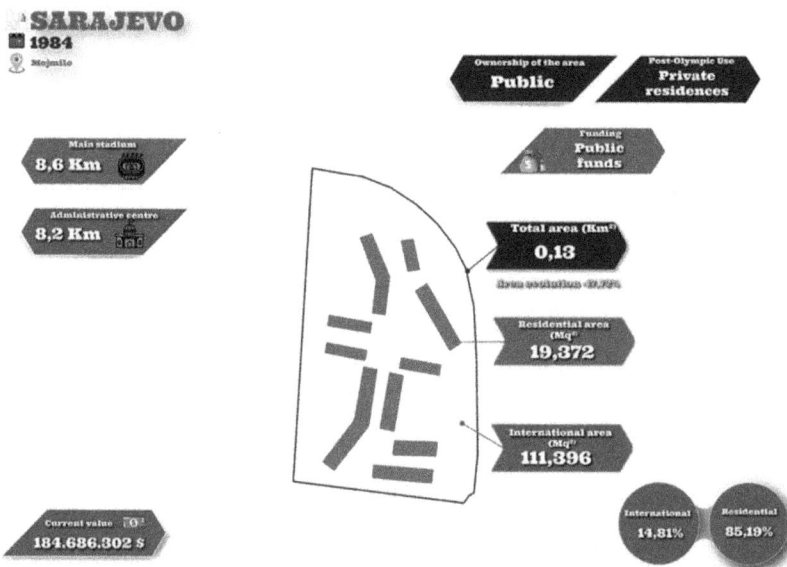

[23.] Organising Committee of the XIVth Winter Olympic Games 1984 at Sarajevo. (1984). *Final report, Sarajevo* (pp. 94, 108, 125, 139).

very close to the Olympic Village, and different transport systems were used to transport the athletes. A hotel was built in Igman to temporarily accommodate the Olympic athletes in the cross-country, biathlon, and Nordic competitions. The new Olympic Village was planned to become a new residential area after the Olympic Games. However, the war with Bosnia-Herzegovina destroyed a large part of the Olympic Village. In 1992, Barcelona aided the reconstruction of the Olympic Village, completed in 1999.

4.2.9 Calgary 1988

The Calgary project is recognized as the first Olympic Village project to be exploited through student accommodation. The Organizing Committee and the University of Calgary agreed to use the campus temporarily. The University Village was expanded through new public funding for the improvement and expansion of the University of Calgary. The residences were included in a multifunctional area comprising all athletic facilities. In addition, the university's sports facilities provided new halls and sporting venues for athlete training. The Village offered administrative, recreational and sanitary services, and a media area was included for the first time.[24]

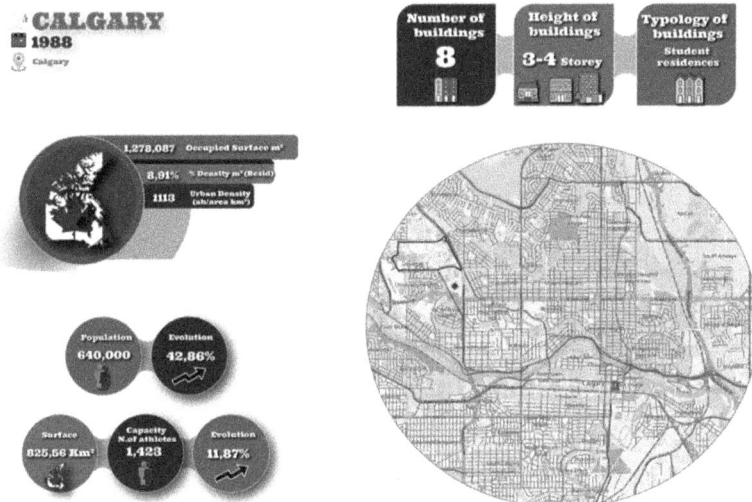

---

[24] Organising Committee for the XV Olympic Winter Games. (1987, April). *Olympic Villages: Information and questionnaire* (pp. 13–16, 21); Comité d'organisation des XVes Jeux Olympiques d'hiver. Calgary [Organising Committee for the XV Olympic Winter Games; Calgary Development Association]. (1988). *Rapport officiel des XVes Jeux Olympiques d'hiver = XV Olympic Winter Games official report* (Vol. 1, pp. 174–181; Vol. 2, pp. 383–394).

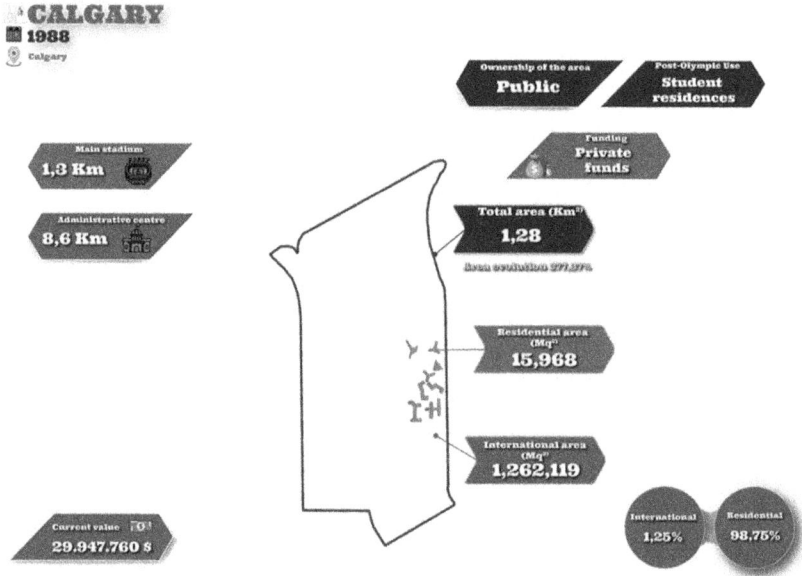

CALGARY
1988
Calgary

Ownership of the area	Post-Olympic Use
Public	**Student residences**

Funding
Private funds

Main stadium
1,8 Km

Administrative centre
8,6 Km

Total area (Km²)
1,28

Area evolution 271,27%

Residential area (Mq²)
15,968

International area (Mq²)
1,262,119

Current value $
29.947.760 $

International **1,25%**   Residential **98,75%**

In the Village of Canmore, temporary accommodation was provided at the golf club. In the post-Olympic period, the University of Calgary acquired the Olympic facilities to offer new services to its students. The Calgary model is recognized as the first university model for the winter editions.

4.2.10 Albertville 1992

The Albertville Olympic Games edition was planned through a regional structure comprising more than seven mountain tourism locations in the Savoie region.

The main village was located in Brides-Les-Bains, about 20 km from Albert-ville. The accommodation organization consisted of existing hotels and other buildings that will be used as resorts in the post-Olympic period. The Olympic Village included a residential and international area offering different services: polyclinic, event area, recreation area, post office, multi-purpose center, restaurants, shops, administrative regions, medical area, and sports facilities.[25] In the

---

[25] Organising Committee of Albertville. (1992). *Rapport Officiel des XVIes Jeux Olympiques d'hiver d'Albertville et de la Savoie* (pp. 406–417).

ALBERTVILLE
1992
Brides-Les-Bains

Number of buildings	Height of buildings	Typology of buildings
8	2-3 Storey	Hotel

124,249	Occupied Surface m²
12,49%	% Density m² (Resid)
14495	Urban Density (ab/area km²)

Population	Evolution
20,000	-96,88%

Surface	Capacity N.of athletes	Evolution
17,54 Km²	1,801	26,56%

ALBERTVILLE
1992
Brides-Les-Bains

Ownership of the area	Post-Olympic Use
Public	Hotel

Main stadium
36,3 Km

Administrative centre
35,1 Km

Funding
Mixed funds

Total area (Km²)
0,12

Area evolution -99,33%

Residential area (Mq²)
14,425

International area (Mq²)
109,824

Current value
783.770 $

International	Residential
11,61%	88,39%

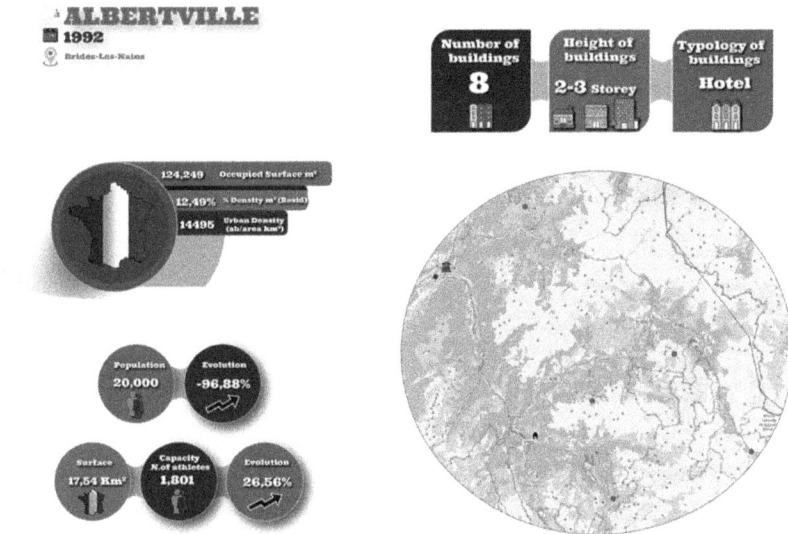

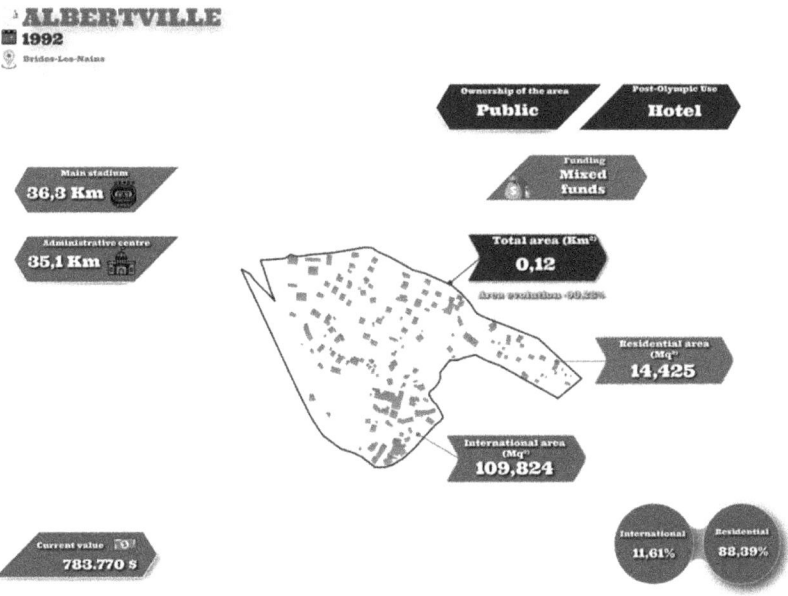

post-event phase, the hotels reverted to private owners, and the accommodation units in the other locations were converted into tourist accommodations. The Albertville edition was inspired by the first winter editions planned in small mountain villages through hotel structures.

4.2.11 Lillehammer 1994

The planning of the Olympic event in Lillehammer was intensely concerned with respecting environmental measures and sustainable development for the future of the winter edition of the Olympic Games. Therefore, the construction of the Olympic Village was geared toward using materials that could be reused in the post-Olympic period. All buildings were constructed in timber, prefabricated components and traditional construction techniques. Of all the houses built, only 185 have been converted into permanent accommodation for the citizens. As the city did not need new homes, the organizing committee decided to transform a vast area of 23 ha into a temporary Olympic Village. Olympic athletes had access to discotheques, a games room, sports facilities, a library, a bookshop, bars, restaurants, shops, cafés, and a medical center.[26] The international part of the Village was retained permanently to offer the new services to the citizens, and the permanent structures were sold to private individuals for the post-Olympic period. In addition, the temporary structures were dismantled and given to Sweden to provide homes for families in difficulty.

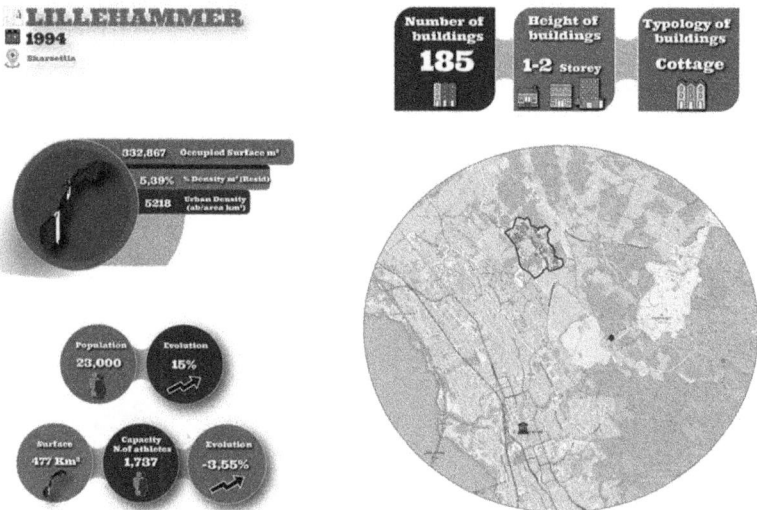

[26.] Lillehammer Olympic Organizing Committee. (1994). *Guide des Villages olympiques* (pp. 39–40); Lillehammer Olympic Organizing Committee. (1995). *Rapport officiel des XVIIes Jeux Olympiques d'hiver Lillehammer 1994* (Vol. 2, pp. 108–116; Vol. 3, pp. 76–79).

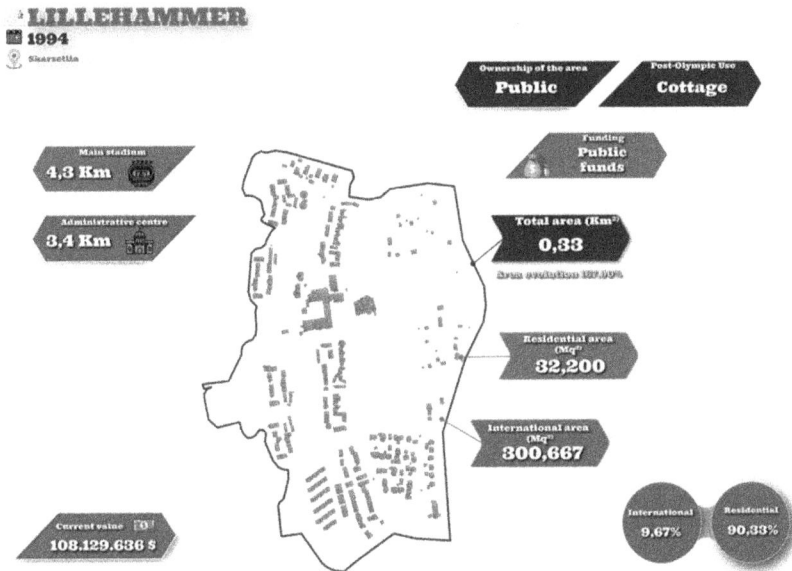

LILLEHAMMER
1994
Skarsetlia

Ownership of the area: **Public**
Post-Olympic Use: **Cottage**

Main stadium: **4,3 Km**
Administrative centre: **3,4 Km**

Funding: **Public funds**
Total area (Km²): **0,33**
Area evolution 117.00%

Residential area (Mq²): **32,200**
International area (Mq²): **300,667**

Current value: **108.129.636 $**

International: **9,67%**
Residential: **90,33%**

The Olympic Village in Lillehammer will be inspiring because of the respect for the environment and the use of temporary accommodation structures that have only been seen in the first editions of the Summer Olympic Games.

4.2.12 Nagano 1998

The Nagano Olympic Village was envisaged through strategic planning of the entire Olympic area. The Olympic Village complex was built to become a residential neighborhood in a peripheral area of the city that, during the Olympic period, could be used for event functions. Therefore, different temporary structures were built during the event, and furniture was rented to save organizational costs. The temporary facilities would include banks, a post office, a meeting area, an internet room, a polyclinic, shops, cinemas, a theater, a discotheque, restaurants, bars, and more.[27] The organizing committee tried to reduce the waste from the Olympic Villages by turning it into fertilizer for the land. Nagano continued to apply and evolve practices to protect the environment and reduce the event's impact. During the post-Olympic period, the entire area became a residential neighborhood managed by the Nagano municipality.

---

[27] Organising Committee for the XVIII Olympic Winter Games Nagano 1998. (1999). *Les XVIIIes Jeux Olympiques d'hiver: rapport officiel Nagano 1998* [The XVIII Olympic Winter Games: Official report Nagano 1998] (Vol. 2, pp. 238–251).

NAGANO
1998
Imai

Number of buildings	Height of buildings	Typology of buildings
23	**2-4** Storey	**Residential**

164,005 Occupied Surface m²

8,88% % Density m² (Resid)

13267 Urban Density (ab/area km²)

Population	Evolution
361,000	**1469,57%**

Surface	Capacity N.of athletes	Evolution
834,81 Km²	**2,176**	**25,27%**

NAGANO
1998
Imai

Ownership of the area	Post-Olympic Use
Public	**Private residences**

Main stadium
3,8 Km

Funding
Public funds

Administrative centre
9,3 Km

Total area (Km²)
0,16

Area evolution -59,78%

Residential area (Mq²)
24,505

International area (Mq²)
139,500

Current value
145.588.687 $

International	Residential
14,94%	**85,06%**

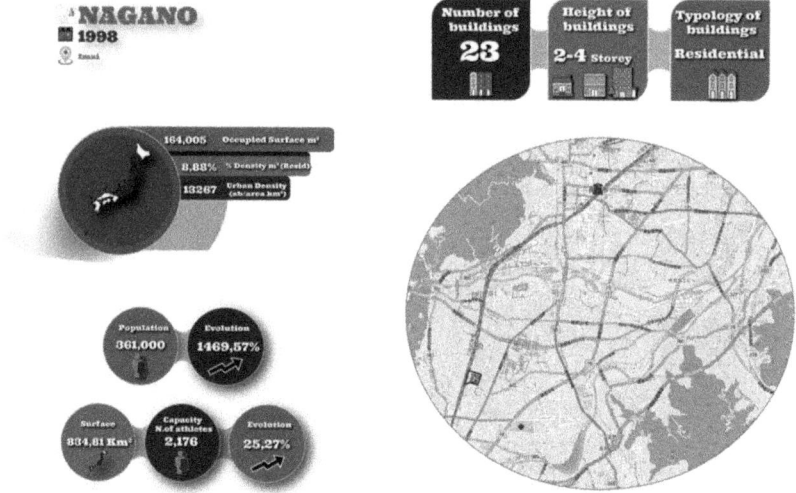

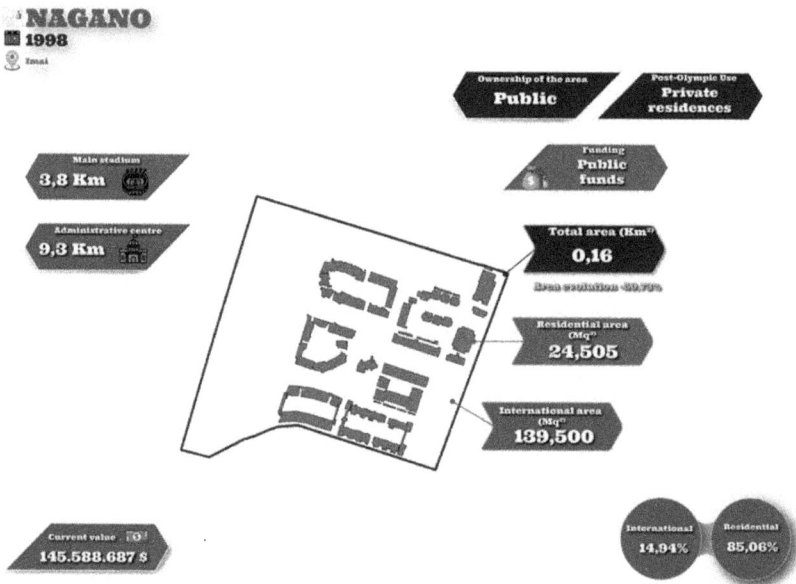

4.2.13 Salt Lake 2002

The Salt Lake Olympic Village was intended for student housing for the University of Utah and the redevelopment of Fort Douglas, a former military area. The Olympic Village could accommodate over 35,000 people, and the international areas included common areas, reception, restaurants, shops, sports facilities, an auditorium, theater, and more.[28]

Meanwhile, other facilities were planned only for the duration of the event and converted in the post-Olympic period. The revaluation of the military allowed the University of Utah to provide new student accommodation and sports facilities.

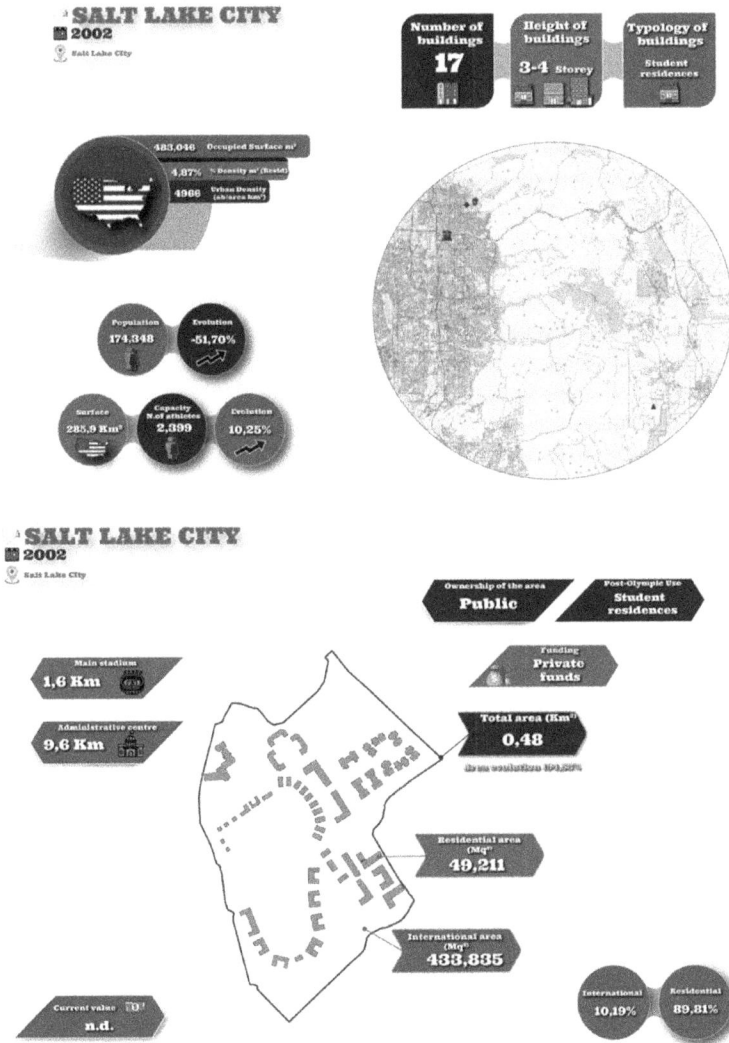

[28] Lake Organizing Committee for the Olympic Winter Games of 2002. (2002). *Salt Lake 2002: Rapport officiel des XIXes Jeux Olympiques d'hiver, Salt* (pp. 140–144).

4.2.14 Turin 2006

The 2006 edition of the Turin Olympics is recognized as the first to include three different Olympic Villages in a territorial space that had never been contemplated before. The construction of an Olympic Village in the city and two other Olympic Villages in the mountain communities will be the catalyst for transformations in the dimensions and organization of the Winter Olympic event. The project envisaged constructing and reusing existing structures to accommodate individuals, students, and tourists. The Olympic Village in the metropolitan city of Turin was in a historic area that was converted into accommodation to become a new residential neighborhood in the post-Olympic period. The construction of the Olympic Village was environmentally friendly with reused materials, solar panels, and independent heating.[29] The Turin Village was close to most of the sports facilities implemented in the city, and the neighborhood had all services and means of transport available.[30]

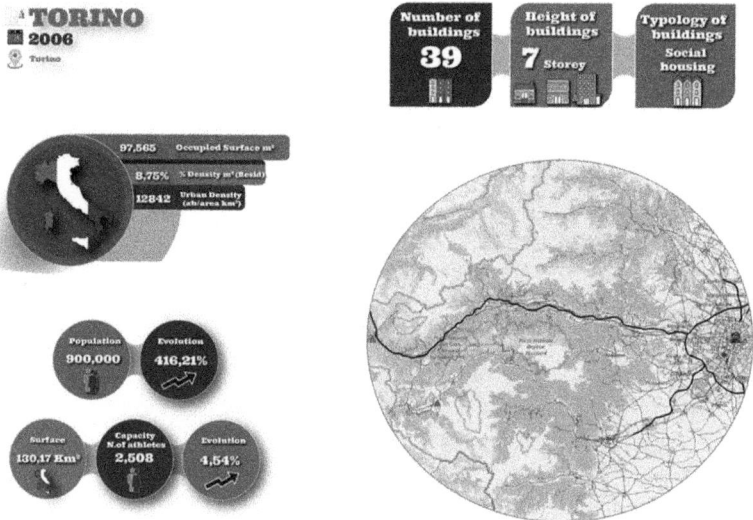

---

[29] Organising Committee for the XX Olympic Games Winter Games. (2007). *XX Olympic Winter Games: Final report* (Vol. 1, pp. 105–110).

[30] sites de competition—Torino, website of Turin. (2006). *"Village olympique de Torino"*.

TORINO
2006
Torino

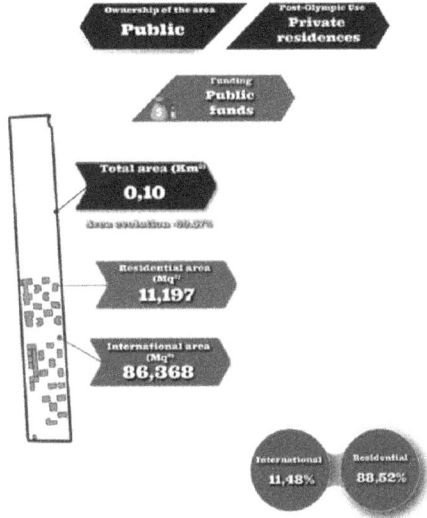

Ownership of the area
Public

Post-Olympic Use
Private residences

Funding
Public funds

Main stadium
2,2 Km

Administrative centre
5,9 Km

Total area (Km²)
0,10
Area evolution -99,97%

Residential area (Mq²)
11,197

International area (Mq²)
86,368

Current value
436.497.230 $

International **11,48%**   Residential **88,52%**

TORINO
2006
Bardonecchia

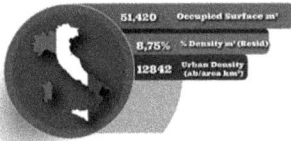

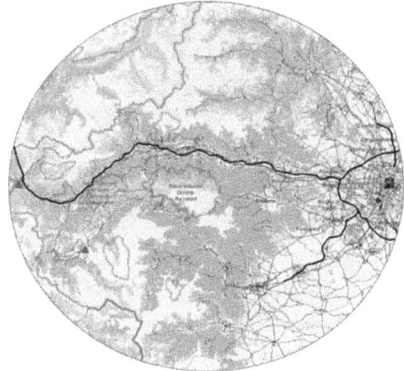

Number of buildings
1

Height of buildings
4-5 Storey

Typology of buildings
Hotel

51,420 Occupied Surface m²

8,75% % Density m² (Resid)

12842 Urban Density (ab/area km²)

Population **900,000**   Evolution **416,21%**

Surface **130,17 Km²**   Capacity N.of athletes **2,508**   Evolution **4,54%**

Meanwhile, the other two Olympic Villas, in Sestriere and Bardonecchia, were planned to be converted into hotel accommodation in the post-Olympic period. The Sestriere Villa was an extension of an existing structure and was sold to private

TORINO 2006 — Bardonecchia

Main stadium: 94,1 Km

Administrative centre: 39,4 Km

Current value: 436.497.230 $

Ownership of the area: Public

Post-Olympic Use: Hotel

Funding: Public funds

Total area (Km²): 0,05 — Area evolution -99,97%

Residential area (Mq²): 7,238

International area (Mq²): 44,182

International: 14,08% — Residential: 85,92%

TORINO 2006 — Sestrière

Occupied Surface m²: 46,304

% Density m² (Resid): 8,75%

Urban Density (ab/area km²): 12842

Number of buildings: 5

Height of buildings: 4-5 Storey

Typology of buildings: Hotel

Population: 900.000 — Evolution: 416,21%

Surface: 130,17 Km² — Capacity N. of athletes: 2,508 — Evolution: 4,54%

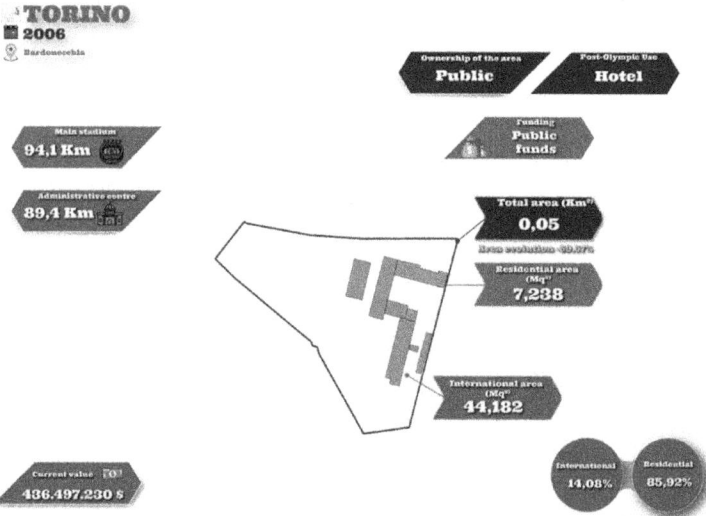

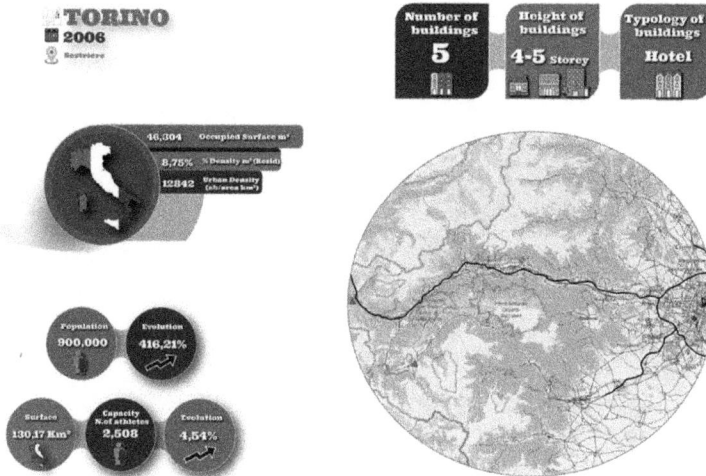

individuals.[31] Meanwhile, the Olympic Village in Bardonecchia[32] was an abandoned hotel complex from the 1930s that was converted and completely renovated. In the post-event period, the aim was to convert the Turin Olympic Village into a mixed

---

[31] sites de compétition—Sestrière, website of Turin. (2006). *"Le Village olympique de Sestrières"*.

[32] sites de compétition—Bardonecchia, website of Turin. (2006). *"Le Village olympique de Bardonecchia"*.

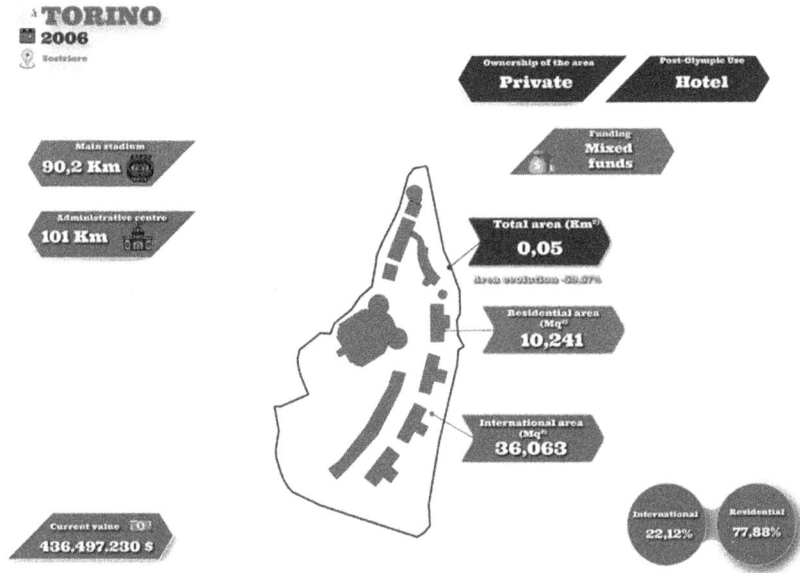

TORINO
2006
Sostriere

| Ownership of the area | Post-Olympic Use |
| Private | Hotel |

Main stadium
90,2 Km

Funding
Mixed funds

Administrative centre
101 Km

Total area (Km²)
0,05
area evolution -99.97%

Residential area (Mq²)
10,241

International area (Mq²)
36,063

Current value [C]²
436.497.230 $

International **22,12%**   Residential **77,88%**

accommodation site, which to this day remains derelict. Meanwhile, the Olympic Villages of Sestriere and Bardonecchia planned to be hotels, have enabled the towns to provide new hotel accommodations for winter tourism. The Turin edition promoted a new type of development and exploitation of the Winter Olympics.

4.2.15 Vancouver 2010

The planning of the Vancouver Olympic Village was included in a significant revaluation project of a disused area: *False Creek*. The *False Creek* area became a vast area of mixed housing developed by private and public funds. The construction of the Village allowed for the implementation of various environmental sustainability initiatives, such as waste collection, new flora and fauna, green roofs, waste treatment, stormwater and wastewater collection, and other projects to implement sustainable practices in the city of Vancouver.[33] The Olympic Village had a compact design and enjoyed all the services needed to reach the city

---

[33.] Comité d'organisation des Jeux Olympiques et Paralympiques d'hiver de 2010 à Vancouver [Vancouver Organising Committee for the 2010 Olympic and Paralympic Winter Games]. (2010). ""Quelle journée.""' *Le Village: Vancouver 2010*.

VANCOUVER
2010
Vancouver, False Creek

Number of buildings	Height of buildings	Typology of buildings
37	5-10 Storey	Residential

256,390 Occupied Surface m²
3,21% % Density m² (Resid)
10008 Urban Density (ab/area km²)

Population 603,400
Evolution -32,96%

Surface 114,97 Km²
Capacity N.of athletes 2,566
Evolution 2,31%

VANCOUVER
2010
Vancouver, False Creek

Ownership of the area **Public**
Post-Olympic Use **Private residences**

Main stadium 1,2 Km
Funding **Mixed funds**

Administrative centre 1,5 Km

Total area (Km²) 0,26
Area evolution 91,35%

Residential area (Mq²) 79,973

International area (Mq²) 176,417

Current value 1.096.905.512 $

International 31,19%
Residential 68,81%

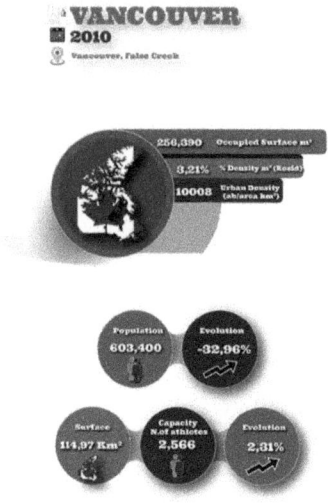

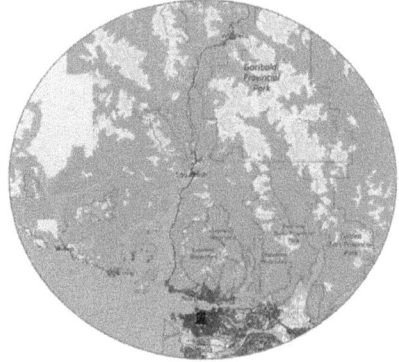

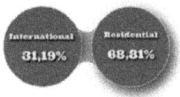

center, the competition areas and the Olympic celebration squares. All Olympic athletes were housed in a large Olympic Village that could accommodate more than 3,000 athletes. The area became communal, and the housing was sold to private individuals. However, some 250 houses were used as social housing. The new area offered a personalized training center, a shopping center, restaurants, services, and transport.

4.2.16 Sochi 2014

The organization of the Sochi Olympics was embedded in a very complex spatial planning where the three Olympic Villages were the three main centers of this spatial model. Each Olympic Village had its own identity and its utmost post-Olympic function. The Sochi Village was in a new area close to the venues and sports halls. In addition, the Village was included in an area with all kinds of services. The other Olympic Villages were arranged in the Village of Rosa Khutor and Sloboda; they had their own identities and the same level of service as the Sochi Olympic Village.[34] The accommodation in the mountain villages in the post-Olympic period was converted into hotels and flats. Meanwhile, the Sochi Olympic Village was reused as a residence. The Sochi edition is considered inspirational for host cities that want to propose a mountain tourism project in a location with a subtropical climate.

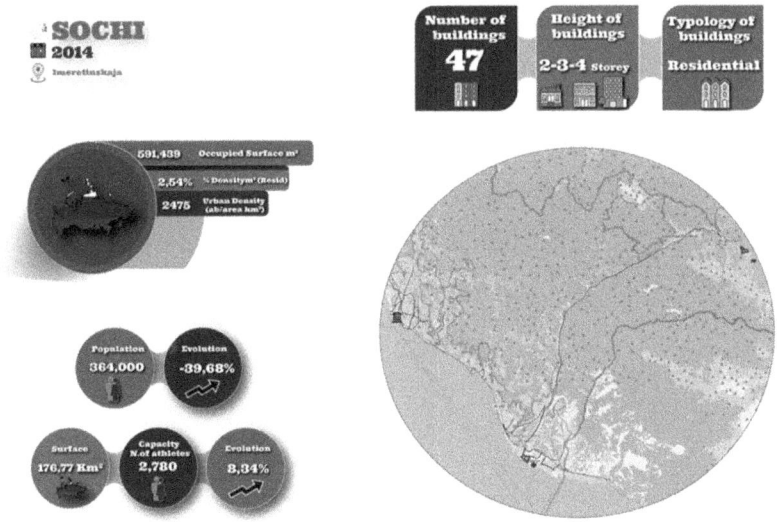

---

[34] Sochi Organising Committee for the 2014 Olympic and Paralympic Winter Games. (2015). *Rapport Officiel: Sochi 2014 Games Olympiques d'hiver* (Vol. 3, pp. 36–38).

SOCHI
2014
Imeretinskaja

Ownership of the area **Public**
Post-Olympic Use **Private residences**

Main stadium **1,4 Km**

Administrative centre **34,2 Km**

Funding **Public funds**

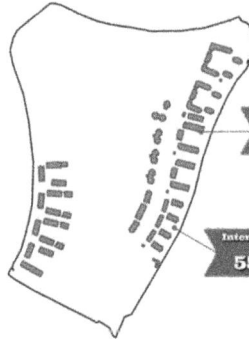

Total area (Km²) **0,59**
Area evolution 988.30%

Residential area (Mq²) **36,980**

International area (Mq²) **554,459**

International **6,25%**
Residential **90,75%**

Current value [€] **1.989.420.169 $**

SOCHI
2014
Rosa Khutor

439,211 Occupied Surface m²
2,54% % Density (Resid)
2475 Urban Density (ab/area km²)

Number of buildings **50**
Height of buildings **2-3** Storey
Typology of buildings **Resort**

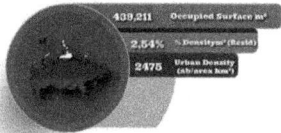

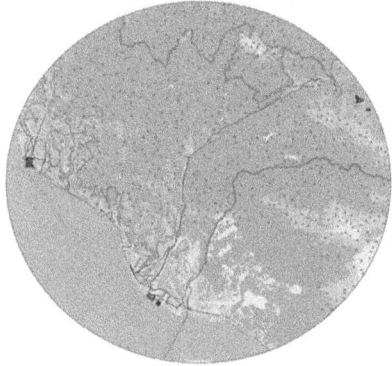

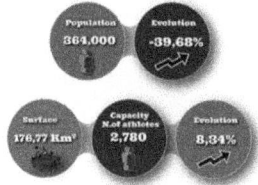

Population **364,000**
Evolution **-39,68%**

Surface **176,77 Km²**
Capacity N.of athletes **2,780**
Evolution **8,34%**

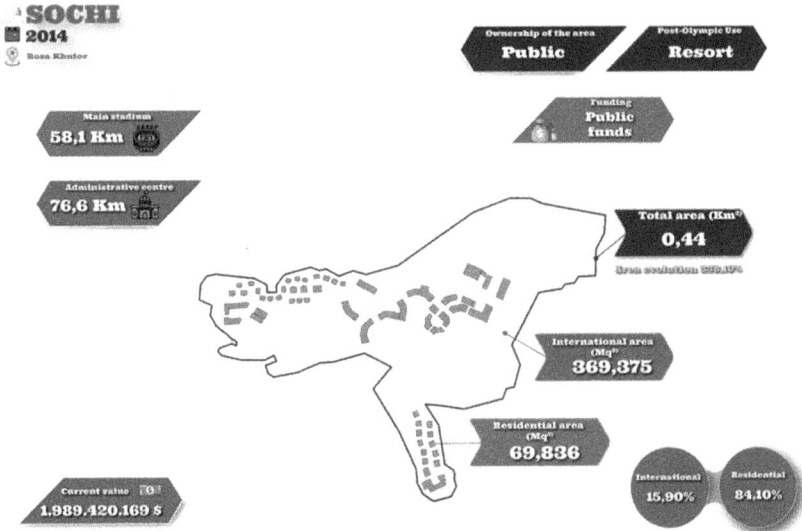

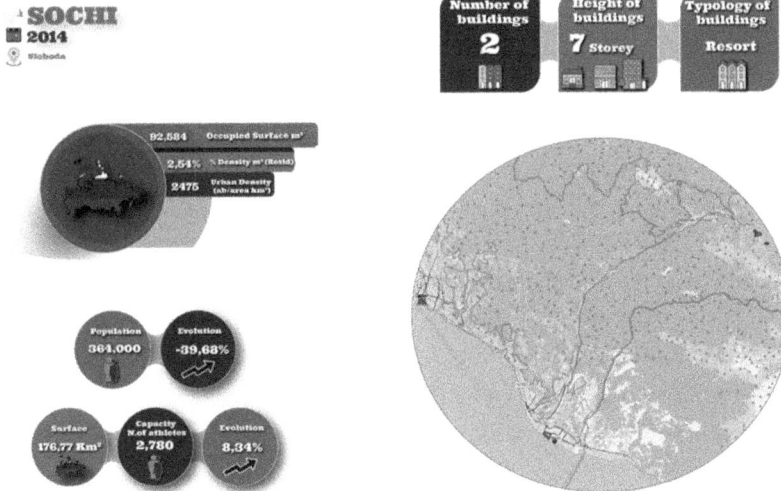

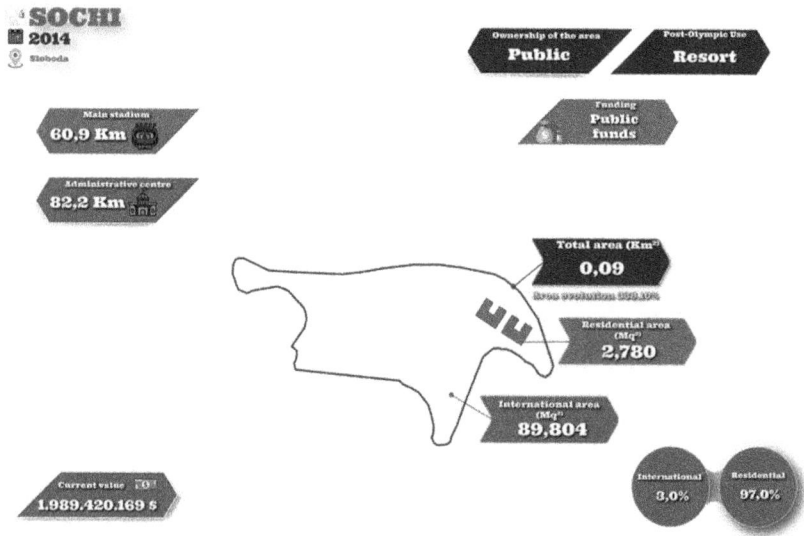

SOCHI
2014
Sloboda

Main stadium
60,9 Km

Administrative centre
82,2 Km

Ownership of the area
Public

Post-Olympic Use
Resort

Funding
Public funds

Total area (Km²)
0,09

Residential area (Mq²)
2,780

International area (Mq²)
89,804

Current value
1.989.420.169 $

International
3,0%

Residential
97,0%

4.2.17 Pyeongchang 2018

The construction of the two Pyeongchang Olympic Villages was included in a housing development plan for the two cities hosting the Olympic competitions: Pyeongchang and Gangneung. The structures were intended to increase the hotel offer and exploit winter tourism in the two cities. The organizers opted for new sustainable measures to respect the environment. The residential area was equipped with all the essential facilities and services for the athletes: a gymnasium, restaurants, polyclinic, leisure area, banks, tourist offices, shops, bars, and more.[35] In the post-Olympic period, the accommodation was converted into private flats and sold to private individuals. However, there was no interest in the tourist exploitation project, so they were converted into accommodation.

[35.] The PyeongChang Organising Committee for the 2018 Olympic & Paralympic Winter Games. (2018). *Olympic Village Guide: PyeongChang 2018* (pp. 6, 9–21, 26–27).

PYEONGCHANG
2018
Pyeongchang

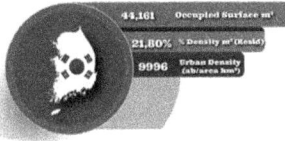

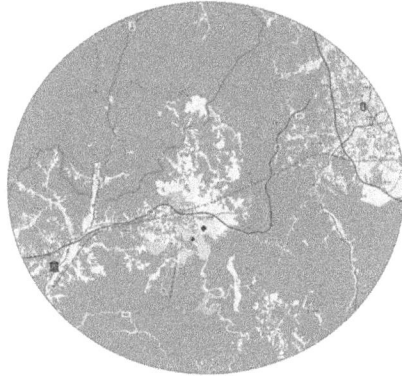

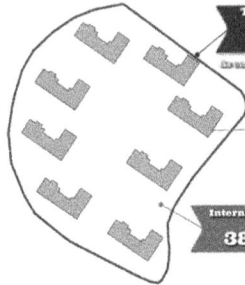

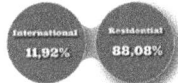

Number of buildings	Height of buildings	Typology of buildings
8	15 Storey	Residential

44,161 Occupied Surface m²

21,80% % Density m² (Resid)

9996 Urban Density (ab/area km²)

Population 43,600

Evolution -88,02%

Surface 116,31 Km²

Capacity N.of athletes 2,833

Evolution 1,91%

PYEONGCHANG
2018
Pyeongchang

Ownership of the area **Public**

Post-Olympic Use **Private residences**

Main stadium 7,2 Km

Administrative centre 23,1 Km

Funding **Public funds**

Total area (Km²) 0,04

Area evolution -91,7%

Residential area (Mq²) 5,265

International area (Mq²) 38,896

Current value 245.452.086 $

International 11,92%

Residential 88,08%

PYEONGCHANG
2018
Gangneung

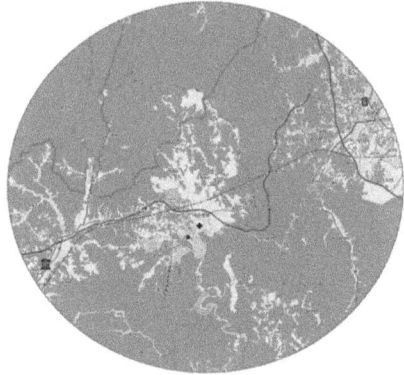

Number of buildings	Height of buildings	Typology of buildings
9	22-25 Storey	Residential

239,245 Occupied Surface m²
21,80% % Density m² (Resid)
9996 Urban Density (ab/area km²)

Population 43,600 Evolution -88,02%

Surface 116,31 Km² Capacity N.of athletes 2,833 Evolution 1,91%

PYEONGCHANG
2018
Gangneung

Ownership of the area: **Public**   Post-Olympic Use: **Private residences**

Main stadium 19,6 Km

Funding **Public funds**

Administrative centre 32,5 Km

Total area (Km²) **0,24**

Area evolution -74,77%

Residential area (Mq²) **7,731**

International area (Mq²) **231,514**

Current value 245.452.086 $

International 3,23%   Residential 96,77%

4.2.18 Beijing 2022

The 2022 Beijing Olympics comprised three different Olympic areas in a territorial space that has reached a distance of 160 km between the central Olympic Village in the city and the Olympic Village in Yanqing. The Olympics would be held in three main hubs: Beijing, Yanqing, and Zhangjiakou.[36] The construction of a central Olympic Village in the metropolis of Beijing was included in the area where the 2008 Summer Olympics were held. Meanwhile, the other Olympic Villages were planned in the two mountainous locations of Yanqing and Zhangjiakou. The Olympic Village in the city had 20 residential buildings and could accommodate 2,338 athletes during the Games. The Village was located in the center of the metropolitan city, close to the National Olympic Sports Centre. During the post-Olympic phase, the project foresees that the residences will be rented from citizens and managed entirely by the central government. Meanwhile, the Olympic Villages in the mountain localities of Chaoyang and Yanqing districts have some 3,500 beds. In contrast, the Zhangjiakou locality would be able to accommodate some 2,800 athletes and Olympic team officials.

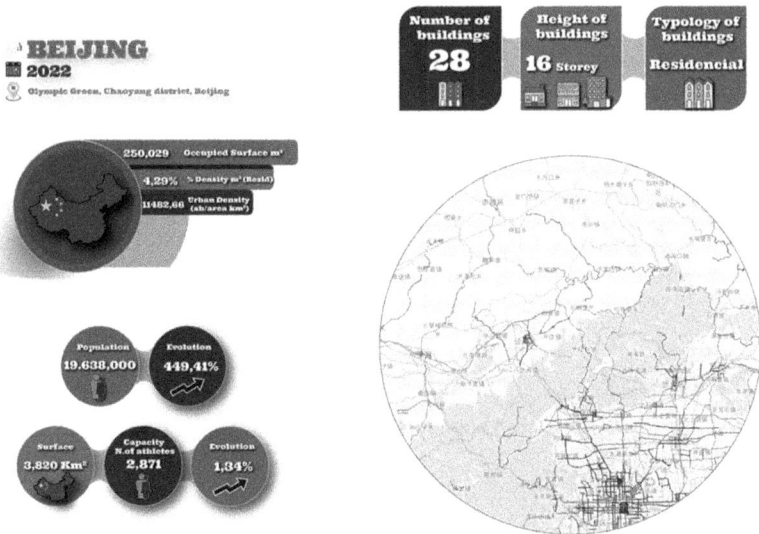

[36.] Beijing Organising Committee for the 2022 Olympic and Paralympic Winter Games. (2019). *The legacy plan of the Olympic and Paralympic Winter Games Beijing 2022.*

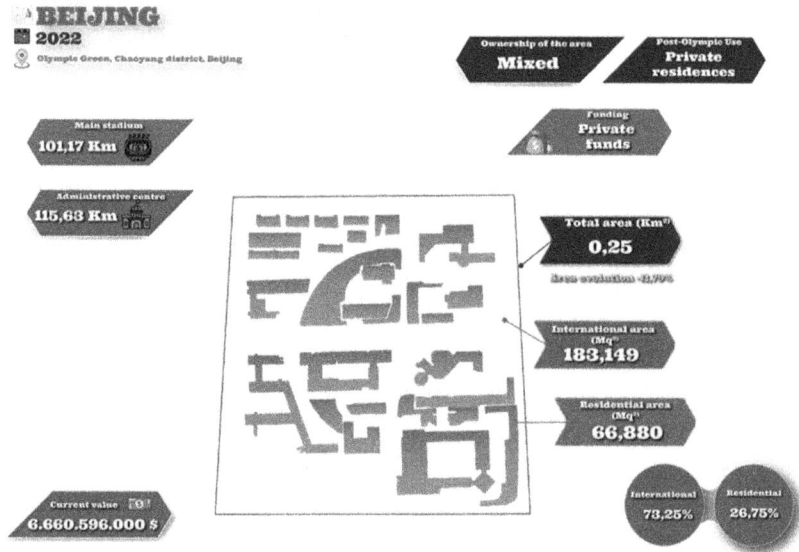

BEIJING 2022
Olympic Green, Chaoyang district, Beijing

Ownership of the area	Mixed
Post-Olympic Use	Private residences
Main stadium	101,17 Km
Funding	Private funds
Administrative centre	115,63 Km
Total area (Km²)	0,25
International area (Mq²)	183,149
Residential area (Mq²)	66,880
Current value	6.660.596.000 $

International 73,25% Residential 26,75%

The Yanqing Olympic Village would predominantly host athletes competing in skating and alpine skiing. Meanwhile, the Zhangjiakou Village would host skiers, snowboarders and ski jumpers. The Yanqing Olympic Village is at the foot of Haituo Mountain, surrounded by mountains and forests. The Village area is located in the center of historical ruins in a diverse geological landscape and ecological environment. The Village consisted of six groups of residences, which, in the post-Olympic period, would be transformed into hotels for the tourism development of Yanqing County.

Meanwhile, Zhangjiakou Olympic Village is in the snow city of Taizicheng and occupies 197,600 m². The Olympic Village space comprises a residential and international area, including restaurants, a clinic, a gymnasium, a religious center, a leisure and training center, a residents' center, a delegation leader room, a service center, and a shared space. The residential area consisted of 31 houses divided into ten groups, which, in the post-Olympic period, would form a new mountain resort for the exploitation of winter tourism in the town of Taizicheng. The Beijing Games would be recognized as the most ambitious project ever in a regional Olympic area, which had never been seen before.

4.2.19 Considerations of the Winter Olympic Villages

As observed from the proposed comparative analysis, the Olympic Village has evolved over the years through different spatial models based on the needs of each venue. However, the first project envisioned a hotel or resort in a location where winter sports are popular. The development of the Olympic Village began in Oslo in 1952 through an urban planning model that envisioned the construction of new accommodation facilities in various cities. However, the Grenoble version implies the development of a regional model, confirmed only by the Turin version and the plan for three permanent Olympic villages in a vast area. However, we observed temporary housing solutions converted into student dormitories in Calgary and Salt Lake City. The Olympic Village continues to inspire different operating models for new host cities. Over time, we have observed various forms, typologies, and structures that have become the heritage of candidate cities and places. However, the number of athletes and the evolution of Olympic sports have increased the difficulty of organizing events using a regional model supported by infrastructure. As mentioned above, since Turin in 2006, the spatial aspects of the event have maintained regional relevance through major structures being built in the candidate metropolises. The holdings in Sochi, Pyeongchang, and Beijing confirm the trend toward regional expansion of the Olympic dimension. Finally, each analyzed element's minimum and maximum values are examined to create a long-term ranking of Olympic Villages.

Table 18: Comparative analysis of Winter Olympic Villages

Main stadium			
Minimum		Maximum	
Grenoble 1968	600 m	Grenoble 1968	101,17 km
Administrative center			
Minimum		Minimum	
Vancouver 2010	1.5 km	Vancouver 2010	115.63 km
Number of buildings			
Minimum		Minimum	
Squaw valley 1960 Innsbruck 1964	4	Squaw valley 1960 Innsbruck 1964	185

(*Continued*)

Urban density (inhabitants/area km²)			
Minimum		Minimum	
Calgary 1988	1,113.40 km²	Calgary 1988	28,356.08 km²
% Density m² (residents)			
Minimum		Minimum	
Grenoble 1968	1.76%	Grenoble 1968	21.80%
Occupied area (m²)			
Minimum		Minimum	
Innsbruck 1964	38,475 m²	Innsbruck 1964	1,278,087 m²
Total area (km²)			
Minimum		Minimum	
Innsbruck 1964	0.03 km²	Innsbruck 1964	1,27 km²
Residential area			
Minimum		Minimum	
Innsbruck 1964	−44.07%	Innsbruck 1964	98.75%
International area			
Minimum		Minimum	
Calgary 1988	1.25%	Calgary 1988	144.07%
Current value			
Minimum		Minimum	
Albertville 1992	$783,770.00	Albertville 1992	$6,660,596,000.00

Source: Own implementation

CHAPTER 5

The Olympic Neighborhoods of the Future

5.1 The permanent transformation of the Olympic Village

The Olympic Games have become a prestigious promotional event (Wernick, 1991) and an urban renewal and regeneration strategy for cities that aims to "strengthen the competitive position of their metropolitan economies in a context of rapidly changing local, national and global competitive conditions" (Swyngedouw et al., 2002).

As noted above, after the 1992 Barcelona Olympics, post-industrial cities began to implement their strategies of urban regeneration and transformation—strategies that, through new processes, accelerated urban development within the major European metropolises. Therefore, the redefinition of spaces permanently has allowed the revaluation and transformation of abandoned or underdeveloped areas to favor the application of new urban practices and strategies. With the construction of a permanent Olympic Village in central regions, modern metropolises will inevitably have to adopt new strategies and solutions. Furthermore, given the location of the Olympic Village in Barcelona, these residential settlements have been transformed into profitable elements catalyzing the creation of new permanent neighborhoods. The construction of the Olympic Village in Barcelona can be considered the first housing project developed through a unique philosophy that integrated elements related to citizens' quality of life. Therefore, the Olympic Village and the Barcelona Olympic Quarter can be defined as multiple applications of new permanent theories capable of catalyzing the development of other neighboring areas.

Furthermore, given the construction costs, the Barcelona project is considered the first housing project developed through mixed financing. In this way, new housing projects integrated new negotiation strategies between public authorities and real estate companies. Handing over public areas, in this case, entire Olympic venues, to private companies for financial exploitation means reevaluating the democratic principles of transparency and community participation in urban planning (Lenskyj, 2012; Owen, 2002). In this way, neighborhood improvement becomes a joint project between public administration and private enterprise, rooted in the urban fabric.

Thus, the organization of public space starts to become a vital element of the host city's infrastructure projects. Moreover, given the new innovative city projects, the Olympic Village may become a pilot model for many cities that intend to align themselves with an integrated development. However, as noted in Barcelona, mixed (public and private) participation is justified as financing that reduces risks for candidate cities. However, looking specifically at the Barcelona project and the subsequent projects in Sydney, London, Tokyo, and Beijing, many common elements related to real estate speculation are observed. The temporary transformation of entire areas and the setting of new priorities induced critical, speculative phenomena to the detriment of the host community. The provision of luxury or speculatively priced housing will certainly not foster the integration of the neighborhood within the host city. Therefore, the following trend must be observed as a negative element for the permanent transformation of host cities.

Creating a new permanent Olympic quarter has become a pretext for transforming places. The transformation will inevitably affect the fabric of the host city permanently in the medium to long term. Ideally, these permanent transformation processes should be supported by master plans, strategic plans, guidelines, actions, and tools, which can mark a fruitful path for the host community. Furthermore, given collaborative planning, decisions and choices linked to the needs of all stakeholders involved in permanent changes within the territory should be implemented. A change of use can entail different socioeconomic issues that can irreversibly transform entire areas of our cities. Therefore, integrating collaborative and informative processes can reduce the adverse effects of temporary transformations. Ideally, these processes should be integrated within ordinary planning. Only through integrating and implementing new planning models will candidate cities reduce their chances of failure.

Furthermore, continuous and accurate information on changes in the overall project and individual interventions will facilitate discussions and reduce risks for the host community. The projects observed in the 21st century have integrated different elements that imply a rethinking of the structure of modern neighborhoods. Creating an Olympic Park with a vast sports infrastructure has become commonplace in candidate cities. The following mega-project changes the scale of permanent intervention within the candidate cities. Therefore, the Olympic Village project can be evaluated before, during, and after the events. In all the following phases, the Olympic project will integrate new design elements that can increase or decrease its permanent impact on the territory. However, in the post-Olympic phase, the Olympic district will nourish new visibility that, given private participation, may favor creating or implementing new housing.

For example, during the 2020 Tokyo Games, the idea was to provide an athletes' village that could become a tangible asset for citizens. However, after the Olympic event, the developer group, with the municipality's support, proposed the construction of two new high-rise buildings in the center of the Olympic Island. Thus, we continue observing how these Olympic areas carry new meanings within a changing host community. A community that will have to decide whether to accept or reject the project put forward by its administration. Although some Olympic cities do not have a democracy, the host communities are the center of the Olympic project. Without citizen acceptance, it will not be easy to open up to the world and thus reap the tangible benefits of the Olympic event. As noted in the first chapter, tourism is the primary real benefit cities can achieve by hosting the Olympic event. However, tourism can undermine the social fabric of our cities. For example, in Barcelona, tourism has led to a radical change in the economic activities and services offered within the city.

Furthermore, the Catalan capital has seen continuous increases in rental costs in observance of the economic possibilities linked to the accommodation market. The emergence of new platforms and the increase in the flow of people have and continue to radically change our cities. Therefore, citizens are subject to continuous pressure and changes related to the socioeconomic transformations induced by mega-events. The Olympic towns are an excellent way to observe the emergence and evolution of the phenomena of segregation and gentrification that are constantly occurring within global metropolises. Therefore, there is no guarantee that informal processes can affect political decisions and objectives during the Olympic bidding phase. However, decisions on housing projects require a broader public dialogue. Only through citizen participation and the sharing of results can the priority issues for our community be discussed. Any artifact that occupies our territory permanently should be interpreted as a common good that can foster the creation, implementation, or transformation of entire areas.

5.2 Future Olympic Villages

As noted above, the Barcelona edition 1992 will mark a milestone in the evolution of Olympic accommodation within central areas of modern metropolises.

Subsequently, in the summer edition, we will observe different spatial models that will lead to the establishment of a purely monocentric model for modern metropolises. After the 2012 London Games, the Olympic Village was transformed into a new multifunctional complex capable of encompassing different meanings and elements in a central area of the British capital. After London, the Olympic accommodation acquired new elements to observe the complexity of designing a main area. Including services, offices, commercial spaces, sports parks, road infrastructure, sports facilities, cinemas, hospitals, schools, and universities has profoundly transformed Olympic design in modern metropolises. Thanks to all these elements, cities can redevelop, redefine, and reshape entire central areas with the help of the best modern technologies. From Barcelona onward, Olympic Village sites, except Rio de Janeiro, have been included in the critical areas identified to explore and implement new elements of the city's new service economy.

Therefore, creating a mix of residential and commercial spaces will lead to creating a new development model for future Olympic accommodation. Furthermore, after integrating the new sports facilities, the entire area will promote a healthy lifestyle within the Olympic city. Over time, the Olympic Village has become a central stage for sport. A place that facilitates the integration of athletes in a new environment.

However, during the 21st century, Olympic accommodation opened up new perspectives for developing new values for the local community. For example, the Olympic Villages in Sydney and Beijing provided new elements related to the landscape and the integration of housing and nature. In this way, Olympic housing carries new meanings that can sensitize future cities in Beijing to adopt sustainable measures. However, as stated above, an ideal model can only be adapted and replicated for some towns. One can only identify spatial models that can inspire future models. Undoubtedly, the application and adoption of each model are strongly linked to each city's socioeconomic and urban context. Current plans for preparing the new Olympic Quarter envisage the construction of 5,000 flats, each for three or four people, within an average total area of 0.10 km^2.

In addition, including various services, infrastructures, and other elements requires an integrated and strategic planning of the new district. The Olympic accommodation model in the 21st century implies the construction of a new district capable of permanently accommodating 15,000 to 20,000 people. A neighborhood that presupposes the provision of hospitals, churches, schools, infrastructure, etc.

So, what will the future Olympic villages look like? Are they just real estate speculation projects, or will they be the engine of a new housing strategy in the host city?

For the projects Paris 2024, Milano Cortina 2026, Los Angeles 2028, and Brisbane 2032, a model Olympic village has been created in the central area, representing a mixed space to host the events. However, as mentioned above, winter events are organized by setting up multiple Olympic villages over a larger area. Therefore, constructing an Olympic Village in a critical area will trigger a rethinking of the construction of new Olympic regions, as it will be integrated into the existing infrastructure system and permanently incorporated into the urban fabric. Thus, the Olympic Village has been transformed into a sports district, but after the Olympics, it could become an area for real estate speculation due to the interest in new housing in sustainable areas and environments with green spaces. The decrease in green spaces in modern metropolises means that developers are increasingly interested in building Olympic Villages in more attractive areas for luxury housing. Thus, the construction or implementation of a vast sports park will be one of the central elements of Olympic Villages shortly.

5.3 Olympic regionalization

As noted in Chapter 2, the different mono/polycentric forms of the Olympic area are the result of the development process of the Olympic space over time. The spatial dimension of functional urban areas can be analyzed with the help of the Olympic space. The Olympic space is a temporary space where members and participants perform synergetic functions within the area of interest. Therefore, competition venues will be regarded as temporary sites of consumption production. Temporary sites must be connected through an infrastructural system capable of meeting the obligations imposed by the International Olympic Committee (IOC). Within this new spatial dimension, transport systems have become a key element in the event's success.

Moreover, given the territory, the road infrastructure is at the center of the transformation of these venues, enabling the redefinition of larger areas within the regional area. The spatial dimension has thus reached a new extension, implying the redefinition and reorganization of public transport. The unique pattern can be observed in the winter edition rather than the summer edition. The winter edition within the Olympic region offers more solutions and options for the host city, solutions and options that can improve or compromise connections within the Olympic region. Therefore, the Winter Olympics provide new projects to implement local strategies for each region.

Moreover, due to the spread of venues across the regional territory, the winter edition can offer many opportunities for local communities. However, we have only sometimes observed positive results. Turin 2006 was the first edition to implement the following spatial model—which over time has had permanent implications for the region, including and excluding places due to the infrastructure system. However, planning a regional territory depends on different factors and entities involved. Therefore, over time, we have observed other regional models that have excluded or integrated different places in consideration of the spatial strategies of each nation. After the failure of Sochi and Pyeongchang, Beijing 2022 reached its maximum spatial dimension by constructing new infrastructure to connect with mountain clusters. Infrastructures that have permanently changed the regional territory.

However, the opportunities arising from improved transport systems and structural changes in the Olympic region will allow new opportunities to be explored by the region. Dimension that may foster local development within the host region.

Therefore, new opportunities must be based on cooperation and public participation to bring tangible benefits to the public (Acioly, 2020). Olympic venues can catalyze significant infrastructural changes, leading to new forms of regionalization that recognize the growing importance of local communities.

5.4 Sustainable planning for the Olympic legacy

According to Ritchie (2000), the Olympic Games must be conceived and designed as a global event in which all participants are included equally. Furthermore, the event must only consider relevant and, above all, reliable and truthful information. However, this will only sometimes be the case. For this reason, the Olympic legacy to be transmitted must include values and meanings accepted by the host community. Programming harmonized with people's values will enable widespread acceptance of the event.

Only the host community can ensure that many people say, "Welcome to the world." Moreover, the Olympic event has its roots in the host city and should be seen as a broader, long-term process (Ritchie, 2000). Olympic sustainability has become an essential element at all organizational levels. Moreover, given the legacy within the host city, sustainability plays a central role in medium- to long-term planning. Since the early 1990s, the Olympic sustainability plan has been the cornerstone of the Olympic bid for many states. This trend started in Lillehammer 1994, Atlanta 1996, Sydney 2000, and continued in all subsequent Olympic Games.

However, it was only after the Turin 2006 event that the strategic assessment of sustainability started to include different elements to assess the holistic impact of the Olympic event. Therefore, cities gradually began incorporating some sustainability aspects into the bidding process—a process that, over the years, has transformed its structure, adapting to the needs of contemporary society. Thus, with its focus on sustainability, the Olympic legacy has become a catalyst for new philosophies of place development and the adoption of shared community practices. In keeping with the historical moment, sustainability planning has proven to be a critical factor in the transformation and regeneration of our territories. However, the Organizing Committees should pay attention to the involvement of community groups, organizations, and companies. Listening to and involving local interest groups means that all priority issues can be included in the post-Olympic sustainability planning process.

On the other hand, Agenda 21 has provided general guidance on measures to be taken to better implement sustainability in mega-events. In the meantime, in the environmental field, the UN calls for minimizing negative impacts on the biosphere (della Sala, 2023c). Key objectives include nature and landscape conservation, energy saving, water recycling, use of sustainable materials, promotion of green technologies, environmentally friendly design techniques, promotion of local resources, public transport, and waste reduction. Agenda 21 emphasizes the importance of conducting comprehensive environmental impact assessments before implementing Olympic construction projects. While in the socioeconomic field, Agenda 21 focuses on social sustainability, combating exclusion and improving people's living spaces.

The following elements highlight the importance of ensuring long-term socio-economic and health benefits for cities and regions. Furthermore, given the IOC guidelines,[1] the Olympic event aims to reduce poverty and involve disadvantaged people in sports and cultural activities. However, in 2015, with the introduction of the 17 Sustainable Development Goals (SDGs)[2] For 2030, the United Nations emphasized the importance of achieving expected outcomes for creating a green and sustainable world. On the other hand, in observance of the Olympic event, it must be emphasized how completely different the summer event is from the winter one. Due to the location, the winter edition inevitably has a more significant environmental impact. Therefore, given competition venues in mountainous areas, the Olympic event should include elements that ensure the preservation and protection of the landscape. Furthermore, using environmental assessment systems, such as the one implemented in Turin in 2006, remains a fundamental tool for optimally evaluating development plans (della Sala, 2022b). Furthermore, the realization, design, and construction of sports facilities must be conducted in such a way as to "ensure their harmonious integration into the local context" (della Sala, 2023a, 2023c). Only through shared and participatory planning will projects integrate the real needs of the local community.

Agenda 21, like the SDGs, emphasizes the importance of including all affected groups, particularly indigenous peoples, women and youth, to ensure democratic decision-making processes at the Olympic Games.

The Olympic Sustainability Analysis prepared by Furrer[3] proposes six main objectives:

- *Equality*—Implication of the sharing of Olympic risks and responsibilities, benefits, and opportunities for the most significant number of tourists, regardless of their social status and geographical location.
- *Strategic planning* means that the Olympics should be used as an opportunity to address severe urban and regional challenges, improving the lives of all citizens. The Games should be integrated into the long-term urban development strategy and catalyze activities and improvements in social policies.

---

[1] IOC. (1999). *Agenda 21 of the Olympic Movement.*

[2] The SDGs are 17 goals introduced by the UN to raise awareness of sustainable development, inclusion, integration, and respect for the environment through a few key points.

[3] Furrer, P. (2002). *Sustainable Olympic Games: A dream or a reality? Bollettino della Società Geografica Italiana, Series XII, Volume VII/4.* https://www.bsgi.it/index.php/bsgi/article/view/6914.

- *Responsible resource management:* Financial, social and environmental resources must be invested to safeguard and enhance the socioeconomic integrity, health systems, and ecosystems vital to the host city and region.
- *A new form of governance for urban sustainability* is characterized by integrity and transparency in decision-making, accountability in the management of public resources, genuine public consultation throughout the planning process and constructive management of opposition.
- *Sustainability monitoring and reporting* is essential to accountability and transparency, helping to maintain dialogue with the Games' diverse audiences, including investors, residents, the nation, etc.
- *Sustainable local design:* When planning Olympic venues for multipurpose and long-term use, special attention needs to be paid to the use of temporary infrastructure.

Furthermore, Furrer (2002) and Frey (2008) argue that partnerships and social networks are essential to developing the long-term sustainability of host cities. Building and expanding the network of stakeholders requires strong synergies between institutions—synergies that, during Olympic planning, can undermine operational project design and execution. This means that businesses, institutions, associations, and society will form a social network that will provide the necessary activities and processes to strengthen the actions to be carried out in the area. Supporting the local network will ensure the execution of sustainable measures within the Olympic region. Furthermore, the population must see and plan sustainability as a collective effort (della Sala, 2023c). The purpose of sustainable planning is to facilitate communication between the public and private sectors.[4] Adopting different shared interests between stakeholders allows new spatial actions and strategies to be implemented and accepted. Therefore, we can only ensure sustainable practices and processes are adopted within host communities through collaborative, sustainable planning.

However, to ensure the sustainability of host communities, citizens must be actively involved in the planning process—a process that must inevitably inform the community about the Olympic event's opportunities, challenges, and risks. Only through continuous information will the Organizing Committee be

---

[4] Frey, M., Iraldo, F., & Melis, M. (2008). *The impact of large-scale sports events on local development: An assessment of the XXth Torino Olympics through the Sustainability Report.* Working Paper No. 10. Universita Commerciale Luigi Bocconi.

able to secure the acceptance and support of the host community. Furthermore, public–private partnerships offer a unique opportunity to solve long-standing problems and large-scale projects that still need to be completed. Therefore, it is essential to streamline the decision-making process by reducing bureaucracy, lowering administrative barriers, and streamlining governmental processes (Furrer, 2002). Conversely, the bureaucratization of processes can lead to the centralization of power and the execution of unfavorable decisions. For example, decentralizing power can prevent local governments from participating in territorial projects.[5] If the government abdicates its responsibilities, it will inevitably suffer conspicuous criticism from the community. Criticism that implies a shared distrust and will inevitably introduce a climate of public dissatisfaction in the territory. Media attention for this event could foment and catalyze negative criticism for central and local governments. Rushing into the planning and design of a mega-event may satisfy only a part of the private sector without considering the public implications and guarantees for the holding of the event.[6] Moreover, the centralized nature of the Olympic organization implies an imbalance in priorities and needs on the part of central and local governments. Cities have different needs and require specific policies and measures to adapt to their situations. Adapting measures and policies requires an in-depth analysis of the socioeconomic specificities of each territory involved in the Olympic event.

The Olympic opportunity, and ultimately the Olympic Games, is entirely possible if the organizers properly consider the risks involved in Olympic planning. It can be "harnessed for positive change, reaping some concrete benefits for most residents."[7]

> "Only careful and realistic strategic planning is essential to achieve positive, rather than negative, legacies."[8]

---

[5] Owen, K. (2001). *The local impacts of the Sydney 2000 Olympic Games: Politics and process of venue preparation* (pp. 2–17). The Center for Olympic Studies, Wales, The University of New South.

[6] Hall, M. C. (2006). Urban Entrepreneurship, Corporate Interests and Sports Mega-Events: The thin policies of competitiveness within the hard outcomes of neoliberalism. In J. Manzenreiter and W. Horne (Eds.), *Sports Mega-Events: Social scientific analyses of a global phenomenon* (pp. 59–70). Blackwell Publishing/*The Sociological Review*.

[7] Furrer, P. (2002). *Sustainable Olympic Games: A dream or a reality? Bollettino della Società Geografica Italiana, Series XII, Volume VII/4*. https://www.bsgi.it/index.php/bsgi/article/view/6914.

[8] Ritchie, J. R. (2000). "Turning 16 days into 16 years through Olympic legacies". *Event Management, 6*(3), 155–165

5.5 Between planning models and urban functions in the post-Olympic period

In observance of the analyses conducted in the previous chapters and considering the theoretical framework offered within the following book, we can make some conclusions regarding the evolution of the Olympic Villages during the 20th and 21st centuries.

The following book highlights several fundamental aspects for the study and analysis of Olympic urbanism. The following concepts have been consolidated through a multidisciplinary and interdisciplinary analysis of the author's doctoral research study.

Therefore, the vast and profound research material has allowed for a valuable and comprehensive analysis of the evolution of Olympic urbanism over time.

This volume considers the mega-event as a great process of transformation, redefinition and reevaluation capable of catalyzing different territories in different ways. Moreover, by specific contexts, as we noted earlier, the Olympic event can favor or disfavor certain territories.

In observance of what is expressed in the following book, the territorial transformations linked to the construction of the Olympic venues imply a physical and imaginary transformation of the host site. Furthermore, the next book highlights the importance of Olympic urbanism as a transformation process that means rethinking housing strategies within the host cities. Through the study of different Olympic experiences, we have observed how Olympic housing over time has evolved to take on multiple dimensions in consideration of the spatial models adopted by Olympic cities.

Therefore, based on the following consideration of Olympic urbanism, the Olympic Village is defined as a unitary corpus capable of reflecting the urban dimension of the sporting event. Moreover, given its spatial dimension, the Olympic Village can be regarded as the only element capable of standing out over time as the fulcrum of urban development associated with the Olympic Games.

On the other hand, Olympic urbanism is part of a transformation process that manifests itself as a representation of different urban realities and considering the specificities of each historical and sociocultural context (della Sala, 2022a, 2022b).

Therefore, through the analysis of the Olympic Villages, we can relate the different Olympic projects with the help of standard parameters that have helped us observe the Olympic accommodations arranged throughout the 20th and 21st centuries.

Through the following book, we want to emphasize how Olympic accommodation is the central element in planning the modern Olympic event. Moreover, as previously noted, the Olympic Village has often become a tangible asset for the host community. However, observing the accommodation built in the 21st century, it was only sometimes provided to the host community. Furthermore, given the abandonments, one must keep the project through the different relationships this urban piece must establish within the existing urban fabric.

Therefore, the following text will advance some reflections on the two research questions posed in the introductory phase.

1.   What types of urban functions have Olympic Villages assumed throughout history, considering their use in the post-Olympic period?
2.   While considering the planning of host cities, we will analyze the different spatial models to answer the following question: Can the Olympic Village be considered a catalyst for urban expansion and/or transformation?

The following questions provide a comprehensive overview of the Olympic Villages built during the 20th and 21st centuries and the spatial models adopted by Olympic cities. In addition, the following conclusions are to be considered fundamental in observance of the results obtained within the comprehensive research study (della Sala, 2022b).

Planning models for Olympic Villages
built in the 20th and 21st centuries.

In observance of what was expressed within the second and third chapters, we could advance different spatial models to advance the first classification of the various Olympic Villages arranged in the 20th and 21st centuries.

Therefore, it is stated that the Olympic accommodations were designed through different spatial models that can be identified as monocentric, satellite, polycentric, cluster, peripheral and metropolitan. Furthermore, the following models allow us to observe a substantial difference between those adopted in the summer and winter editions.

In the summer edition, the Olympic Villages took different forms of the context territory and in consideration of the Olympic project proposed by the host city. Within the analysis, the monocentric model stands out as the standard model capable of recognizing the existence of an urban strategy. An urban strategy must inevitably respect the urban structure of the host cities. Moreover, as noted in Chapter 3, the 1992 Barcelona edition, adopting the monocentric model, inspired and bore a new planning model for Olympic accommodation within the modern metropolis. Therefore, by observing the proposed spatial models, we can affirm that the different experiences of the Olympic Villages in the summer edition took a form capable of fitting within the central strategies of the host metropolises.

Meanwhile, in the winter edition, the Olympic Villages, after Oslo 1952, were planned using multiple strategies involving different spatial models.

Chapter 3 notes that the polycentric model can be identified as the standard model adopted by Olympic cities. Hence, adopting the polycentric model implies the existence of a regional strategy that, starting with Turin 2006, asserts itself as the primary solution for planning the winter edition.

The following spatial strategy in the 21st century has established itself as the new planning model for multiple accommodations in an ever-expanding Olympic space. Thus, the continuous and growing size of the winter edition allows us to observe how the polycentric model is a catalyst for regionalization processes within the host territories.

Therefore, through the following statements, common patterns can be identified in both Olympic editions. Observing spatial patterns makes it possible to classify and analyze Olympic accommodations through the spatial dimension that each Olympic Village assumed during the planning of the Olympic event. Furthermore, thanks to the following spatial models, it is possible to make assessments of the profound transformations that occurred within the Olympic territories in the post-event phase.

Finally, in light of the theoretical framework provided, we stress the importance of the proposed models as inspiring examples for planning future events. Therefore, the spatial model of the Olympic Village, and thus of the temporary accommodation facilities, can establish different relationships considering each local context. Therefore, in each local context, the following models produce acts of territorialization by creating connections and interconnections that will inevitably affect existing networks.

On the other hand, the planning and spatial organization of the winter event implies reconsidering existing relations in a much wider area than the summer edition.

For this reason, the planning of the winter edition is much more complex than the local development system. Adopting a regional spatial model may contribute to and favor the creation of different spatial imbalances. Spatial imbalances that may cause the reconsideration of inland areas. Furthermore, the regional dimension may favor the emergence of internal competition between intermediate areas, excluding and favoring certain territories included in spatial planning.

The urban functions of Olympic villages in the post-Olympic period

Considering the different solutions adopted and the functions assumed by the Olympic Villages in the post-Olympic period, we can consider the different urban strategies related to the housing needs of the host cities. Throughout Olympic history, housing has assumed other urban functions that can be analyzed by considering its uses: temporary or permanent.

Therefore, through the classification related to the Olympic Villages' character, we can clearly distinguish between the two editions.

In the summer edition, except for the initial and American editions, permanent accommodation was the model most used by the host cities.

Whereas, in the winter edition, temporary accommodation was only adopted in those localities that had accommodation available in advance. However, some localities had prepared a tourism enhancement project so that the facilities could be included within the areas involved in the organization of the Olympic event.

Subsequently, observing the evolution in the post-event phase, the Olympic Villages can be analyzed in consideration of their reuse and abandonment.

In the summer edition, as mentioned in Chapter 3, most Olympic Villages were reused as available accommodation for the host population. Only the cases of Berlin 1936, Athens 2004 and Rio de Janeiro 2016 are in a state of abandonment and disuse by the local community.

On the other hand, in the winter edition, the Olympic accommodation facilities were mainly used to foment the construction of hotels, resorts, or tourist accommodations.

Thus, the winter edition within the mountain resorts could have accommodations added or included in the tourist circuits, transforming in the post-event phase into an asset available for the exploitation of winter sports tourism. Therefore, it is stated that including accommodation facilities within a tourism plan reduces the uncertainties linked to abandonment phenomena in the post-event period.

Furthermore, in the winter edition, except for the Sarajevo bombing, only the Olympic accommodation in Turin can be recognized as the only abandoned facility.

Thus, observing the urban functions of the Olympic Villages in the post-event phase, it is stated that the Olympic lodgings arranged in the mountain resorts were always reused. Whereas, in the summer edition, different abandonments were observed in the post-event phase in consideration of size. Abandonments in several locations catalyzed other problems and forms of social deviance, such as squatting and occupation.

The following classification of Olympic Villages advanced within the text allows us to consider the importance of post-Olympic planning. Planning must be carried out to observe the spatial pattern, use and dimensions that the accommodation complexes assume in the post-event phase. A delicate phase that implies much uncertainty for the host cities and the community. Therefore, it is argued that functions must be planned in advance to reuse the Olympic Village. Land consumption within increasingly fragile territories can be avoided through strategic planning and adherence to community priorities.

BIBLIOGRAPHY

Acioly, C., Aubrey, D., Betancourth, C., Bland, S., Caglin, P., Chong, J., … Torres, C. (2020). *Participatory Incremental Urban Planning. A Toolbox to support local governments in developing countries to implement the New Urban Agenda and the Sustainable Development Goals-Edition for fast growing small cities*. www.unhabitat.org

Andranovich, G., & Burbank, M. (2011). *Contextualizing Olympic legacies: Urban geography*. Taylor & Francis Group.

Andranovich, G., Burbank, M. J., & Heying, C. H. (2001). Olympic cities: Lessons learned from mega-event politics. *Journal of Urban Affairs, 23*(2), 113–131.

Andreff, W. (2012). The winner's curse: Why is the cost of mega sporting events so often underestimated? In W. Maenning (Ed.), *International handbook on the economics of mega sporting events*. Elgar.

Arsen, D. (1997). Is there really a link between infrastructure and economic development? In R. D. Birmingham & R. Mier (Eds.), *Dillemas of urban economic development: Issues in theory and practice* (pp. 82–98). Sage Publishing.

Auruskeviciene, V., Pundziene, A., Skudiene, V., Gripsud, G., Nes, E. B., & Olsson, U. H. (2010). Change of attitudes and country image after hosting major sports events. *Inzinerine Ekonomika–Engeneering Economics*, 21(1), 53–59.

Baldassarri, M. (1993). *Privatization processes in Eastern Europe: Privatization processes in Eastern Europe*. Palgrave Macmillan.

Bale, J., & Christensen, M. K. (2004). *Post-Olympic? Questioning sport in the twenty-first century*. BERG.

Beijing Organizing Committee for the Games of the XXIX Olympiad. (2010). *Official report of the Beijing 2008 Olympic Games*.

Benevolo, L. (1968). *Le Origini Dell'urbanistica Moderna*. Universale Laterza.

Billings, S. B., & Holladay, J. S. (2012). Should cities go for the gold? The long-term impacts of hosting the Olympics. *Economic Inquiry, 50*(3), 754–772.

Blunden, H. (2012). The Olympic Games and housing. In H. J. Lenskyj et al. (Eds.). *The Palgrave handbook of Olympic studies* (pp. 520–532). Palgrave Macmillan.

Bondonio, P. (2006a). Carocci (Ed.) *Olimpiadi, oltre il 2006: Torino 2006: Secondo rapporto sui territori olimpici.*

Bondonio, P. (2006b). *Proceedings: International Symposium for Olympic research* (pp. 355–381).

Bondonio, P. (2007). *A giochi fatti: Le eredità di Torino 2006* (p. 374).

British Olympic Council. (1909). *The Fourth Olympiad: Being the official report of the Olympic Games of 1908 celebrated in London.*

Brunet, F. (1995). An economic analysis of the Barcelona'92 Olympic Games: Resources, financing, and impact. In de Moragas M., Botella M. (Eds.), *The Keys to Success: The Social, Economic and Communications Impact of Barcelona'92* (pp. 203–237). Servei de Publicacions de la UAB.

Brunet, F. (2005). *The economic impact of the Barcelona Olympic Games, Barcelona*: The legacy of the games 1992–2002 (pp. 1–27). Centre d'Estudis Olímpics (UAB).

Cashman R. (1999). *Staging the Olympics*. Centre for Olympic Studies, UNSW Press.

Cashman, R. (2002). *What is "Olimpic Legacy"?* The Legacy of the Olimpic Games, Losanna, International Olympic Committee.

Cashman, R. (2005). *The bitter-sweet awaking: The legacy of Sydney 2000 Olympic Games*. Walla Press.

Cashman, R. (2010). *Impact of the games on Olympic host cities*. Centre d'Estudis Olímpics (UAB).

Chalip, L. (2010). *Leveraging the Sydney Olympics for tourism*. Centre d'Estudis Olímpics, UAB.

Chalkley, B., & Essex, S. (1999). Urban development through hosting international events: A history of the Olympic Games. *Planning Perspectives, 14*(4), 369–394.

Chappelet, J. L. (2002). From Lake Placid to Salt Lake City: The challenging growth of the Olympic Winter Games since 1980. *European Journal of Sport Science, 2*(3), 1–21.

Chappelet, J. L. (2010). *A short overview of the Olympic Winter Games.* CEO-UAB.

Charlesworth, E. (Ed.). (2005). *Cityedge: Case studies in contemporary urbanism* (p. 244). Routledge.

Clark, G. (2008). *Local development benefits from staging global events: Achieving the local development legacy from 2012, (2011)* (p. 89). LEED.

COJO 76. (1978). *Montreal 1976: Games of the XXI Olympiad Montreal 1976: Official report.*

Comitato Giorgio Rota. (2000). *Rapporti su Torino—Lavori in corso.*

Comitato Giorgio Rota. (2001). *Rapporti su Torino—La mappa del mutamento.*

Comitato Giorgio Rota. (2002). *Rapporti su Torino—Voglia di cambiare.*

Comitato Giorgio Rota. (2003). *Rapporti su Torino—Count down.*

Comitato Giorgio Rota. (2004). *Rapporti su Torino—Le radici del nuovo futuro.*

Comitato Giorgio Rota. (2005). *Rapporti su Torino—L'immagine del cambiamento.*

Comitato Giorgio Rota. (2006). *Rapporti su Torino—Giochi aperti.*

Comitato Giorgio Rota. (2007). *Rapporti su Torino—Senza rete.*

Comitato Giorgio Rota. (2008). *Rapporti su Torino—Solista e solitaria.*

Comitato Giorgio Rota. (2009). *Rapporti su Torino—10 anni per un'altra Torino.*

Comitato olimpico nazionale italiano. (1957). *VII Giochi olimpici invernali, Cortina d'Ampezzo, 1956 = VII Olympic Winter Games, Cortina d'Ampezzo, 1956.*

Comitato per l'Organizzazione dei XX Giochi Olimpici Invernali Torino 2006. (2007). *XX Giochi Olimpici invernali Torino 2006 = XX Olympic Winter Games Torino 2006.*

Comité de candidature de Beijing aux Jeux Olympiques d'hiver de 2022. (2014). *Beijing 2022: Candidate city.*

Comité d'organisation des Jeux Olympiques et Paralympiques d'hiver de 2010 à Vancouver[Vancouver Organising Committee for the 2010 Olympic and Paralympic Winter Games]. (2010, February 21). *VANOC official Games report = Rapport officiel des Jeux COVAN.*

Comité d'organisation des Xèmes Jeux Olympiques d'hiver. (1969). *Rapport officiel [Xèmes Jeux olympiques d'hiver] : Official report [Xth Winter Olympic Games].*

Comité d'organisation des XVes Jeux Olympiques d'hiver. Calgary. (1988). *Rapport officiel des XVes Jeux Olympiques d'hiver = XV Olympic Winter Games official report.*

Comité exécutif des jeux d'Anvers ; Comité olympique belge. (1920). *XVIIème Olympiade Anvers 1920.*

Comité Olímpico Brasileiro. (2010). *Passion unites us: Rio 2016 bid official report = Unis par la passion: Rapport officiel de la candidature de Rio 2016.*

Comité olympique français. (1924). *Les Jeux de la VIIIe Olympiade: Paris 1924: Rapport officiel.*

Comité Olympique Suisse. (1951). *Rapport général sur les Ves Jeux Olympiques d'hiver, St-Moritz 1948.*

Comité organisateur des Jeux de la XIX olympiade. (1969). *Mexico 68: Official report.*

COOB'92. (1992). *Official report of the games of the XXV Olympiad Barcelona 1992.*

Dansero, E. (2002). *I "luoghi comuni" dei grandi eventi: Allestendo il palcoscenico territoriale per Torino 2006* (pp. 861–894). IRIS.

Dansero, E. (2014). *I grandi eventi: Spazi per una discreta geografia del cambiamento continuo: Atti del XXXI Congresso Geografico Italiano* (Vol. II). Mimesis.

Dansero, E., & de Leonardis, D. (2006). Torino 2006: La territorializzazione olimpica e la sfida dell'eredità. *Bollettino della società geografica italiana, XI*, 611–641.

Dansero, E., & Mela, A. (2007). Olympic territorialization. The case of Torino 2006. *Journal of Alpine Research / Revue de géographie alpine*, 95(3), 16–26.

Dansero, E., & Maroni O. (2003). *Cercando SLoT per le Valli Chisone e Germanasca, in Rossignolo C.* SLOT.

Dansero, E., Maroni, O., & Ricciardi, C. (2003). Cercando SLOT per le Valli Chisone e Germanasca. In Una geografia dei luoghi per lo sviluppo locale. Approcci metodologici e studi di caso, Slot quaderno 3, 111 -145. Baskerville.

Dansero, E., & Mela, A. (2007). Olympic territorialization. *Revue de Géographie Alpine, 95–3*, 16–26.

Dansero, E., & Mela, A. (2012). Bringing the Mountains into the City: Legacy of the Winter Olympics, Turin 2006. In H. J. Lenskyj, & S. Wagg (Eds.), *The Palgrave handbook of Olympic Studies* (pp. 178–194). Palgrave Macmillan.

Dansero, E., & Puttilli, M. (2010). Mega-events tourism legacies: The case of the Torino 2006 Winter Olympic Games—A territorialisation approach. *Leisure Studies, 29*(3), 321–341.

Davidson, M., & McNeill, D. (2012). The redevelopment of Olympic sites: Examining the legacy of Sydney Olympic Park. *Urban Studies*, 49(8), 1625–1641.

Decreto Legge. (2003). *Torino 2006—La legge n. 48 del 2003*.

della Sala, V. (2022a). The Olympic Village and the Olympic Urbanism: Perception and expectations of Olympic Specialists. *Bollettino della Società Geografica Italiana* serie *14, 5*(2), 51-64.

della Sala, V. (2022b). *The Olympic Villages and Olympic urban planning: Analysis and evaluation of the impact on territorial and urban planning (XX-XX I centuries).* Doctoral thesis. UAB, Polito.

della Sala, V. (2023a). Olympic Games and expectations: The factor analysis model about Olympic Urbanism and Olympic Villages. *Sociologia e Ricerca Sociale, 132*(3), 127–147.

della Sala, V. (2023b). Olympic games: Between expectations and fears—Factor analysis model applied to Olympic urbanism and Olympic Villages. *Rivista Internazionale di Scienze Sociali, 132*(1), 55–86.

della Sala, V. (2023c). Sustainable planning for the Olympic Legacy. *Environmental Analysis & Ecology Studies, 11*(2), 1237–1239.

della Sala, V. (2023d). The legacy of the Turin 2006 Olympic Games through a long-term development perspective: Reflection and opinion about the physical and social change in the post-Olympic period. *Cambio: Rivista sulle trasformazioni sociali, 25*(1), 229–247.

Deloitte. (2012). *Lessons from London 2012.*

Delorme, F. (2014). Du Village-station à la station-Village. Un siècle d'urbanisme en montagne. *In Situ. Revue des patrimoines, 24.* https://journals.openedition.org/insitu/11243.

Dematteis, G. (1995). *Progetto implicito: Il contributo della geografia umana alle scienze del territorio.* Franco Angeli.

Dematteis, G., & Governa F. (a cura di). (2005). *Territorialità, sviluppo locale, sostenibilità: Il modello SLoT.* Franco Angeli.

Dematteis, G., & Guarrasi V. (1995). *Urban networks, Heo-Italy, Italian committee for international geographical union* (Vol. 2-1994). Patron Editore.

Department for Communities and Local Government (DCLG). (2015). *London 2012 Olympics regeneration legacy evaluation framework.*

Department for Communities and Local Government (DCLG). (2012a). *Department for culture, media and sport London 2012 Olympic and Paralympic games impacts and legacy evaluation framework final report.*

Department for Communities and Local Government (DCLG). (2012b). *Plans for the legacy from the 2012 Olympic and Paralympic games.*

Department for Communities and Local Government (DCLG). (2015). *Olympic Games impact study-London 2012 post-games report.*

Essex, S. (2017). *The Winter Olympics-Driving urban change, 1924-2022, in Olympic cities, City agendas, planning and the World's Games*. Routledge.

Essex, S., & Chalkley, B. (1998). Olympic Games: Catalyst of urban change. *Leisure Studies, 17*(3), 187–206.

Essex, S., & Chalkley, B. (2004). Mega-sporting events in urban and regional policy: A history of the Winter Olympics. *Planning Perspectives, 19*(2), 201–204.

Essex, S., & Chalkley, B. (2010). *Urban transformation from hosting the Olympic Games*. Centre d'Estudis Olímpics (UAB).

European Commission. (2011). *Cities of tomorrow*.

European Commission. (2016). *The State of European Cities 2016 Cities leading the way to a better future*.

Evans, G. (2009). Creative cities, creative spaces and urban policy. *Urban Studies, 46*(5&6), 1003-1040.

Ferrari, S. (2002). *Event marketing: I grandi eventi e gli eventi speciali come strumenti di marketing*. CEDAM.

Flyvbjerg, B., & Stewart, A. (2012). Olympic proportions: Cost and cost overrun at the Olympics 1960-2012. *SSRN Electronic Journal*, June, 1–23.

Frey, M., Iraldo, F., & Melis, M. (2008). *The impact of wide-scale sport events on local development: an assessment of the XXth Torino Olympics through the sustainability report*. http://dx.doi.org/10.2139/ssrn.1117967.

Furrer, P. (2002). Giochi Olimpici sostenibili: Utopia o realtà?. *Bollettino della Società Geografica Italiana, serie XII, VII*, 4.

Getz, D. (1989). Special events: Defining the product. *Tourism Management, 10*(2), 125–137.

Getz, D. (1997). *Trends and issues in sport event tourism*. Tourism Recreation Research, Taylor & Francis.

Getz, D. (2004). Bidding on events. *Journal of Convention & Exhibition Management, 5*(2), 1–24.

Getz, D., & Fairley, S. (2008). Media management at sport events for destination promotion: Case studies and concepts. *Event Management, 8*(3), 127–139.

Getz, D., & Page, S. J. (2016). *Event studies: Theory, research and policy for planned events* (3rd ed.). Routledge.

Gold, J. R., & Gold, M. M. (2008). Olympic cities: Regeneration, city rebranding and changing urban agendas. *Geography Compass, 2*(1), 300–318.

Gold, J., & Gold, M. M. (2016). *Olympic cities: City agendas, planning, and the World's Games, 1896* (3rd ed.). Routledge.

Governa, F. (1999). *Il milieu urbano: L'identità territoriale nei processi di sviluppo.* Franco Angeli.

Gratton C. (2002). *Sport in the city. Routledge.*

Greslery, G. (1994). *La Ciutat Mundial in Visions Urbanes. Europa 1870-1993. La ciutat de l'artista. La ciutat de l'arquitecte.* Centre de Cultura Contemporània de Barcelona, Electa, 164–166.

Guala, C. (2002a). Per una tipologia dei mega eventi. In E. Dansero, & A. Segre (a cura di), *Il territorio dei grandi eventi. Riflessioni e ricerche guardando a Torino 2006* (VII, pp. 743-755). Bollettino della società geografica italiana, Roma.

Guala, C. (2002b). *International Society of City and Regional Planners 38th Congress-"The Pulsar Effect" Monitoring Torino 2006 Winter Olympic Games.*

Guala, C., & Crivello, S. (2006). Mega events and urban regeneration: The background and numbers behind Turin 2006. In N. Muller, M. Messing, & H. Preuss (a cura di), *From Chamonix to Turin: The Winter Games in the scope of Olympic research* (pp. 323-342). Agon.

Guarrasi, V. (2002). Ground zero: Grandi eventi e trasformazione urbane. *Bollettino della Società Geografica Italiana, serie XII, volume VII, 4.*

Hall, C. M. (1992). *Hallmark tourist events: Impacts, management & planning.* Belhaven Press.

Harvey, D. (1991). *The condition of postmodernity: An enquiry into the origins of cultural change.* Wiley.

Harvey, D. (2002). *Spaces of capital*. Routledge.

Heine, M. (2018). Olympic commodification and civic spaces at the 2010 winter Olympic Games: A political topology of contestation. *International Journal of the History of Sport, 35*(9), 898–910.

Hiller, H. H. (1990). The urban transformation of a landmark event. *Urban Affairs Quarterly, 26*(1), 118–137.

Hiller, H. H. (2000). Toward an urban sociology of mega-events. *Research in Urban Sociology, 5*, 181–205.

Hiller, H. H. (2003). *Towards a science of Olimpic outcomes: The urban legacy*. The Legacy of the Olimpic Games, Losanna (pp. 32-38). International Olympic Committee.

Hiller, H. H. (2014). *Host cities and the Olympics: An Interactionist Approach* (1st ed.) Routledge.

Hodges, J., & Hall, C. (1996). The housing and social impacts of mega events: Lessons for the Sydney 2000 Olympics. In G. Kearsley (Ed.), *Tourism down under II; towards a more sustainable tourism* (pp. 152–166). Centre for Tourism, University of Otago.

Holden, M., Mackenzie, J., & Vanwynsberghe, R. (2008). *Sports Mega-Events: Social scientific analyses of a global phenomenon*. The Sociological Review, Blackwell Publishing.

Insolera, I. (1978). *La città e la crisi del capitalismo*. Tempi Nuovi Laterza.

International Olympic Committee. (1996). *Technical manual on Olympic village*. Author.

International Olympic Committee. (1999). *Olympic charter*. Author.

International Olympic Committee. (2005a). *International Olympic Committee manual for candidate cities for the games of the xxix Olympiad 2008*. Author.

International Olympic Committee. (2005b). *Technical manual on Olympic Village (November 2005)*. Author.

International Olympic Committee. (2005c). *Technical manual on planning, coordination & management of the Olympic Games (November 2005)*. Author.

International Olympic Committee. (2005d). *Technical manual on sport (November 2005)*. Author.

International Olympic Committee. (2005e). *Technical manual on venues—Design standards for competition venues (November 2005)*. Author.

International Olympic Committee. (2007). *Technical manual on Olympic Games impact*. Author.

International Olympic Committee. (2008). *Manual for candidate cities for the games of the xxix Olympiad 2008*. Author.

International Olympic Committee. *(2010a). Candidature procedure and questionnaire xxiii Olympic Winter Games*. Author.

International Olympic Committee. (2010b). Jeux Olympiques: Héritages et Impacts [Olympic Games: Legacies and impacts]. *Legacy*, December, pp. 1–64.

International Olympic Committee. (2011a). *Candidature acceptance procedure games of the xxxii Olympiad*. Author.

International Olympic Committee. (2011b). *Internationalism in the Olympic Movement*. VS Verlag für Sozialwissenschaften. Author.

International Olympic Committee. (2012). *Olympic legacy*. Author.

International Olympic Committee. (2013a). *Factsheet: Legacies of the games* (pp. 1–11). Author.

International Olympic Committee. (2013b, October). *The games of the Olympiad* (pp. 1–8). Author.

International Olympic Committee. (2014). *Factsheet the Olympic Winter Games*. Author.

International Olympic Committee. (2015a). *Factsheet legacies of the games*. Author.

International Olympic Committee. (2015b). *Olympic Winter Games Strategic Review Working Group*. Author.

International Olympic Committee. (2015c). *Part ii : Candidature file*. Author.

International Olympic Committee. (2015d). *Technical manual on Olympic Village (November 2005)*. Author.

International Olympic Committee. (2016). *Key OGKM activities*. Author.

International Olympic Committee. (2017). *Celebrate capture partner embed legacy strategic approach moving forward*. Author.

International Olympic Committee. (2017a). *Host city contract operational requirements*. Author.

International Olympic Committee. (2017b). *Host city contract principles games of the xxxiii Olympiad in 2024*. Author.

International Olympic Committee. (2017c). *Report Evaluation Commission 2024*. Author.

International Olympic Committee (2017d). *The Olympic Winter Games in numbers: Vancouver 2010, Sochi 2014 and PyeongChang 2018.* Author.

International Olympic Committee. (2018a). *Host city contract operational requirements*. Author.

International Olympic Committee. (2018b). *Olympic Agenda 2020 Olympic Games: The new norm report by the Executive Steering Committee for Olympic Games delivery*. Author.

International Olympic Committee. (2018c). *Olympic Summer Games Villages from Paris 1924 to Rio 2016.* Author.

International Olympic Committee. (2018d). *Sharing history, enriching the future Olympic Winter Games Villages from Oslo 1952 to*. Author.

International Olympic Committee. (2019). *Sustainability progress update a review of our 2020 objectives*. Author.

International Olympic Committee. (2020). *Olympic charter*. Author.

International Olympic Committee. (2021). *Marketing fact* (pp. 8 -21). Author.

International Olympic Committee. (2022). *Olympic Games*. olympics.com

Jennings, W. (2012). *Olympic risks*. Palgrave Macmillan.

Kagaya, S. (1991). Infrastructural facilities provision for Sapporo's winter Olympic of 1972 and its effects on regional developments. *Revue de Géographie Alpine*, *79*(3), 59–71.

Kasimati, E. (2003). Economic aspects and the Summer Olympics: A review of related research. *International Journal of Tourism Research*, *5*(6), 433–444.

Kasimati, E. (2006). *Macroeconomic and financial analysis of mega-events: Evidence from Greece* (p. 249).

Kassens-Noor, E. (2013). Transport legacy of the Olympic Games, 1992–2012. *Journal of Urban Affairs*, *35*(4), 393 -416. https://doi.org/10.1111/j.1467-9906.2012.00626.x

Kassens-Noor, E. (2016). From ephemeral planning to permanent urbanism: An urban planning theory of mega-events. *Urban Planning*, *1*(1), 41–54.

Kassens-Noor, E., & Lauermann, J. (2017). How to Bid Better for the Olympics: A participatory mega-event planning strategy for local legacies. *Journal of the American Planning Association*, *83*(4), 335–345.

Lake Organizing Committee for the Olympic Winter Games of 2002. (2002). *Salt Lake 2002: Rapport officiel des XIXes Jeux Olympiques d'hiver, Salt* [Official report of the XIX Olympic Winter Games Salt Lake 2002]: 8-24 February 2002.

Lefebvre H. (1991a). *Critique of everyday life*. Verso.

Lefebvre H. (1991b). *The production of space—Wiley*. Wiley.

Lenskyj, H. J. (2006). The Olympic (affordable) housing legacy and society responsibility. *Eighth International Symposium for Olympic Research* (pp. 191–199).

Lenskyj, H. J. (2012). The Winter Olympics: Geography is destiny? In *The Palgrave handbook of Olympic Studies* (pp. 88–102). Palgrave Macmillan.

Liao, H., & Pitts, A. (2006). A brief historical review of Olympic urbanization. *The International Journal of the History of Sport, 23*(7), 1232–1252.

Lillehammer Olympic Organizing Committee. (1995). *Rapport officiel des XVIIes Jeux Olympiques d'hiver Lillehammer 1994* [Official report of the XVII Olympic Winter Games Lillehammer 1994].

Maenning, W., & Zimbalist, A. (2012). *International handbook on the economics of Mega Sporting Events*. Elgar.

Magnaghi, A. (2000). *Progetto locale*. Bollati Boringhieri.

Magnaghi, A. (2001). *Rappresentare i luoghi*. Alinea Editrice.

Matheson, V. A. (2006). *Mega-events*: *The effect of the world's most significant sporting events on local, regional, and national economies*. College of the Holy Cross, Department of Economics.

Matheson, V. A., & Baade, R. A. (2004). Mega-sporting events in developing nations: Playing the way to prosperity? *South African Journal of Economics*, *72*(5), 1084–1095.

McDonogh, G. (1991). Discourses of the city: Policy and response in post-transitional Barcelona. *City and Society*, *5*(1), 40–63.

Metropolis. (2002). *Commission 1 the impact of major events on the development of large cities*. Author.

Milano Cortina. (2019). *Milano Cortina 2026 candidate city Olympic Winter Games*. Author.

Millet i Serra, L. (1997). *Olympic Villages after the games Lluís Millet*. Centre d'Estudis Olímpics, UAB.

Montanari A. (2002). Grandi Eventi, marketing urbano e realizzazione di nuovi spazi turistici. *Bollettino della Società Geografica Italiana*, serie XII, VII, 4.

Moragas, M. (1996). *Olympic Villages: A hundred years of urban planning and shared experiences: International Symposium on Olympic Villages*. Autonomous University of Barcelona (Ed.).

Müller, M. (2011). State dirigisme in megaprojects: Governing the 2014 Winter Olympics in Sochi. *Environment and Planning A: Economy and Space*, *43*(9), 2091–2108.

Müller, M. (2014). After Sochi 2014: Costs and impacts of Russia's Olympic Games. *Eurasian Geography and Economics, 55*(6), 628–655.

Muñoz, F. (1996). Historic evolution and urban planning typology of Olympic Villages. In Miquel de Moragas, Montserrat Llinés, & Bruce Kidd (Eds.), *Olympic Villages: A hundred years of urban planning and shared experiences: International Symposium on Olympic Villages, Lausanna* (p. 28). IOC.

Muñoz, F. (2006). Olympic urbanism and Olympic Villages: Planning strategies in Olympic Host Cities, London 1908 to London 2012. *The Sociological Review, 54*(2_suppl), 175–187.

Muñoz, F. (2011). I grandi eventi nella città del XXI secolo: Variazioni sull' esperienza di Barcellona. *Rivista di sociologia urbana e rurale, 96*, 46-71.

Muñoz, F. (2015) Urbanalisation and city mega-events: From "copy & paste" urbanism to urban creativity. In Valerie Viehoff & Gavin Poynter (Eds.), *Mega-event cities: Urban legacies of global sports events* (pp. 11-21). Ashgate.

Nakamura, H., & Suzuki, N. (2017). Reinterpreting Olympic legacies: The emergent process of long-term post-event strategic planning of Hakuba after the 1998 Nagano Winter Games. *International Journal of Sport Policy, 9*(2), 311–330.

Netherlands Olympic Committee (Committee 1928). (1928). *The Ninth Olympiad: Being the official report of the Olympic Games of 1928 celebrated at Amsterdam* (Van Rossem (Ed.), Sydney W. Fleming, Trans.).

NSW Treasury: Office of Financial Management. (November 1997). *The economic impact of the Sydney Olympic Games*. Author.

Oben, T. (2011). *Sport and the environment: An UNEP perspective* (pp. 25–33).

OECD Regional Outlook 2011. (2011). *OECD regional outlook 2011*. OECD.

OECD. (2020). *Cities in the World* (OECD urban studies).

Olds, K. (1998). Urban mega-events, evictions and housing rights: The Canadian case. *Current Issues in Tourism, 1*(1), 2–46.

Olympic Winter Games Committee Lake Placid. (1932). *III Olympic Winter Games, Lake Placid 1932: Official report.*

Organisasjonskomiteen. (1953). *VI Olympiske Vinterleker Oslo 1952 = VI Olympic Winter Games Oslo 1952.*

Organisationskomitee der IX. Olympischen Winterspiele in Innsbruck 1964. (1967). *Offizieller Bericht der IX. Olympischen Winterspiele Innsbruck 1964.*

Organisationskomitee für die IV. Olympischen Winterspiele 1936 Garmisch-Partenkirchen. (1936). *IV Olympische Winterspiele 1936: Garmisch-Partenkirchen 6. bis 16. Februar : Amtlicher Bericht.*

Organisationskomitee für die XI. Olympiade Berlin 1936. (1937). *The XIth Olympic Games Berlin, 1936: Official report.*

Organising Committee. (1928). *Rapport général du Comité exécutif des IImes Jeux olympiques d'hiver et documents officiels divers.*

Organising Committee. (1955). *The official report of the Organising Committee for the Games of the XV Olympiad.*

Organising Committee. (1958). *The official report of the Organising Committee for the Games of the XVI Olympiad Melbourne 1956.*

Organising Committee. (1960). *VIII Olympic Winter Games Squaw Valley, California, 1960: Final report California Olympic Commission.*

Organising Committee. (1966). *The games of the XVIII Olympiad, Tokyo 1964: The official report of the Organising Committee.*

Organising Committee. (1974). *Die Spiele: The official report of the Organising Committtee for the Games of the XXth Olympiad Munich 1972.*

Organising Committee. (1995). *Official report of the XVII Olympic Winter Games Lillehammer 1994.*

Organising Committee. (1996). *Official Report of the Games of the XXVI Olympiad.* Atlanta Committee for the Olympic Games.

Organising Committee. Organising Committee of Lake Placid 1980. (1980). XIII Olympic Winter Games Lake Placid 1980: Official results = XIII Olympic Winter Games Lake Placid 1980: résultats officiels = XIII Olympic Winter Games Lake Placid 1980: offizielle Ergebnisse.

Organising Committee for the Games of the XVII Olympiad. (1963). *The Games of the XVII Olympiad Rome, 1960 : The official report of the Organising Committee.*

Organising Committee for the XIIth Winter Olympic Games 1976 at Innsbruck. (1976). *Endbericht : XII. Olympische Winterspiele Innsbruck 1976 = Rapport final: Innsbruck '76 = Final report : Innsbruck '76.*

Organising Committee for the XIth Olympic Winter Games Sapporo 1972. (1973). *The XI Olympic Winter Games Sapporo 1972 : Official report = Les XI Jeux olympiques d'hiver Sapporo 1972 : Rapport officiel.*

Organising Committee for the XIV Olympiad. (1951). *The official report of the Organising Committee for the XIV Olympiad.*

Organising Committee of Albertville. (1992). *Rapport officiel des XVIes Jeux Olympiques d'hiver d'Albertville et de la Savoie = Official report of the XVI Olympic Winter Games of Albertville and Savoie.* Olympic Winter Games, Organising Committee.

Organising Committee of Lake Placid 1980. (1980). *XIII Olympic Winter Games Lake Placid 1980 : Official results = XIII Olympic Winter Games Lake Placid 1980 : Résultats officiels = XIII Olympic Winter Games Lake Placid 1980 : Offizielle Ergebnisse.*

Organising Committee of Los Angeles Olympic. (1985). *Official report of the Games of the XXIIIrd Olympiad Los Angeles 1984.*

Organising Committee of the Games of the XXII Olympiad. (1981). *Games of the XXII Olympiad: Official report.*

Organising Committee of the XIVth Winter Olympic Games 1984 at Sarajevo. (1984). *Final report = Rapport final = Završni izvještaj.*

Organising Committee of the XXII Olympic Winter Games and XI Paralympic Winter Games of 2014 in Sochi. (2015).

Owen, K. A. (2002). The Sydney 2000 Olympics and urban entrepreneurialism: Local variations in urban governance. *Australian Geographical Studies, 40*(3), 323–336.

Paris Candidate City Olympic Games 2024. (2016). *Candidature file: Paris Candidate City Olympic Games 2024.*

Payne, M. (2007). A Gold-Medal partnership. *Strategy + Business.*

Poynter, G. (2009). *London Assembly Economic Development, Culture, Sport and Tourism Committee Literature Review : Olympic Legacy Governance arrangements Professor Gavin Poynter November 2009*, November, pp. 1–47.

Poynter, G. (2010). *Mega Events and the Urban Economy: What can Olympic Cities learn from each other?* Centre d'Estudis Olímpics (UAB).

Poynter, G. (2012). The Olympics: East London's renewal and legacy. In *The Palgrave handbook of Olympic Studies* (pp. 505–519). Palgrave Macmillan.

Poynter, G. (2015). *Urbanism: Space, planning and place-making, in Mega-Event Cities: Urban Legacies of Global Sports Events.* Routledge.

Preuß, H., Andreff, W., & Weitzmann, M. (2019). *Cost and Revenue Overruns of the Olympic Games 2000–2018.* Springer.

Preuss, H. (2000). *Economics of the Olympic Games: Hosting the games 1972–2000.* Walla Press. University of Germany.

Preuss, H. (2004). *The economics of staging the Olympics: A comparison of the games 1972–2008.* Edward Elgar Publisher.

PwC. (2001). *Business and economic benefits of the Sydney 2000 Games: A collation of evidence.* Author.

PwC (2010, June). *Public-Private partnerships: The US perspective.* Author.

PyeongChang Organising Committee for the XXIII Olympic and Paralympic Winter Games. (2019). *PyeongChang 2018 Official Report.*

Raffestin, C. (1981). *Per una geografia del potere.* Unicopli.

Raffestin, C. (1984). *Territorializzazione, deterritorializzazione, riterriteritorializzazione e informazione,* in A. Turco (a cura di), *Regione e regionalizzazione* (pp. 69-82). Franco Angeli.

Regione Piemonte. (2006). *Regione Piemonte, Torino 2006, Le olimpiadi del territorio piemontese.*

Ritchie, J. R. (2000). Turning 16 days into 16 years through Olympic Legacies. *Event Management, 6*(3), 155–165.

Ritchie, J. R. B., & Smith B. H. (1991). The impact of a mega-event on host regional awareness: A longitudinal study. *Journal of Travel Research, 30*(1), 3-10.

Roche, M. (1992). Mega-Events and Micro-Modernisation: On the Sociology of the New Urban Tourism. *British Journal of Sociology, 43,* 563-600.

Roche, M. (2000). *Megaevents and modernity: Olympics and Expos in the Growth of Global C.* Routledge.

Roche, M. (2002). Olympic and Sport Mega-Events as Media-Events: Reflections on the globalisation paradigm. *Symposium a Quarterly Journal in Modern Foreign Literatures* (pp. 1–12).

Roche, M. (2003). The Olympics and the Development of "Global Society." In M. De Moragas, C. Kennett, & N. Puig (a cura di), *The Legacy of the Olympic Games*, Document of the Olympic Museum, International Olympic Committee.

Roche, M. (2006). Mega-Events and modernity revisited: Globalization and the case of the Olympics. *The Sociological Review, 54*(2_suppl), 27–40.

Rose, A., & Spiegel, M. (2009). *The Olympic effect.* National Bureau of Economic Research.

Sands, L. M. (2008, July -August). The 2008 Olympics' impact on China. *The China Business Review.*

Sassen, S. (1991). *The Global City. New York, London, Tokyo.* Princeton University Press.

Savitch, H. V. (1988). *Post-Industrial cities, politics and planning in New York, Paris and London.* Princeton University Press.

Scherer, J. (2011). Olympic Villages and large-scale urban development: Crises of capitalism, deficits of democracy? *Sociology, 45*(5), 782–797.

Scott, D., Steiger, R., Rutty, M., & Johnson, P. (2015). The future of the Olympic Winter Games in an era of climate change. *Current Issues in Tourism,* 18(10), 913–930.

Segre, A., & Scamuzzi, S. (2004). Aspettando le Olimpiadi: Torino 2006 : Primo rapporto sui territori olimpici.

Seoul Olympic Organizing Committee. (1989). *Official report: Games of the XXIVth Olympiad Seoul 1988.*

Short, J. R. (2008). Globalization, cities and the Summer Olympics. *City, 12*(3), 321–340.

Skarveli, Efharis. (2004). Athens 2004 Organising Committee for the Olympic Games (Ed.) *Official report of the XXVIII Olympiad: Athens 2004.*

Smith, A. (2009). Theorising the relationship between major sport events and social sustainability. *Journal of Sport and Tourism, 14*(2–3), 109–120.

Smith, A. (2012). *Events and urban regeneration.* Routledge.

Smith, A. (2014). "De-Risking" East London: Olympic Regeneration Planning 2000–2012. *European Planning Studies, 22*(9), 1919–1939.

Smith, C. J., & Himmelfarb, K. M. G. (2007). Restructuring Beijing's social space: Observations on the Olympic Games in 2008. *Eurasian Geography and Economics, 48*(5), 543–554.

Smith, M. (2008). When the Games Come to Town: Host Cities and the local impacts of the Olympics Games and Paralympics on host cities, December, pp. 1–95.

Soja, E. (2000). *Postmetropolis: Critical studies of cities and regions—Wiley.* Wiley-Blackwell.

Sordet, P. (1996). *The Olympic Village of Albertville' 1996. In Hundred years of urban planning and shared experiences.* International Symposium on Olympic Villages. IOC.

Sorkin, M. (1992). *Variations on a Theme Park.* Hill and Wang.

Spilling, O. R. (1996). Mega event as strategy for regional development the case of the 1994 Lillehammer Winter Olympics. *Entrepreneurship and Regional Development, 8*(4), 321–344.

Spilling, O. (1998). Beyond Intermezzo? On the long-term industrial impacts of mega-events: The case of Lillehammer 1994, *Festival Management & Events Tourism, 5,* 101-122.

Spooner, E. D., Morphett, D., Watt, M. E., Grunwald, G., & Zacharias, P. (2000). Solar Olympic Village case study. *Energy Policy, 28*(14), 1059–1068.

Swyngedouw, E. (2004). Globalisation or "glocalisation"? Networks, territories and rescaling. *Cambridge Review of International Affairs, 17*(1), 25–48.

Swyngedouw, E., Moulaert, F., & Rodriguez, A. (2002). Neoliberal urbanization in Europe: Large-scale urban development projects and the New Urban Policy. *Antipode, 34*(3), 542–577.

Sydney Organizing Committee for the Olympic Games. (2001). *Official report of the XXVII Olympiad: Sydney 2000 Olympic Games.*

Terret, T. (2008). The Albertville Winter Olympics: Unexpected legacies—failed expectations for Regional Economic Development. *The International Journal of the History of Sport, 25*(14), 1903–1921.

The London Organising Committee of the Olympic Games and Paralympic Games. (2013). *London 2012 Olympic Games: The official report.*

The Organizing Committee for the XVIII Olympic Winter Games Nagano 1998. (1999). *The XVIII Olympic Winter Games: Official report Nagano 1998.*

Tokyo 2020 Olympic Games Bid Committee. (2013). *Tokyo 2020: Discover tomorrow.*

Turco, A. (1984). *Regione e regionalizzazione*: Scritti di Roger Brunet. Franco Angeli.

Turco, A. (1988). *Verso una teoria geografica della complessità.* Unicopli.

UK Government. (2011a). *The Green Book: Appraisal and evaluation in central government*—GOV.UK.

UK Government. (2011b). *The Magenta Book.*

UN. (1980). *Patterns of urban and rural population growth.*

UN (1992). *Agenda 21.*

UN. (2005). *United Nations Development Program.*

UN. (2016). *Culture: Urban future—diversity of cultural expressions.*

UNEP. (2005). *World resources 2005: The wealth of the poor—managing ecosystems to fight poverty.* London Word Resources Institute.

UN-Habitat. (2009). *Planning sustainable cities: Global report on human settlements.*

UN-Habitat. (2015). *International guidelines on Urban and Territorial Planning.*

United Nations. (2019). *The future is now.*

Vancouver Organizing Committee for the 2010 Olympic and Paralympic games (VANOC). (2009). *Olympic Games Impact (OGI) study for the 2010 Olympic and Paralympic Winter Games Pre-Games results report The Vancouver Organizing Committee for the 2010 Olympic and Paralympic Games.*

Vanolo, A. (2008). The image of the creative city: Some reflections on urban branding in Turin. *Cities, 25*(6), 370–382.

Vanwynsberghe, R. (2015). The Olympic Games Impact (OGI) study for the 2010 Winter Olympic Games: Strategies for evaluating sport mega-events' contribution to sustainability. *International Journal of Sport Policy, 7*(1), 1–18.

VanWynsberghe, R., Derom, I., & Maurer, E. (2012). Social leveraging of the 2010 Olympic Games: "sustainability" in a City of Vancouver initiative. *Journal of Policy Research in Tourism, Leisure and Events, 4*(2), 185–205.

Venturi, R. (1966). *Complexity and contradiction in architecture. MOMA.*

Venturi, M. (1994). *Grandi Eventi, La festivalizzazione della politica urbana.* Il Cardo.

Viehoff, V., & Poynter, G.(2018). *Mega-event cities: Urban legacies of global sports events* (1st ed.). Routledge.

Weicker, F., & Company Management Consultants. (2003). *Vancouver agreement community assessment of 2010 Olympic Winter Games and Paralympic games on Vancouver's inner-city neighbourhoods final report February 2003 prepared for the Vancouver agreement in conjunction with the Vancouver 2010 bid Corporation.*

Wernick, A. (1991). Global promo: The cultural triumph of exchange. *Theory, Culture & Society, 8*(1), 89–109.

Whitson, D., & Macintosh, D. (1996). The global circus: International sport, tourism, and the marketing of cities. *Journal of Sport and Social Issues, 20*(3), 278–295.

Westerbeek, H. M., Turner, P., & Ingerson, L. (2002). Key success factors in bidding for hallmark sporting events. *International Marketing Review, 19*(3), 303–322.

Wimmer, W. (1976). *Olympic buildings*. Edition: Leipzig.

World Economic Forum. (2010, January). *Global risks 2020: A global risk network report*. Author.

Xth Olympiade Committee of the Games of Los Angeles. (1933). *The Games of the Xth Olympiad Los Angeles 1932: Official report*.

Zou, Y., Mason, R., & Zhong, R. (2015). Modeling the polycentric evolution of post-Olympic Beijing: An empirical analysis of land prices and development intensity. *Urban Geography, 36*(5), 735–756.

www.ingramcontent.com/pod-product-compliance
Lightning Source LLC
Chambersburg PA
CBHW040423110426
42814CB00008B/335